JUDGMENT
DAY

*A compilation of biblical facts regarding
God's judgment of His creation.*

JERRY RICHARDSON

CONTENTS

ACKNOWLEDGEMENTS

The New King James version of the Bible is
used except where otherwise noted

First of all, and above all others in this world, my thoughts are still on Bev, my wife of 52 years. She went away on March 13, 2019---while the book was still in progress. She was my inspiration; not only for the book, but in every way. To her memory this book is dedicated. She was indeed the wind beneath my wings.

To my beloved brother in Christ, John Nichols, my early mentor; who encouraged me for many years to share my thoughts on the things I had studied. John always inspired me to look to the scriptures only.

To my lifelong friend, Roger Bell; for his many years of encouragement and friendship I will always be indebted.

To my kids; Rachel, Becky, Todd and Travis; who were my sounding boards all along the way during the writing of the book.

In large part I write the book for my twelve grandkids, along with my four great-grandkids—and perhaps others to come. My desire and prayer is that the book will help to point them closer toward a love for God's Word.

I want to especially thank Madalyn Richardson, my granddaughter, who lovingly did the pictorial illustrations for each chapter.

But above all my gratitude is to the Lord, who did all the heavy lifting. To Him I give all glory forever!

Contacts in reference to the book can be made at (*jrichardsoncoll@ hotmail.com*)

FORWARD

The best books may not be the ones with all the answers, so to speak. I think the best ones are the books written by honest, searching authors whose lives have already been profoundly impacted by what they are writing about. That would be Jerry Richardson.

I don't think I've known anyone more honestly unbiased in their Bible study than Jerry. When my wife, Shirley, and I met Jerry and his late wife Beverly, it didn't take us long to realize they were authentically Christian people who would impact our lives as well. Since that time many years ago, Jerry's grace-filled spirit—void of sectarian attitudes—and his communication of God's kindness toward all people has only expanded. You may not agree with everything Jerry writes, but you will find in insightful and never mean-spirited.

This is not a casual read. We have to pay attention, if we are to follow Jerry's development of the important topics under consideration from chapter to chapter. This book is the result of a lifetime of study and tempered by the wisdom of an uncommonly spiritual man. But, the humility in which Jerry offers his book to the world is found in the hope that his studies will encourage people to examine their ideas, to look more deeply into the scriptures themselves, and, if need be, to rethink some of their beliefs that may not have been helpful to their spiritual formation.

Don Prantl

PREFACE

I never intended to write a book. There are so many books on every subject, and so many authors who are far superior to me as professional writers. The contents of "Judgment Day" covers a wide variety of subjects, but all are for the purpose of viewing the ultimate judgment of God on His creation. My purpose is to show the reality and the surety of eternal judgment for humanity and all of God's creation.

But in order to understand things that are scripturally revealed we must first think about the Revealer and establish a relationship with Him. Traditional religion, in my opinion, has not only done a poor job in bringing God's revelation to the world, but in many cases has blocked its view by allowing sectarian dogma to obscure the revelation of God's counsel. As it was when Jesus walked the earth, the assumed sanctity of the religious sects have diminished and hindered the relationship of the people with their God. And the end result is the same as in the day of Jesus. His rebuke was strong to the most religious. Woe to you, scribes and Pharisees, hypocrites! For you travel land and sea to win one proselyte, and when he is won, you make him twice as much a son of hell as yourselves. Matthew 23:15

My ultimate goal in this writing is to point out in a simple way that church doctrines built on religious tradition will not please the Creator of the world. Following tradition is easy, but it is so spiritually dangerous. We have only two options when it comes to whom we worship and trust in religious matters; either the Creator or the created. The first commandment makes clear that only worship of the Creator will be acceptable.

I will acknowledge that there will be mistakes in the book. My purpose is not to prove "who" is right. I do not think in terms of me or the group I am affiliated with religiously as having "cornered the market" on the righteousness of God. This is the religion of "who" is right. This is the prideful sectarian way of assuming doctrinal perfection through perfect knowledge. My goal is rather to point the readers of this book to "what" is right by pointing them to God's Book. As Paul told the Athenians, He is not far from any of us if we seek to find Him. Every one of us will give a personal accounting to God. When we sincerely reach out to Him, He will always reach back for us, and will give us what we need in order to know His will for our lives.

My goal is not to win proselytes to "my" religion, but to point souls to God that they might become disciples of Jesus Christ. My prayer is that you might read this with a mindset of seeking to find God, rather than looking for another religion. Thank you for taking the time and the interest in reading the book. May THE GREAT I AM, the one and only Lord God Almighty of the entire created universe....bless you as you seek His guidance and counsel.

~Jerry Richardson~

CHAPTER 1
CHILDHOOD THOUGHTS

"Look! What is it?" my younger sister, Carolyn, asked me, pointing toward the northern horizon.

I was about seven years old at the time. Looking up in the direction Carolyn pointed caused a fear to instantly come over me. It seemed as if the whole world on the north side of our farm was on fire! I had seen some pretty big fires—especially when my dad would burn off a field of sage grass at the end of winter—but nothing like this!

"I don't know," I said to my sister in a voice lacking courage. "Let's go tell Dad and Mom."

The location was our family farm in southern Missouri near the Arkansas line. My sister and I had been playing out in the backyard near the chicken house. We had become so preoccupied with our games that we hadn't looked up into the sky as the evening shades turned into night. The scene was an awesome display of weird scarlet and crimson light across the northern sky.

We ran as fast as we could back to the house and around to the front door. I scrambled through the door and saw Dad sitting in the room. "Dad," I said as I pointed north, "there's a big fire back there." He instantly became concerned, probably thinking a fire had gotten out on his place or our neighbors' place to the north. He quickly arose from his chair and followed me outside with Mom and the rest of the kids following.

I felt assured once Dad had investigated the situation that he would somehow put things into a more manageable perspective, which should lower my fear level. This was the way it usually happened. But this wasn't the way it happened this time.

"What on earth is that?" Dad exclaimed, unable to hide the anxiety in his voice.

My fear level instantly doubled! There we all were, the whole family, standing huddled in the backyard, waiting for what seemed certain calamity to overtake us.

It was always Mom who would bring the Bible into a discussion. Dad seldom invoked the scriptures (except in principle). But he rarely argued with Mom's interpretation of the details. The kids could sometimes see by the look he gave Mom he wasn't sure her scriptures were all rightly divided. But her kids never ever doubted her interpretation of the Bible. She was Moses the lawgiver as far as we were concerned.

That night as Mom stood there with the light from the north shining on her face, and with a very reverent and somber facial expression, tears began to well up in her eyes. Now when Mom cried, her kids always felt they were witnessing their condition being transitioned from normal to catastrophic. I had no idea what we were witnessing in the northern sky, but I knew it was something bigger and greater than a field on fire.

Dad hadn't said another word. He just stood there looking at the awesome sight in amazement. Mom was now gently wringing her hands and weeping softly. After what seemed like an eternity Mom finally spoke and announced her scriptural verdict of the mystery we were witnessing. Turning her head toward my dad, she said in a hushed voice, "I think this is the end of the world! The Bible says that before the end comes, the moon will be turned into blood."

I and my family went to bed with great fear and anxiety that night. But the sun came up as usual the next morning, which made the entire family much happier. We later heard on the radio that the "northern lights" sometimes naturally happened. What a relief to a fragile young mind! So as long as the moon kept coming out at night in its normal way, I felt satisfied the world would go on a little while longer!

THE POWER OF TRADITION

Beware lest anyone cheat you through philosophy and empty deceit, according to the tradition of men, according to the basic principles of the world, and not according to Christ. (Col. 2:8)

The fearful event of my childhood that I just described now seems a bit amusing. But it points out a very important fact that sometimes gets lost in our busy day-to-day life. When we exist in a low-information environment, we are operating at a disadvantage. And because of this, especially when danger approaches, the situation can only be dealt with to the extent that our knowledge and experience allows. In other words, we cannot deal with a problem or situation any better than we have the knowledge to do so.

During my childhood, and as my story about the northern lights indicate, I was both intrigued by and fearful of thoughts of Judgment Day. I'm sure most kids feel the same way. This is especially true with kids brought up in religious homes. The first reason is that they are subjected to more biblical information. Another major factor is the trust they have in the religion of their parents. Because of these things, they naturally would have a greater interest in God's judgment. For the most part, and for most people, religious teachings are received primarily as a result of ancestral or religious traditions handed down from generation to generation. These traditions often quench a desire for a more informed truth and can lead to a mistaken way of thinking. Ultimately they will lead to mistaken words and actions.

To be sure, accepting without question the information you are given is the easiest way to obtain information. But it's definitely not the smartest way. Information can come from unbelievable sources. Some tales and conspiratorial notions are relatively easy to dismiss because of their absurdity. However, information becomes more difficult to dismiss when it comes through a smoothly polished religious system. And when this happens, it sometimes becomes especially difficult to detect the errors. Mainly, once again, this is because the information comes from a trusted source. But no matter the source, secondhand information is a bad way of being informed. If we're smart, we'll check it out carefully before we pass it on.

In a letter to Timothy, Paul indicates that looking to "myths and old wives' tales" can get in the way of seeking the truth of God's will.

Have nothing to do with godless myths and old wives' tales; rather, train yourself to be godly. (1 Tim. 4:7) (NIV)

Myths and tales take us out of spiritual training for truth. They put our minds into a carnal cesspool of superstition and misinformation. Almost any information will seem plausible when there's no way to test its validity. The scriptures warn against accepting unproven ideas. Many times, because of our preconceptions, the truth of a matter may seem unreasonable when first presented. A friend once told me that truth is usually received only after a three-stage process. First, it is ridiculed. Next, it is violently opposed. And then, finally, it is accepted as self-evident. *Self-evident* was the position the writers of the Declaration of Independence took as they drafted the document that became one of our most treasured national literary works. They wrote, "We hold these truths to be self-evident: that all men are created equal; that they are endowed by their Creator with certain unalienable rights; that among these are life, liberty, and the pursuit of happiness." Today, we would hope most

Americans do hold these truths regarding being created equal as self-evident, although these truths have been ridiculed and violently opposed over and over throughout the nation's history and remain so today among many people.

There have always been false prophecies from men whose standards of truth are far removed from the God-breathed language of the Spirit. Paul's advice to the early Christian church was basically to listen, then test, and then hold on to what passes the spiritual test of God's inspired Word.

Do not quench the Spirit. Do not treat prophecies with contempt but test them all; hold on to what is good. (1 Thess. 5:19–21)

Most inherited traditions evolve from the wholesale acceptance of unreliable information. According to the *Merriam-Webster Dictionary*, the primary definition of *tradition* is "an inherited, established, or customary pattern of thought, action, or behavior (such as a religious practice or a social custom)."

Traditional influence is a very powerful force. Jesus likened the bad influences of tradition to the leaven that would be put in bread dough made of unleavened flour or meal. He taught it takes only a very small amount of leaven to change or leaven the complete lump of dough. He then likened this leavened dough to the religious influences of the Jews, who bound their traditions on the people as sacred law. He once told His disciples to beware of the leaven of the Pharisees and also the Jewish king, Herod. Most of the time, religious tradition and political affiliation come from the same wellspring of the mind.

Then He charged them, saying, "Take heed, beware of the leaven of the Pharisees and the leaven of Herod." (Mark 8:15)

The Jewish religious and political leaders in Jesus' day, by virtue of their lofty positions, had a great ability to influence the minds of God's people. The same is true regarding the people of God in our day. Beware! Beware of the hypocritical influences of spiritual leaders who prophecy falsely and bind unnecessary burdens on the people. The Lord said these influences lead to traditions of men that make the Word of God ineffective. Listen to Jesus speak about this as He talks to the Jewish religious leaders.

He answered and said to them, "Why do you also transgress the command-ment of God because of your tradition? For God commanded, saying, 'Honor your father and your mother'; and, 'He who curses father or mother, let him be put to death.' But you say, 'Whoever says to his father or mother, "Whatever profit you might have received from me is a gift to God"— then he need not honor his father or mother.' Thus you have made the commandment of God of no effect by your tradition. (Matthew 15:3–6)

Recently I read an article about a scientific view that pointed out both good and bad things connected with keeping traditions. Among other things, the article talked about the positive effects family tradition has on the stabil-ity and well-being of children. And although the author generally had posi-tive things to say, I was struck by the following part that seemed to serve as a warning for those who would blindly follow traditions.

Human traditions exists, it turns out, largely due to our fear and a determination to do what other people are doing. According to a series of experiments on traditions and imitation conducted in 2015 by the Emotion Lab in Sweden, we're far more likely to obey a tradi-tion (that is, something we observe other people doing) if our choices come with a threat of punishment. We don't follow all traditions just because we enjoy them; subconsciously, we may follow them because we're afraid. (Why We Love Traditions, According to Science. J. R. Thorpe, Dec. 23, 2015) https://www.bustle.com/articles/131377-why-we-love-traditions-according-to-science

Two thousand years ago Jesus Christ came into the world to bring a doctrine by which people could be steered toward godliness by being moti-vated to love. Only in this way will people be able to espouse a higher nature, a self-denying nature predicated on the higher spiritual calling. Paul referred to this way as "the unleavened bread of sincerity and truth" in his first letter to the Corinthian church.

Therefore let us keep the feast, not with old leaven, nor with the leaven of malice and wickedness, but with the unleavened bread of sincerity and truth. (1 Cor. 5:8)

Human nature promotes a doctrinal system gravitating toward fear, doubt, and the things opposed to love. This is the natural course of un-regenerated humanity—always rooted and grounded in self-serving desires and ambitions. After a few generations any idea embraced and promoted becomes a tradition. This is true whether it is from heaven or from men. Those who receive and embrace the tradition do so by receiving and embracing the folks who advocate and promote it. This is almost always the case. In other words, it's really trust in the one who promotes the teaching that makes people fearful to turn it loose. And it's always either because of a fear of the Lord or a fear of men that people embrace a tradition connected with religion.

Most religious teachings are passed down from generation to generation. They finally evolve into family religious traditions. It's sometimes a difficult thing for people to see and to admit this obvious situation. We all want to think "our doctrine" is Bible based. But if our parents and grandparents have adhered to the teachings of a particular religious sect, chances are we will follow it as well. For example, if our parents are Catholic, it's unlikely that we'll wind up being Protestant or Jewish. We will likely be of the same persuasion. And this will hold true no matter what the religious denomination or sect might be. But it doesn't have to be this way.

Of course it is natural for children to follow the religion of their parents. This is true not because there is necessarily a greater amount of scriptural truth in the parents' doctrine, even though the children will usually believe there is. It's very difficult for people to see the errors of their family teachings. So in actuality it is much more about the power of the religious tradition within the family teaching than about the perfection of Bible knowledge within the family. So what causes the influence of family religious teaching to have this much power over its captive members? Just that! They are captive members. But those who are involved think it is because of doctrinal perfection. We have faith that the family has wisely followed the scriptures and has therefore perfected the doctrine. This is the thing one would naturally want to believe. But it is simply not the case! Doctrinal perfection is not what causes a tradition to be perpetuated through many successive generations. This should be obvious to even the most casual observer who is only seeking after truth. This should be seen by the fact that most people cling blindly to the doctrinal positions of their parents without ever really looking much into the Bible for themselves.

I once heard about a preacher who was sent to work with a small congregation in a remote, rural area in the northern part of this country. The church there had struggled for many years and the number of members was gradually decreasing as time passed. But the remaining members were very welcoming, friendly and accepting.

When the preacher got there on his first Sunday, and as he got up to speak, he noticed something very strange, which bothered him more than a little! All of the people were sitting on the same side of the building. This made him quite uncomfortable and was very distracting to him, but he assumed there must be a reason for it. He wondered what that reason could possibly be and proceeded with his message as if all was normal.

After he had ended his sermon and the invitation song had been sung, an even stranger thing happened. Every single one of the parishioners suddenly moved to the other side of the building! The next Sunday when he got up to preach, the same thing happened. All of the people were once again seated on the same side of the building where they began the previous Sunday. The preacher was absolutely bewildered! It was difficult for him to believe this actually was happening. Then again, just as the Sunday before, they all moved to the other side at the end of the sermon.

After the services were over, he took one of the young men aside and asked him why all of the members had sat on one side at the beginning of the services and then later moved to the other side. The young man said, "I really don't know—it's just always been that way—all my life." The preacher then stopped a middle-aged church leader to ask him the same question. The man responded with the same answer.

The preacher then vowed to himself he would get to the bottom of the situation. Noticing a very old sister of the congregation who was well into her nineties, he decided to ask her for the answer to the mystery. Approaching her, he presented her with the same question he had asked the young man and the middle-aged church leader. With a sweet but feeble voice she smiled and said, "Well, I'll tell you why. When I was just a child, over eighty years ago, the church met in this same building. Back then we had an old wood stove for our heat." Pointing, she said, "The stove was on that side of the building. When we would first come in, we all gathered to the side where the stove was—until we got too hot. Then we moved to the other side. After years had passed the wood burning stove was replaced with a more modern heating system, but by that time everybody was so used to moving in the middle of the service that they just kept on doing it."

Tradition is established by a myriad of conditions and circumstances. It's very easy for almost any kind of tradition to become an important part of the established norm for any group or organization. However, once the purpose of the tradition is forgotten and as time passes, it is next to impossible to distinguish the difference between it becoming an unnecessary tradition or being a vital part of the organization's work or doctrine. Some confess to knowingly keeping a religious tradition, even though they realize it has nothing to do with any biblical principle, example or rule. When asked why, they may say it is done out of love and respect for their parents, their organization or their religious affiliation. In effect, they are admitting they personally have no regard for the particular tradition, but they go along with it in order to not rock the boat shared with family and peers. But it is highly unlikely that anyone continues in a tradition only out of love or respect for parents, family or church. It is far more likely to be because of their pride, or fear of rejection from their family or the church.

The vast majority of people greatly value time-honored family traditions. These kinds of traditions usually have the strongest and most lasting influence on the lives of those keeping them. But once again, the value of the tradition is primarily determined by the value placed on those who have passed it down.

I think we all will admit that, at least to a degree, we are the product of traditions. And even though religious family traditions are usually the most sacred, they often are the most difficult to overcome. One reason for this is because traditions passed on to us through our families are from the most valued sources. Family traditions are the ones most indelibly programmed in our mind. From infancy we are constantly and repeatedly taught these ideas, many times almost to the point of being brainwashed. And at the same time we are usually taught either explicitly or by example to close our mind to all rival teachings.

According to an article I read in the Pew Forum, 72 percent of American adults follow their parents' religion in their own lives. And because of some of the reasons already mentioned, these traditions become the most difficult to reject. But sometimes rejection of them is absolutely necessary in order to seek truth. The rejection of a family tradition, especially one passed down for several generations, can feel a lot like the rejection of family itself. There are many reasons why family religious traditions are dangerous, but the greatest reason is because they can create barriers between us and God and His Word.

CHILDHOOD TEACHING

The traditional teaching I received in childhood about Judgment Day seemed very plain and simple to my young and trusting mind. As I grew up it all seemed to make perfect sense. In fact I felt a sense of comfort and security in the teaching because of the confidence I had in those who taught me. Tradition almost always gives a feeling of safety. Many times the fear of abandoning a tradition is actually spawned from insecurity. The thought of being forsaken by family, friends or the church is scary. Loyalty to tradition without resistance is usually much more comfortable.

Keeping long-held traditions will often cause folks to feel sure they are walking down the correct path. One reason is because we know those we love are walking down that same path with us. It feels right when we all walk together with no argument or dissention. We have a tendency to believe everything is okay when we know our parents and the loved ones gone before have already checked things out for us.

We also have a tendency to believe that as long as we are faithful to our tradition (which is in effect being faithful to family, church, etc.) our heart must be right with God because of our loyalty to "the faith." But fidelity to God is one thing whereas loyalty to friends and families is quite another. We must be willing to forsake everyone and everything in order to serve God. Listen to the words of Jesus.

So likewise, whoever of you does not forsake all that he has cannot be My disciple. (Luke 14:33)

Surrendering to the will of people will never prove our heart is pure before God. It will only prove loyalty to people. Our heart can only lead us in the right direction when it is programmed with the right information. Only by our faithfulness to the dictates of divine inspiration can we be assured of the proper condition of our heart. It really makes no difference how we feel about the direction we're headed if we're headed in the wrong direction. We can still wind up in the wrong place.

The heart is deceitful above all things, and desperately wicked; who can know it? (Jer. 17:9)

It is natural that children feel comfortable in believing the teaching they have received from parents and others. They are children. They are expected to embrace these teachings without question in most cases. In fact, to question a traditional teaching can feel like rebellion to a young child. After all, family and religious instructors are those whom they believe love them. Therefore, my personal acceptance of the traditions I learned in childhood was largely due to the fact that I trusted in the knowledge of those who taught me. I believe that to be true for most others as well.

I eventually came to realize that the bottom line causing me to cling so tightly to my childhood teaching was the fact that somewhere down deep inside me was a fear of being rejected by people. This was not so much of a problem during my early childhood because I never considered there might be major flaws in the teachings I had received. But it grew to be a problem as I began to mature. I began to become confused. I was beginning to realize I was mistaking love for loyalty. Again, nothing is wrong with placing a certain amount of trust in those we love. This must happen in order to establish many proper and necessary relationships in life. It is usually necessary for a child to trust his or her parents. And they will trust them as long as they experience love from them. In fact, it is completely natural for a child to believe and trust in anyone who would take care of them and love them. In my opinion, the greatest way trust is eroded or destroyed in any relationship is by a dishonest party. Truth is always the key to love and trust. If children don't trust the honesty of their parents, usually it is because of the dishonesty they detect in them. Parental dishonesty is a sure way to have a problem in a parent–child relationship. We listen most closely to those who are closest to us, and what we hear matters!

Parents and church leaders are almost always well intentioned as they pass information on to the younger generation. But good intentions don't always translate into wise counsel. A trusting heart is cultivated and molded by the reception of truth. We should always understand there is nothing particularly right or spiritual in clinging blindly to traditional information, which may or not be true. This becomes especially true when children reach a point of maturity where they can reason for themselves. When parents fail to be honest, even the maturity of a child is compromised.

There is a simple way to gauge the value or infallibility of the information we are receiving. It is by realizing all teaching comes from one of two sources. The information is received either from an *inspired* source or from one of many *uninspired* sources. The counsel of God is the only inspired source. And it is for this reason that information received from human sources must be constantly checked in light of the divine counsel of Almighty God.

As I now think of my parents and others who came before me regarding passed-down traditional beliefs, I have been made to realize we all face a similar dilemma. It is the dilemma of secondhand and unchecked information. Most of the teaching given to me by my parents was the same teaching they had received from their parents and grandparents. And when the source is someone like a parent it is easily embraced without question or further investigation. This is the natural inclination of children, and rightly so, but eventually we need to mature.

When I was a child, I spoke as a child, I understood as a child, I thought as a child; but when I became a man, I put away childish things. (1 Corinthians 13:11)

It is also true that just because our initial indoctrination comes from a parent, this does not mean it is wrong. Parents are our first and usually best human teachers. But they are only human. And because they are human, as we mature a little common sense should teach us they could be wrong. It's simply not worth taking risks about the most important matters of life. And it's never wise to allow any religious teaching to go unchallenged.

I later grew to understand that some of my childhood teaching was indeed wrong. This was not because my teachers were bad, but because they were human. Now as I entertain the idea that a traditional doctrine may be wrong, I almost always think about a statement made by the apostle Paul.

Certainly not! Indeed, let God be true but every man a liar. As it is written; "That you may be justified in your words, and may overcome when you are judged." (Romans 3:4)

The fact is that unchecked scriptural sources are the primary reason well-intended traditions gradually harden into unscriptural human doctrines. We will all individually give an account to God. Therefore we need to have a personal rather than a secondhand relationship with Him.

PREMATURE CONCLUSIONS

An incomplete set of facts will either lead us to search harder for more information or lead us to an incomplete and premature conclusion. I am completely convinced there are two vital ingredients in arriving at a more perfect conclusion, especially in spiritual matters: (1) keeping our mind open and (2) trusting in God and His Word.

See then that you walk circumspectly [i.e., "careful to consider all circumstances and possible consequences," Merriam-Webster Dictionary], not as fools but as wise. (Ephesians 5:15)

A great danger of blindly following a tradition is the possibility of coming to a conclusion prematurely. When a person believes strongly in a particular tradition and feels comfortable in the teaching that flows from it, the desire to search further is diminished. It therefore becomes much more difficult to view it in any another way than the way faith in the traditional view concludes. This leads to an incomplete set of facts.

Undiscovered and incomplete evidence is a big problem with a *closed-minded* approach to following tradition. But it doesn't have to be. We have been given the power to reason by our Creator. Reasoning occurs only when minds are opened. Then we can consume information; the information can

14

then be judged as credible or not by reasoning with what we already know. A closed mind chokes off the normal flow of information. We are only able to consider evidence we allow ourselves to be subjected to in a search for truth. It is impossible to do otherwise. So we need always to question whether we have exhausted the entire body of evidence in any matter. Reasoning, along with a sincere mind, will create an honest curiosity. We must have a *discerning* mind in our search for truth.

In his first letter to the church at Corinth, Paul talked about the proper way to participate in the Lord's Supper. He specifically elaborated on the need to "discern" the Lord's *body* by indicating this discernment is to be accomplished through self-examination or judgment.

Therefore whoever eats this bread or drinks this cup of the Lord in an unworthy manner will be guilty of the body and blood of the Lord. <u>But let a man examine himself, and so let him eat of the bread and drink of the cup.</u> For he who eats and drinks in an unworthy manner eats and drinks judgment to himself, not <u>discerning</u> the Lord's body. (1 Corinthians 11:27–29)

> *Vines Expository Dictionary* gives the following thought on the word *discerning* in verse 29, saying it "signifies to separate, discriminate; then, to learn by discriminating, to determine, decide … in 1 Cor. 11:29, with reference to partaking of the bread and the cup of the Lord's Supper unworthily, by not discerning or discriminating what they represent." (*Vines Expository Dictionary of New Testament Words*, https://studybible.info/vines)

The apostle continues in the next verse by telling the church a lack of discernment was the reason many in the church were weak, sickly and sleeping.

For this reason many are weak and sick among you, and many sleep. (1 Cor. 11:30)

No doubt Paul was speaking of a spiritual situation rather than a physical condition. The point is this: those lacking in *diligence* failed to do what was needed to "discern" the Lord's body. This caused a spiritual illness to inflict the church. The failure was clearly due to a spiritual lack of concern, which led to a state of spiritual unawareness. But it was ultimately all due to a self-inflicted inability to *discern* (learn by discriminating, determining, deciding) brought on by a failure of diligence.

Arriving at a conclusion without all of the evidence does not necessarily make our motive impure, but it always delays our finding out the whole truth of a matter. Once again, we can only consider and reason on the things we already know. And because of this, we should always keep our minds open to receive more evidence. When evidence is left undiscovered we are unlikely to arrive at the correct or complete conclusion. Many times we think we have sufficient evidence to rest our case and make a concluding decision when a lot of scriptural evidence is left behind. In other words, there may be a lot of other facts that would have a great bearing on the matter if we only knew about them. It's that simple.

We must believe God's Word has the answers to the questions that need to be answered. The truth will begin to come together as we exercise a more *diligent* effort. Diligence is an important key to finding any truth, as well as establishing our fidelity to God and His Word.

But without faith it is impossible to please Him, for he who comes to God must believe that He is, and that He is a rewarder of those who <u>diligently</u> seek Him. (Hebrews 11:6)

If additional evidence is left undiscovered, then our conclusion will probably be a premature one. So why conclude prematurely? If God has given us time for anything in the world, surely it should be used in the search for truth. The truth should be priceless to a child of God. The scriptures show truth to be invaluable, and the sale of it is forbidden.

Buy the truth and do not sell it, also wisdom and instruction and understanding. (Proverbs 23:23)

God's servants have been given access to spiritual wisdom and enlightenment. We should ask, seek and knock before arriving at a premature conclusion.

If any of you lacks wisdom, let him ask of God, who gives to all liberally and without reproach, and it will be given to him. (James 1:5)

So I say to you, ask, and it will be given to you; seek, and you will find; knock, and it will be opened to you. (Luke 11:9)

Many premature conclusions are reached because we overvalue our time-honored family or church traditions while at the same time failing to grasp the pricelessness of truth. The question is, how important is truth to us?

FLESHLY VERSUS SPIRITUAL MOTIVATION

The natural impulse of humans is to do the will of our human or fleshly nature. This is always our natural tendency. This impulse is the nature-driven response of all humanity. But it is only our personal desire or self-driven will, and it will never bring us closer to God. And, unlike being motivated by love, it only seeks out the fulfillment of its own desire. The natural self always stands in opposition to being guided by the Spirit through a love for the will of God.

Fleshly motivation causes people to insist they are correct about their religious beliefs in the face of scriptural evidence to the contrary. Natural desires, when conceived and nurtured, are invariably manifested in a self-serving attitude tantamount to a pride-filled nature. There is nothing inherently evil in desiring to be correct in our beliefs as long as the motive is pure. But pure motives are not found among those who desire and continually exercise selfish pride.

Whoever secretly slanders his neighbor, him I will destroy; the one who has a haughty look and a proud heart, him I will not endure. (Psalms 101:5)

We as humans are proud of being right in our views. But the important thing is not who is right, but what is right! Our motives must be driven by a desire for truth into the will of God!

The will of the flesh can never supply a selfless motive. No motive can be pure without love. The will of the flesh is always about what we want at the expense of everybody and everything else. A godly motive generated by love is bigger than oneself. It will be for what is true and right. It will be for what the Lord wants for our lives.

As true disciples of Jesus we can be driven by what will please the Lord. Once again, the scriptures put much more emphasis on "what is right" than on "who is right." Ultimately no one has a claim on legal or moral doctrinal perfection. Being doctrinally correct might seem all-important, but the most important value should be put on being pure in heart. Only purity of heart can take us in the direction of sound doctrine.

Blessed are the pure in heart, for they shall see God. (Matthew 5:8) Let us draw near with a true heart in full assurance of faith, having our hearts sprinkled from an evil conscience and our bodies washed with pure water. (Hebrews 10:22)

Since you have purified your souls in obeying the truth through the Spirit in sincere love of the brethren, love one another fervently with a pure heart. (1 Peter 1:22)

Even having great faith and knowledge without being motivated by love always results in dire consequences.

And though I have the gift of prophecy, and understand all mysteries and all knowledge, and though I have all faith, so that I could remove mountains, but have not love, I am nothing. (I Corinthians 13:2)

In order to find out the truth about anything, we need to care enough about the thing to sacrifice for it. Chances are we will not exert ourselves in the investigation of facts to the shedding of blood, sweat and tears unless something is very important to us. Once again, we need to understand we will only value evidence to the same degree as we value the source of the evidence. For example, if we hold our traditional church doctrine in high esteem, we will then prioritize the evidence supported by our particular fellowship or sect. The same is true with the ideas of our parents or others. We will always consider and value the evidence to the same degree as we value the source.

Many important foundational biblical truths were used and emphatically taught in my childhood for which I am very thankful. Many of these truths have given me a firm foundation on which to build and to be able to go on and learn further. But I must confess the traditional teachings of my upbringing were not always the whole counsel of God. And with traditional teaching this will always prove to be the case. The source of our counsel must be a divine source—the Word of God!

Through the years, after my spiritual rebirth and as my love and reverence for the Bible grew, my love and reverence for Jesus grew as well. I began to strongly believe it was because of Jesus that God's Word was living in me and making me alive to His will. I quit trying so hard to separate God the Father from the Holy Spirit and Jesus, and Jesus from God the Father and the Holy Spirit. In a word, I realized there was, as Paul told the Ephesians, "one God and Father of all, who is above all, and through all, and in you all" (Eph. 4:6). I also began to lose my dependency on men and traditional religion to furnish me knowledge in the things of God. I would listen to all, but I was gradually learning to put my trust in the power of the Word!

A CHILDHOOD VIEW OF JUDGMENT DAY

As I have previously indicated, a mental portrait of Judgment Day seemed very clear to my innocent childhood mind. In fact, the mental scene back then was so vivid that to further speculate or question it seemed totally unnecessary. My unwavering faith in the interpretation and analysis passed down to me through traditional teaching was my final authority in religious matters at that time.

As a child, I was especially sure my mom was correct in her views of the Bible. But even if I had not been schooled at her feet from birth to receive her bits of knowledge and instructions, I was generally fed the same regular spiritual diet at church services every Sunday. However, whether it was family teaching or at a church service, almost no one ever seemed to offer up many opposing views or questions in regard to what was being taught. This caused me to be even more certain of my childhood thinking. At the time I honestly believed in the doctrinal infallibility of the teaching I received. In actuality it was because of the confidence I had in *my* people. Almost everyone in my family and in our church circle seemed satisfied as well. And so, because of these reasons, I felt absolutely spiritually secure with the religious teachings of my childhood.

I strongly believed my early teaching was deeply rooted in the scriptures. Most everyone around me seemed to believe this as well. For example, I felt certain all of the conversations and sermons I heard about Judgment Day were backed up with solid scriptural evidence. But because of my limited biblical knowledge, I failed to see lots of other scriptures that could have further substantiated or refuted the things I was being taught about it. I could have learned many things by studying just a little deeper. But a lot of scriptures were not used. And in fact some were avoided by the preachers and teachers like the plague. Later I came to realize this happened in order to ensure that *our doctrine* could be defended.

After my conversion to Christ I continued to be surprised that much scripture that could have shed additional light on many important biblical truths was not even considered. This was no doubt due in part to what had been lost as tradition was passed down the generational ladder. But I soon began to see another reason for it. It was because of the need for doctrinal purity of the sect. Only the scriptures needed to substantiate an already existing belief are deemed necessary when we already have it all figured out. This way of presenting God's Word to the world can become a way of life. Verses are isolated and passages are circumvented in order to maintain the traditional thinking of a religious group or sect. By operating in this fashion we can boast our doctrine is pure and soon we will come to believe we have a monopoly on God and His Word. Jesus categorically condemned the Jewish religious leaders for this attitude. God doesn't require that we possess all knowledge. If that were the case no one could be acceptable to Him. But He does require a pure heart that seeks "the whole counsel of God," as well as a heart that comes to know and surrender to Him Who does have all knowledge. He requires a heart that loves truth!

Regarding the hereafter there was always one simple scripture that stuck in my mind from my youth on. This scripture was used to show how all would be judged according to their works, and it included both the saved and unsaved. This verse created a kind of foundational fact for my belief in the final judgment. In my mind at that time, and now as well, few things could have been as important in shedding scriptural light on the subject of the final judgment as this one verse.

For we must all appear before the judgment seat of Christ; that every one may receive the things done in his body, according to that he hath done, whether it be good or bad. (2 Cor. 5:10) (KJV)

There it is! Nothing could be clearer. "We must *all* appear ... that *everyone* may receive the things done in his body, *according to that he hath done, whether it be good or bad.*" This is perhaps the most emphatic and explicit verse of scripture speaking to God's judgment on the human race. But still it must be studied in light of other scriptures in order to see a complete picture of judgment. This verse gives the literal, true and plain foundational facts of God's judgment on the world. But it brings up many other questions. In other words, without knowing the whole story from the scriptures, we are prone to fill in the blanks with our own (or someone else's) traditional reasoning. This happens in many cases, and it creates a big problem!

But even by taking this verse alone we can be sure of several things. First, according to all of God's counsel on the subject, God's judgment on sin in this world will be a reality. We can be assured of this. And we can also be assured no one will escape this judgment. Another fact is that the basis for judgment on sin is in connection to the good or bad done in the life of each individual. And in addition to these simple facts, and most importantly, we must never doubt the standard for determining what is good and bad will be the Word of God and nothing else! This is an undeniable fact clearly borne out by the inspired scriptures.

So with the few scriptural evidences I had in my possession, my childish mind would continue to imagine the Judgment Day. I also clearly understood there will be a *bodily resurrection* of all of the dead, both saved and unsaved.

For the hour is coming in which all that are in the graves shall hear his voice, and shall come forth; they that have done well, unto the resurrection of life; and they that have done evil, unto the resurrection of damnation. (John 5:28–29) (KJV)

The bodily resurrection of all of the dead is a scriptural fact. I was correctly taught this from my earliest recollection and found it irrefutably confirmed by God's Word. This is simple, but very important to understand. It may sound like a no-brainer because most everyone believes it in the Christian world today. But it was a controversial issue among some of the Jews when Jesus was on earth, which may have been the reason Jesus said what He said in the verse just quoted. So the bodily resurrection of both saint and sinner is a scriptural fact that cannot be denied and will provide a lot of intriguing thought to deal with in the overall scheme of redemption as we continue. We now have foundational facts on which to begin to build.

As time continued the Judgment Day picture in my mind began to be somewhat redrawn. Although I continued to draw from my earlier scripturally confirmed evidences as I envisioned Judgment Day, I also began to examine other passages that were equally clear and undeniable. At first I only looked for the clear and literal things that were explicit and without controversy. I was still unaware of the fact that while using other scriptural evidences more and more for my proof, I was also still inadvertently adding in things already stored in my traditional mindset. I was unintentionally trying to connect the dots with centuries of traditional thought steeped in philosophy, heathen custom and scriptures not rightly divided.

But, as a child, and with the information I had, this is the way I saw Judgment Day in my mind. First, Jesus would come back and everyone living would see Him. Next, all of the dead would be resurrected from their graves. Then in my mind's eye I would always see a long line of people stretching across the sky. To me, at that time, this line of humanity represented all of the people who had ever lived on the earth. They waited until their time came to appear before the judgment throne of Almighty God. And when their turn finally came, they stood trembling and completely humbled before the awesome power of the Almighty Judge of the earth. They were waiting to see whether they would be saved or lost. Next came the opening of the books of the Bible. The books contained all of the laws of God. It was at that time that all of life's deeds, both good and bad, were revealed by God in the presence of the entire world! It was in this way that all of the works of every life were compared with the law of God.

This was the way my mind envisioned all humanity being judged. All individuals were judged as to whether they were worthy to be saved or lost. I believed this was to be determined by the amount of good versus the amount of bad in their life. If there were more good deeds in their lives than bad, they would be eternally saved and get to go to heaven. If there were more bad deeds in their lives than good, they were condemned to hellfire to suffer forever! After the pronouncement of judgment by the Almighty, the righteous souls were placed on the right-hand side of the throne and the unrighteous on the left. The saved were then allowed to enter heaven for eternity, but the wicked were cast alive into the lake of fire to be tortured or tormented forever. This was my traditional thinking about Judgment Day.

I doubt my childhood idea of the final judgment varies drastically from what millions of other children have grown up believing. I feel certain Christian human masses have accepted a handed-down, traditional, orthodox view of Judgment Day without much investigation as to its validity. It has been sprinkled down with carefully selected scriptures in order to strengthen its already codified doctrinal views. This is always the end result of binding religious traditions that do not proceed from the counsel of God. Paul, in writing to the Galatian Christians, made an interesting observation of his own life before his conversion by the following statement.

And I advanced in Judaism beyond many of my contemporaries in my own nation, being more exceedingly zealous for the traditions of my fathers. (Gal. 1:14)

Many people never see what the scriptures really teach in connection to Judgment Day and many other important truths. A lot of people blindly follow their sectarian practices and spiritual leaders. And there are those in religious leadership roles who knowingly will profit in a fleshly way by perpetuating the traditional sectarian teachings of the fathers of their sect. But there will always be those who take the Word seriously and look to God rather than man for instructions in righteousness.

CONCLUDING THOUGHT

I was one of twelve kids born to my parents. I was not the most talented or the smartest, nor was I the best looking. But I think perhaps I was the one with the greatest curiosity. As a four-year-old kid, I would follow my mom around the house as she busily did her housework, asking her questions by the score. She would usually patiently answer them to my satisfaction. But on a few occasions she would pause, turn toward me and say, "You ask too many questions." When this happened, I sometimes never received an answer to my question. It was only when I got older that I realized she didn't have all the answers!

When I was a child, I spoke as a child, I understood as a child, I thought as a child; but when I became a man, I put away childish things. (1 Corinthians 13:11)

CHAPTER 2
THE GREAT I AM

It is written: "'as surely as I live,' says the Lord, 'every knee will bow before me; every tongue will acknowledge God.'" (Romans 14:11)

Someday all of creation will yield to the almighty power of the Creator. Someday all of creation will kneel before Him. And someday all tongues will confess that only through and by Him is all power and honor and glory derived. He alone is the Great I Am!

THE NAME OF GOD

Then Moses said to God, "Indeed, when I come to the children of Israel and say to them, 'The God of your fathers has sent me to you,' and they say to me, 'What is His name?' what shall I say to them?" And God said to Moses, "I AM WHO I AM." And He said, "Thus you shall say to the children of Israel, 'I AM has sent me to you.'"(Exodus 3:13–14)

Moses was the man God chose to deliver the children of Israel from their long and agonizing bondage in Egypt. The scriptures record that while Moses was tending the flock of his father-in-law, Jethro, and leading the flock to the back of the desert he came to Horeb, the mountain of God. It was there he observed a flame burning from the midst of a bush without causing the bush to be harmed or consumed. The awesomeness of the scene aroused his curiosity and caused him to turn toward the bush to observe the sight. It was at that time the Lord spoke to him from the burning bush.

So when the Lord saw that he turned aside to look, God called to him from the midst of the bush and said, "Moses, Moses!" And he said, "Here I am." Then He said, "Do not draw near this place. Take your sandals off your feet, for the place where you stand is holy ground." Moreover He said, "I am the God of your father—the God of Abraham, the God of Isaac, and the God of Jacob." And Moses hid his face, for he was afraid to look upon God. (Exodus 3:4–6)

During this fearful and unnerving encounter with the Lord God, Moses was informed he would be sent to Pharaoh of Egypt to convince Pharaoh to let God's people go free from their bondage and leave Egypt.

And the Lord said: "I have surely seen the oppression of My people who are in Egypt, and have heard their cry because of their taskmasters, for I know their sorrows. So I have come down to deliver them out of the hand of the Egyptians, and to bring them up from that land to a good and large land, to a land flowing with milk and honey, to the place of the Canaanites and the Hittites and the Amorites and the Perizzites and the Hivites and the Jebusites. Now therefore, behold, the cry of the children of Israel has come to Me, and I have also seen the oppression with which the Egyptians oppress them. Come now, therefore, and I will send you to Pharaoh that you may bring My people, the children of Israel, out of Egypt." (Exodus 3:7–10)

At first Moses was hesitant to accept this mission. He seemed unable to fathom being God's deliverer of this great multitude of people. The following verses give us an account of the conversation between Moses and the Lord. Moses is finally convinced to go to Pharaoh. This was the time and place God declared to Moses the great name of the Almighty, which was to be His name forever.

But Moses said to God, "Who am I that I should go to Pharaoh, and that I should bring the children of Israel out of Egypt?" So He said, "I will certainly be with you. And this shall be a sign to you that I have sent you: When you have brought the people out of Egypt, you shall serve God on this mountain." Then Moses said to God, "Indeed, when I come to the children of Israel and say to them, 'The God of your fathers has sent me to you,' and they say to me, 'What is His name?' what shall I say to them?" And God said to Moses, "<u>I AM WHO I AM</u>." And He said, "Thus you shall say to the children of Israel, '<u>I AM has sent me to you</u>.'" Moreover God said to Moses, "Thus you shall say to the children of Israel: 'The Lord God of your fathers, the God of Abraham, the God of Isaac, and the God of Jacob, has sent me to you. This is My name forever, and this is My memorial to all generations." (Exodus 3:11–15)

God seemed to have had at least two purposes in telling Moses to inform the children of Israel that "I AM has sent me to you." First, God wanted His people to know that there was still a "God of their fathers" after more than four hundred years in Egypt. Second, He wanted them to know the true name of the God of their fathers. "I am" was to be the answer to their question as to the name of the God of their fathers.

The Lord God Almighty is designated by a great number of names and titles in the Bible. However, in God's conversation with Moses it is made clear there is to be a supreme name or designation, and the Lord wanted His people to know that name and what it means. This name was to be used to designate the <u>ONLY</u> one true Lord God Almighty, completely ruling out all other gods or powers. God told Moses, "This is my name forever." He also told him, "This is my memorial to all generations." It seems that now, when Israel is about to be delivered from Egypt, it would be imperative for the Israelites to fully understand who it was who brought them out of bondage and established them as a nation of the people of God.

Listen now as the Lord gives further details to Moses concerning the deliverance of Israel from Egyptian bondage, while at the same time impressing on the mind of Moses the importance of Israel knowing His name.

Then the Lord said to Moses, "Now you shall see what I will do to Pharaoh. For with a strong hand he will let them go, and with a strong hand he will drive them out of his land." And God spoke to Moses and said to him: "I am the Lord (or YHWH). I appeared to Abraham, to Isaac, and to Jacob, as God Almighty, but by My name Lord (YHWH) I was not known to them." (Exodus 6:1–3)

God tells Moses He is *YHWH*. This is a unique Hebrew word translated simply as Lord in these two places in the passage just quoted. Why was God so insistent about establishing His name as *YHWH* at this particular time for Moses and the children of Israel? And why was the Lord not known to Abraham, Isaac and Jacob by the name *YHWH* when He had conversed with them hundreds of years before the time of Moses? Obviously it was not because God had failed to tell them His name. More than likely it was the failure of Abraham, Isaac and Jacob to comprehend His awesome and uniquely powerful characteristics, characteristics of the one and only almighty power that was intended to be conveyed by the name. Today the concept of an almighty being remains a problem for many professing Christians.

From the time of Moses the Jews actually did use the word *YHWH* for God's name. Later they began to use it with vowels added, making it *YAHWEH*. Finally the name came to be regarded by Jews as too sacred to be spoken. Then it was only written, rather than orally uttered. The Jews finally completely replaced *YHWH* with other names when speaking of God.

Following is a brief article from *Encyclopedia Britannica* on *Yahweh (YHWH)*.

Yahweh, name for the God of the Israelites, representing the biblical pronunciation of "YHWH," the Hebrew name revealed to Moses in the book of Exodus. The name YHWH, consisting of the sequence of consonants Yod, Heh, Waw, and Heh, is known as the tetragrammaton.

After the Babylonian Exile (6th century BCE), and especially from the 3rd century BCE on, Jews ceased to use the name Yahweh for two reasons. As Judaism became a universal rather than merely a local religion, the more common Hebrew noun Elohim (plural in form but understood in the singular), meaning "God," tended to replace Yahweh to demonstrate the universal sovereignty of Israel's God over all others. At the same time, the divine name was increasingly regarded as too sacred to be uttered; it was thus replaced vocally in the synagogue ritual by the Hebrew word *Adonai ("My Lord"), which was translated as Kyrios ("Lord") in the Septuagint, the Greek version of the Hebrew Scriptures.* "Yahweh" (*Encyclopedia Britannica*, www. britannica.com/topic/Yahweh)

It was in the conversation God had with Moses as recorded in the third chapter of Exodus that the name *Yahweh* is best known from the scriptures. From this great "I am" conversation God's all powerful, eternal and ever-present existence becomes evident with the words "I am." God has always existed and will always exist. Even though this is true, His eternal existence is not the only point of fact in the understanding of the meaning of *Yahweh*.

In the ancient world names communicated something about a person's character. So a name carried great meaning. In God's infinite sovereignty He chose to reveal Himself in the name *Yahweh*. Consequently it could be expected that this name was given in order to communicate a more full understanding about the eternal power in the character of *Yahweh*. To understand something of the true characteristics of the one and only Creator is to understand the greater purpose for His name. According to Exodus 3:13–14, Moses asks God, "Whom should I say has sent me?" God responds by saying, "I AM that I AM… You must say this to the Israelites, 'I AM has sent me to you.'"

I AM HE

Jesus used similar language when speaking with the Pharisees. The Pharisees were a Jewish religious sect. In His conversation with them Jesus says the following: "Your father Abraham rejoiced to see My day, and he saw it and was glad." Then the Jews said to Him, "You are not yet fifty years old, and have You seen Abraham?' Jesus said to them, 'Most assuredly, I say to you, before Abraham was, I AM." (John 8:56–58).

Jesus here is referring to Himself in the same way as the Lord instructed Moses to reintroduce the "God of their fathers" to the children of Israel in Egypt. Jesus says, "…before Abraham was, I AM." Jesus obviously wanted the Jewish leaders to understand that His prior, pre-earthly existence was in some way the same as His Father's existence. His was an existence as one with God, and as God as well. This truth is borne out in the two following verses recorded by His disciple John.

In the beginning was the Word, and the Word was with God, and the Word was God. (John 1:1) That which was from the beginning, which we have heard, which we have seen with our eyes, which we have looked at and our hands have touched—this we proclaim concerning the Word of life. (1 John 1:1)

The preexistence of that which became Jesus can only be identified with the Word, which was with God and was God. It would also be identified with the power of life through the Word. As John states, "this we proclaim concerning the Word of life." Jesus also later said, "I am the way, the truth and the life" (John 14:6).

In addition to this, Jesus wanted the Jewish religious leaders to know Abraham had witnessed what Jesus referred to as "My day" and rejoiced. This was incomprehensible to them since Abraham had been dead for hundreds of years. It would seem to mean either that Abraham existed at the time Jesus was speaking, or that Jesus was old enough to have known Abraham. Jesus seemed to be referring to His earthly existence by speaking of "My day."

But He also said, "...before Abraham was, I am." Listen as Jesus confirms the conscious present existence of Abraham, Isaac and Jacob after physical death, as he speaks of them in the present tense.

I am the God of Abraham, the God of Isaac, and the God of Jacob. God is not the God of the dead, but of the living. (Matt. 22:32)

Abraham, Isaac and Jacob were physically dead (disembodied) at the time the Lord spoke these words. When we say they were dead, we speak only of the condition of their physical bodies. Their spirits had departed from their bodies long before this time. The New Testament writer James says the body without the spirit is dead. But the spirit remains alive after it exits the body. The spirit of humans departs from the body at the time of physical death. Humans remain in a disembodied state until the time of the resurrection of the body at the return of Jesus to earth.

That which eventually became Jesus had existed as the Word, with God, in the days of Abraham. The spirit of Abraham remained conscious after his physical death and therefore could rejoice in seeing Jesus' day, or the time of His life. This is also seen in the narration of Lazarus and the rich man's death. The rich man, after physical death, spoke to Abraham about the condition of his brothers still on the earth. He was conscience and aware of things on earth.

Then he said, "I beg you therefore, father, that you would send him to my father's house, for I have five brothers that he may testify to them, lest they also come to this place of torment." Abraham said to him, "They have Moses and the prophets; let them hear them." And he said, "No, father Abraham; but if one goes to them from the dead, they will repent." But he said to him, "If they do not hear Moses and the prophets, neither will they be persuaded though one rise from the dead." (Luke 16:27–31)

When Jesus was betrayed by Judas, and as He was being captured by the Roman soldiers and the Jewish officers, He spoke, using this most powerful phrase of declaration, saying, "I am He." Upon hearing these words his pursuers were momentarily stunned as though they had been afflicted by a supernatural power.

Jesus therefore, knowing all things that would come upon Him, went forward and said to them, "Whom are you seeking?" They answered Him, "Jesus of Nazareth." Jesus said to them, "I am He." And Judas, who betrayed Him, also stood with them. Now when He said to them, "I am He," they drew back and fell to the ground. (John 18:4–6)

It would be foolish for anyone to claim to understand all of the implications of this statement regarding the Great I Am. But we can know this was a very powerful statement proclaimed by God to Moses, and later by Jesus to those seeking to destroy Him. The statement was obviously meant to convey a more complete picture regarding the unique power of God. And when the message of God's name was conveyed to the people of Israel, it was to allow them to know it was a power without exception and without limit. And it ultimately was meant to show the unlimited power of the Father being transferred to His only begotten Son through the power of the Word as well.

I am persuaded that the most basic implication of the words "I am" would be that God dwells in a realm far beyond our human existence in a state of being that is far beyond what human minds have the ability to comprehend. His existence is one that is continually ever present, not governed by the limitations of mortal existence. Mortal existence is only temporarily maintained. It is limited through the destructive effects of the human system of time. These temporal things have no effect on the Great I Am.

Once while talking about Abraham's faith being the reason the Almighty accepted and blessed him, Paul speaks about God having the power to exist in the past, present and future without regard to the effects of time. Things such as this are things we can only accept. We cannot understand them. By accepting what the scriptures say, it seems that in the realm of God's domain nothing is really past or future, but His existence and knowledge are always in the present—*I am.*

At a certain point in time, which could also be referred to as a place in the history of human time or endurance, God promised Abraham He would bless him with many nations of posterity because of his faith. But before any of the promise had been carried out through the chronicles of finite time, the Lord made reference to the fulfillment of the promise as having already happened.

(As it is written, "I <u>have</u> made you a father of many nations") in the presence of Him whom he believed—God, who gives life to the dead and calls those things which do not exist as though they did. (Romans 4:17)

God tells Abraham "I have" made (rather than "I will" make) him a father of many nations. He could do this because the Almighty is not limited by time, space or matter. Simply put, the existence of *deity* is not governed or affected by time. This obviously was the pre-earthly existence of "that" as stated in 1 John 1:1. "That" was called the Word. "That" was with God and was God in a pre-earthly existence. "That" became flesh and became the Son of God in His earthly existence. This allowed "that" (the Word) to be heard and seen and touched.

<u>That</u> which was from the beginning, which we have heard, which we have seen with our eyes, which we have looked upon, and our hands have handled, concerning the Word of life— the life was manifested, and we have seen, and bear witness, and declare to you that eternal life which was with the Father and was manifested to us. (1 John 1:1–2)

"That" which became Jesus had always existed. That (the Word) was without beginning. And that was the Word that became flesh. The Word that became Jesus was with God and was God, as John recorded in his gospel. "That" was the Word (Greek *logos*) and it was that which was with God (though not existing independently as the Son or a separate person at the time, but was God). That was the Great I Am, Creator of all things.

I see no indication that the Word of life, although existing with God from the beginning, was separate from God in any way in a pre-earthly existence. Jesus could say He was with God and that He came from His Father because the Word was with God and was made flesh to become the only begotten of the Father. I believe the scriptures are absolutely silent in order to show that the Word existed separately from God before it became flesh as Jesus the Son. By the power of this same Word the worlds were framed. But it was not necessary for the Word to be separated into more than one being of deity to accomplish the work of creation. Therefore to say the worlds were framed by the Word of God is to say they were formed by the Word that became flesh— that which became Jesus, the Son of God.

By faith we understand that the worlds were framed by the word of God, so that the things which are seen were not made of things which are visible. (Heb. 11:3)

The unique *inherent ability* to create something from nothing was possible only through the absolute power and deity of a single Creator. And in the same manner, the unique procreative or generative ability to join deity with humanity was achieved only through the power of the Great I Am. I believe this to be the unequivocal testimony of God's Word.

Prior to the birth of Jesus, both God and the Word (which was God) were the Great I Am. The Word was with God, and the Word was God. The Word (which was God) existed as one being by virtue of the power and deity of God only. But now God has a Son. This happened through the unique procreation of deity and humanity having commingled. It was in this way Jesus became the only begotten Son of the Father—*the Word was made flesh.* The Son of God is now reigning in all the power and glory of His Father.

Now in God's kingdom, Jesus upholds all things (the creation) by the Word of His power. This can only be accomplished by Him being the express *image of God's person* (the only begotten Son and the only true heir of deity).

Therefore the unique name of *YAHWEH* or *I Am* would apply to the Son as well as the Father by way of the power of procreative deity.

[God] has in these last days spoken to us by His Son, whom He has appointed heir of all things, through whom also He made the worlds; who being the brightness of His glory and the express image of His person, and upholding all things by the word of His power, when He had by Himself purged our sins, sat down at the right hand of the Majesty on high. (Hebrews 1:2–3)

This would also account for Jesus being referred to as "that … concerning the Word of life." John did not use the words "Son" or "Jesus" in the following verse, but he chose to use the word "that" in reference to the Word of life. After His birth Jesus was referred to as both the Son of Man and the Son of God.

* <u>That</u> which was from the beginning, which we have heard, which we have seen with our eyes, which we have looked upon, and our hands have handled, concerning the Word of life (1 Jn. 1:1)

The Merriam-Webster Dictionary defines *deity* in the following way: "(a) the rank or essential nature of a god." Some English translations of the Bible use the word *Godhead* while others use the word *deity*. Traditional use of the word *Godhead* creates the connotation of a pluralistic deity, which in my estimation was not the intention of the writers of inspiration. An example of this can be seen in the New King James Version (NKJV) of the Bible in Colossians 2:9. Here it is translated as follows:

For in Him (Christ) dwells all the fullness of the Godhead bodily (in bodily form).

The true meaning of the verse is to convey the idea that in the body of Jesus all of the fullness of God or *deity* is present. In translations that use *deity* the verse would in no way indicate that God or *deity* is pluralistic, but rather show the completeness or fullness of the deity of God in Christ. It would simply be stating that all of the fullness of the deity of God dwells in Jesus. In Christ resides an unlimited measure of the power of the Holy Spirit of God.

He who has received His testimony has certified that God is true. For He whom God has sent speaks the words of God, for God does not give the Spirit by measure. The Father loves the Son, and has given all things into His hand. (John 3:33–35)

The use of *deity* or *divinity* gives a clearer understanding. For this reason I primarily use *deity* or *divinity*. In the days of my childhood, however, I never thought much about the Godhead. I occasionally heard the word *Godhead* in the reading of the scriptures, but I really didn't have much of an idea as to what it meant. I never thought of God as being three persons or beings, all coequal, but together making up one God. I believed there was one God, in one being, and that He had a Son named Jesus. In other words, I was brought up to believe there was simply one God, and that He, through Mary, produced His Son, Jesus.

As I wrote about quite extensively in the first chapter, tradition has always played a major part in what we think, say and do. Our view of God, when disconnected from scripture, is a product of an evolving web of tradition beginning all the way back with Adam and Eve in the Garden of Eden. In Eden God had commanded Adam and Eve to abstain from eating of the tree of knowledge of good and evil.

Then the Lord God took the man and put him in the Garden of Eden to tend and keep it. And the Lord God commanded the man, saying, "Of every tree of the garden you may freely eat; but of the tree of the knowledge of good and evil you shall not eat, for in the day that you eat of it you shall surely die." (Genesis 2:15–17)

Immediately after this single, explicit command the subtle serpent of godlessness deceived our first parents with the first lie the scriptures record. This was no doubt done by Satan in order to cast a negative reflection of God into the minds of our first human ancestors.

Now the serpent was more cunning than any beast of the field which the Lord God had made. And he said to the woman, "Has God indeed said, 'you shall not *eat of every tree of the garden'?" And the woman said to the serpent, "We may eat the fruit of the trees of the garden; but of the fruit of the tree which is in the midst of the garden, God has said, 'You shall not eat it, nor shall you touch it, lest you die.'" Then the serpent said to the woman, "<u>You will not surely die</u>. For God knows that in the day you eat of it your eyes will be opened and you will be like God, knowing good and evil." So when the woman saw that the tree was good for food, that it was pleasant to the eyes, and a tree desirable to make one wise, she took of its fruit and ate. She also gave to her husband with her, and he ate. (Genesis 3:1–6)*

It was through this manipulative deception that the purpose of Satan was revealed as twofold. The first purpose was his desire that humans would forfeit living in peace and harmony with their Creator. He accomplished this aim by deceiving Mother Eve into believing his lie and breaking God's commandment, and at the same time he sought to convince her the Creator was the real manipulator.

But perhaps the chief goal of the devil was to show a diminished love and mercy of God toward His creation in the minds of Adam and Eve. This he achieved by casting the shadow of a less than loving and compassionate Creator. In both these endeavors the devil is still at work today. Satan deceived humanity into believing the truth was a lie and a lie was the truth. And in doing so, the devil cast an unholy reflection on the love of God. Satan then defied God and deceived man with the lie that has resounded throughout all future ages—*you will not surely die!*

After Adam and Eve sinned God subjected all of creation to the cursed consequences of sin. This was actually the beginning of the work of redemption and restoration to be accomplished through His Son who would come into the world. Not only humanity but all of creation was made to partake of the pain and death that could only be alleviated by the Redeemer. I take up the task of proving God's love for His creation in more depth in one of the following chapters, entitled "The Restoration of All Things."

Without the love of God manifest through the innocent sacrifice of His only begotten Son, the law of sin and death would condemn the entire world forever. This law governing the consequences of sin, without Christ, is as sure as the law of sowing and reaping. The result of sowing is to reap that which is sown, and the result of sin is death. But the mind of a loving and merciful Almighty Creator had predetermined that redemption and restoration would be made available through the innocent sacrifice of His only begotten Son. Because of His plan of redemption He spoke the following words (about the Redeemer to come) to that old serpent almost immediately after man's sin and subsequent fall.

And I will put enmity between you and the woman, and between your seed and her Seed; He shall bruise your head, and you shall bruise His heel. (Genesis 3:15)

Redemption and restoration! Redemption would be for the people who had sinned like Adam and Eve. They could find redemption from the law of sin and death through the redemptive work of Jesus. Those obtaining redemption were and are those whom God foreknew, and by His foreknowledge He knew they would be conformed to the image of His Son. Restoration would be for the rest of the creation that was innocently subjected to the curse of one man's sin. Paul beautifully summed up God's plan for man's redemption in his letter to the Roman church. This loving act of God's sovereign power would allow freedom from the law of sin and death through the law of the Spirit of life in Jesus.

There is therefore now no condemnation to those who are in Christ Jesus, who do not walk according to the flesh, but according to the Spirit. For the law of the Spirit of life in Christ Jesus has made me free from the law of sin and death. (Romans 8:1–2)

Those who were predetermined through God's foreknowledge to become conformed to the image of His Son had been chosen in Christ before the foundation of the world. This could have been accomplished only through the sovereign power of the foreknowledge of God. These who were predetermined were to be forever glorified with His Son. However, this would in no way rule out the power of choice of those He would sanctify, but it would show the power of God in devising redemption for them through the omnipotent foreknowledge of a loving Creator.

Just as He chose us in Him before the foundation of the world, that we should be holy and without blame before Him in love. (Eph. 1:4)

In the eighth chapter of Romans Paul makes plain God's plan of grace through the divine foreknowledge of God.

And we know that all things work together for good to those who love God, to those who are the called according to His purpose. For whom He foreknew, He also predestined to be conformed to the image of His Son, that He might be the firstborn among many brethren. Moreover whom He predestined, these He also called; whom He called, these He also justified; and whom He justified, these He also glorified. (Romans 8:28–30)

Those who were foreknown and thereby predestined for redemption were known only to God through the complete foreknowledge possessed by His divine power.

Nevertheless the solid foundation of God stands, having this seal: "The Lord knows those who are His," and, "Let everyone who names the name of Christ depart from iniquity." (2 Tim. 2:19)

Things that are impossible for the creation, such as foreknowledge, are fully possible through the deified power of the Creator.

Even though Adam and Eve were mortals, as long as they would have continued to obey God and remain sinless their lives would have continued. However, the entrance of sin into the world changed all that. Because Adam and Eve ate of the tree and rejected the counsel of God, without redemption they would die. It was by the sin in eating of the forbidden tree that death entered into the world. This was the law of sin and death. From that time forward death and the consequences of sin continued for all. All of creation was placed under sin's curse. Without redemption freeing humanity from the law of sin and death the result would be eternal death.

Therefore, just as through one man sin entered the world, and death through sin, and thus death spread to all men, because all sinned. (Romans 5:12)

The wages (price paid) for sin would be death, either of the sinner or of the redeemer. This law of sin and death would affect the relationship of the Creator and the creation in a very profound way. In order to satisfy divine justice, the only penalty for sin would be the just sentence of death. Without a plan of redemption satisfying the only justice acceptable to the Creator, all creation would be sentenced to death without remedy. Divine justice was completely satisfied and the debt was completely paid by Jesus on the cross. Those trusting in the blood of Christ would be redeemed.

THERE IS ONLY ONE GOD

In examining whether the concept of one God is truth or fallacy, I can see only three possible options.

1. *There is no god.*

2. *There is more than one god.*

3. *There is only one God.*

Our only source of proof is the authenticity of the Bible. There is no doubt as to the testimony of the scriptures in connection to whether there is a true, living God. God's eternal existence is explicitly taught in the scriptures in a thousand ways. The story of God is what the Bible is all about. The holy words of inspiration are clear, teaching there is only *one* true and living God.

However, within the minds of some, ideas of no god and many gods continue to be entertained and promoted. Paul, as he writes to the Roman church, speaks of the rejection of God in the minds of a part of humanity. In this discourse he deals with the awful consequences of that rejection as well. The primary goal for my writing this particular chapter is to establish and promote the one, true and living God of the Bible.

Paul begins to build his case on the premise that to reject the existence of God is inexcusable, willful ignorance. Man was created with a fleshly nature and therefore subject to temptation and sin. However, man was not created with an inherent nature to reject the idea of a Creator. Actually the Bible teaches quite the opposite.

An interesting statement is made in John 1:9. The writer seems to indicate that all people born are given *light* or enlightenment in some way.

That (Jesus) was the true Light which gives light to every man coming into the world. (NKJV)

Translations vary regarding this verse. The King James Version (KJV) says, "That was the true Light, which lighteth every man that cometh into the world." This would seem to indicate that Jesus *lights* each person at birth. The NKJV version, although worded somewhat differently, indicates the same. But many, perhaps most, translations indicate that it is Jesus who is coming into the world, giving light to all. For example, the translation of the Modern Literal Version (MLV) is worded, "There was the true light, the light which illuminates every man, coming into the world." Here, it is difficult to determine whether the phrase "coming into the world" refers to Jesus or every man. The Modern English Version (MEV) says, "The true Light, which enlightens everyone, was coming into the world." This version shows Jesus, who was coming into the world, would enlighten everybody. Many versions agree with this wording.

But whether it is Jesus or everyone coming into the world, there is no disagreement as to *every man* being enlightened or illuminated. The light received could not mean natural physical life. Jesus' coming into the world only caused spiritual life or enlightenment. Humanity already possessed natural physical life or enlightenment. So Jesus in some fashion has given spiritual enlightenment to everyone. I believe this enlightenment must have been faith in a Creator; created inherent in the individual. Faith in God is not something to acquire just by knowledge, but it is inherently created within each individual. Each individual will either follow that faith into a relationship with his Creator or finally reject it.

Paul shows the existence of a Creator is made glaringly obvious and inexcusable by the visible facts in the power of creation. He maintains that the invisible attributes of the Creator are clearly seen by the things that are made, thus proving the eternal power and deity of the Almighty. To reject these evidences is *inexcusable* before a just and all-knowing supreme Creator. To reject the evidences is also to *suppress* the source of all spiritual truth.

For the wrath of God is revealed from heaven against all ungodliness and unrighteousness of men, who <u>suppress</u> the truth in unrighteousness, because what may be known of God is manifest in them, for God has shown it to them. For since the creation of the world His invisible attributes are clearly seen, being understood by the things that are made, even His eternal power and Godhead, so that they are without excuse. (Romans 1:18–20)

Paul strongly asserts that this willful rejection of God will invariably result in the degeneration of the human conscience into shameless moral depravity as long as an ongoing and continual rejection of God is cultivated within the mind.

Because, although they knew God, they did not glorify Him as God, nor were thankful, but became futile in their thoughts, and their foolish hearts were darkened. Professing to be wise, they became fools, and changed the glory of the incorruptible God into an image made like corruptible man—and birds and four-footed animals and creeping things. (Romans 1:21–23)

Man has always desired to worship someone or something. He will either seek after the Almighty and the singular power of his Creator by striving to please and worship Him, or he will seek to worship something else, sometimes even multiple powers, in order to please himself. Since the eternal power and deity of God are clearly seen and understood by viewing God's creative power, the rejection of the Almighty is inexcusable.

When the human mind goes down this slippery slope of depraved infidelity, anything and everything can become an object of perverted worship through lust. Worship that is truly spiritual and holy comes by knowing and glorifying God and by possessing a heart filled with love and gratitude to and for Him. When worship is turned from the Creator to the creature, God will eventually allow these depraved hearts to be given over to their own impenitent, lustful desires. These hearts have purposely been cultivated in opposition to love and reverence for the Almighty.

Therefore God also gave them up to uncleanness, in the lusts of their hearts, to dishonor their bodies among themselves, who exchanged the truth of God for the lie, and worshiped and served the creature rather than the Creator, who is blessed forever. Amen. (Romans 1:24–25)

There is no bottom to the depths of evil to which the mind of created man can descend when the dictates of a godless mindset are pursued. There is a point, known only to God, when man's Creator will withdraw His presence from that mind and allow only its natural course to continue. During the antediluvian period God saw that *the imaginations of men were only evil continually.* At that time some people were living almost a thousand years on the earth. This may account not only for the proliferating number of people on the planet but also for the proliferated effects of degenerated imaginations. In other words, there was plenty of time for the complete degeneration of minds. After the flood God drastically shortened the lifespan of humanity.

However, in His great mercy, God will only allow this natural course of depravity to be turned over to its own wicked devices when every other recourse of a loving Creator has been exhausted. Today God's only presence and assistance to humanity is through His Son, Jesus. How far will Jesus go in helping us remain faithful to God? He, as the prophet has told us, will not give up as long as any bit of hope remains.

A bruised reed He will not break, and smoking flax He will not quench; He will bring forth justice for truth. (Isa. 42:3)

A dear brother in Christ once told me that departing from the knowledge of God is like venturing out into an ocean. He said at first it may seem pleasant. You can easily wade out for a considerable distance. Finally, if you continue onward, you must swim. Even swimming may seem enjoyable for a while. But then a point will come where you will not have the physical ability to return. When this happens, and when there is nothing or no one to rescue you, you will perish.

Beware, brethren, lest there be in any of you an evil heart of unbelief in departing from the living God. (Heb. 3:12)

The most obvious and flagrant example of suppression of truth is suppressing the truth of the existence of the one and only true God as Creator of all things. Every false religion, as well as every evil, develops as a result of the rejection of God. Man's defiance and rebellion against God originate from a mind that stubbornly rejects truth. It is the desire of God that no one should perish, but God's Spirit will not continue with man when man's will is to suppress truth by denying God's existence and power.

THE HOLY SPIRIT OF GOD, IS GOD

Through the years, one thing that has continued to bother me greatly is the traditional view of deity. The first thing I would like to discuss is whether the Holy Spirit of God is a separate person or a distinct being from Almighty God, the Father of Jesus. I fail to find this "separate but equal" doctrine taught within the inspired pages of holy writ. In fact, I believe the exact opposite is taught. However, this idea has evolved into a nearly universal belief within professing Christianity, affecting the vision of folks in seeing God's sovereignty.

In the beginning of the Christian age there were no differing opinions among the New Testament writers about the Holy Spirit of God. In the inspired gospel writings and letters, all of the writers seem in harmony about what or who the Holy Spirit of God was and is. In the scriptures the Holy Spirit is conveyed to the mind of readers in both the Old and New Testaments as the Spirit of God. It was not until the post-apostolic period that the separate being controversy began to gain strength among church leaders. By the time of the Roman emperor Constantine the Holy Trinity concept began to be codified in creedal form within the Roman church.

> The Council of Nicaea, the first ecumenical debate held by the early Christian church, concludes with the establishment of the doctrine of the Holy Trinity. Convened by Roman Emperor Constantine I in May, the council also deemed the Arian belief of Christ as inferior to God as heretical, thus resolving an early church crisis. www.history.com/this-day-in-history/council-of-nicaea-concludes; Council of Nicaea concludes - HISTORY

The decision of the church to mandate a creed of faith in the Trinity was added after the death of the inspired apostles of Christ. It was also clearly aided and sanctioned by Constantine and the Roman state. I deal more with the origin of the Trinity later on.

I have never had a problem in understanding that Jesus, from His birth forward, is a separate entity from God, His Father. All of the scriptures attest to this truth. He was Jesus Christ, the begotten Son of God. But in contemplating the possibility of the Holy Spirit being a separate person from God Almighty, I honestly fail to find that the Bible teaches or infers any such separation.

However, with Jesus, even though the Bible doesn't talk about Jesus as God the Son, it does talk about Jesus as a different being or person than His Father. The Father was God, whereas Jesus was the Son of God. But this separation is spoken of only after the birth of Jesus. There is no separation of being, in my opinion, ever spoken of in connection with the Holy Spirit of God and God, the Father of Jesus.

I have heard people talk about the Holy Spirit (or Holy Ghost [KJV]) all of my life. But never once in my growing up years do I remember hearing the phrase "God the Holy Spirit." Not that it would be incorrect to refer to God as the Holy Spirit, because certainly He is that. And it would be correct as well to refer to the Holy Spirit as God, because the Holy Spirit is the Spirit of God.

God is Spirit, and those who worship Him must worship in spirit and truth. (John 4:24)

It would be incorrect to refer to God the Holy Spirit in order to convey the idea of the Holy Spirit being separated from God into another being or person. In talking about the Spirit of God we might use this analogy. It would be like talking about the spirit of John as opposed to talking about John's body. In either case we would be talking about one single person, John. The Holy Spirit of God is God in the same way that John's spirit is John. "God is spirit …"

But John also has a body, and because of this we would also refer to John's body as John. God not only is Spirit, but the Word was God as well. The Bible teaches the Word of God is the sword of the Spirit.

And take the helmet of salvation, and the sword of the Spirit, which is the word of God. (Eph. 6:17)

The Word of God is the sword of the Spirit. The Word of God and the Spirit of God are inseparable and interdependent, just as it is with a human body and spirit before physical death. The Spirit gives living power to the Word and the Word is the sword or executing instrument of the life-giving power of the Spirit of God. These two qualities or characteristics are, I believe, the essence of God.

For the word of God is living and powerful, and sharper than any two-edged sword, piercing even to the division of soul and spirit, and of joints and marrow, and is a discerner of the thoughts and intents of the heart. (Heb. 4:12)

These, the Word and Spirit, are the two most essential attributes used to describe and define God in scripture. But just because there are two separate characteristics of God doesn't mean God is two separate persons or beings. Neither my spirit nor my body is a separate being from me. They are me—my essence in one person.

I have concluded, as much as my reasoning ability allows, that the Holy Spirit has to do with the power of eternal life only God possesses. God not only is alive, but He alone is the giver and sustainer of life. His life is inherent eternal life. What I mean by *inherent eternal life* is that this life is of infinite or eternal quality, without beginning or end, and possessed only by the Creator. God is the only source of eternal life and therefore only He can give life.

The Spirit of God has made me, and the breath of the Almighty gives me life. (Job 33:4)

It is the Spirit who gives life; the flesh profits nothing. The words that I speak to you are spirit, and they are life. (John 6:63)

Paul tells the Ephesians there is only one Spirit.

There is one body and one Spirit, just as you were called in one hope of your calling. (Eph. 4:4)

Before the church age began, when the Bible spoke of the Spirit of the Lord, the Spirit of God or simply the Spirit, it referred to God only. However, now, after Jesus has been given all power by the Father, the Spirit of Christ is one and the same as the Holy Spirit of the Father. Chapters 3 and 4 deal with Jesus coming in the Spirit of His Father to sit upon the throne in God's kingdom.

Notice Paul's writings to the Roman church. There he uses *God, Christ* and *the Holy Spirit* interchangeably.

But you are not in the flesh but in the Spirit, if indeed <u>the Spirit of God</u> dwells in you. Now if anyone does not have the <u>Spirit of Christ</u>, he is not His. And if Christ is in you, the body is dead because of sin, but the Spirit is life because of righteousness. But if <u>the Spirit of Him</u> who raised Jesus from the dead dwells in you, He who raised Christ from the dead will also give life to your mortal bodies through <u>His Spirit</u> who dwells in you. (Romans 8:9–11)

The Spirit of Him who brought Christ up from the dead was the Holy Spirit of God. It is this same Spirit, through Christ, who will change the believer's mortal body into an immortal body at the resurrection. Notice once again:

But if the <u>Spirit of Him</u> who raised Jesus from the dead dwells in you, He who raised Christ from the dead will also give life to your mortal bodies through <u>His Spirit</u> who dwells in you. (Romans 8:11)

Jesus was given an immortal body at His resurrection, and after He ascended back to the Father He was glorified in His immortality. He then was crowned king of God's kingdom and given all power in heaven and on earth by the Father (Matthew 28:18–20). From that time forward the Lord Jesus could Himself give eternal life through the power of His Father's Holy Spirit to those He chose. No one else had or would ever be given this power except the Son of God. By the same token, no one but King Jesus would ever be given the authority to execute eternal judgment.

For as the Father has life in Himself, so He has granted the Son to have life in Himself, and has given Him authority to execute judgment also, because He is the Son of Man. (John 5:26–27)

Earlier in the fifth chapter of John, Jesus talks to the Jews seeking to kill Him. They were accusing Him of breaking the Sabbath. Here the Lord addresses the question of His power in relationship to the power of the Father.

The Jews were also accusing Him of claiming equality with God because of His testimony as the Son of God. Listen to what Jesus tells them.

Therefore the Jews sought all the more to kill Him, because He not only broke the Sabbath, but also said that God was His Father, making Himself equal with God. Then Jesus answered and said to them, "Most assuredly, I say to you, the Son can do nothing of Himself, but what He sees the Father do; for whatever He does, the Son also does in like manner. For the Father loves the Son, and shows Him all things that He Himself does; and He will show Him greater works than these, that you may marvel. For as the Father raises the dead and gives life to them, even so the Son gives life to whom He will. For the Father judges no one, but has committed all judgment to the Son, that all should honor the Son just as they honor the Father. He who does not honor the Son does not honor the Father who sent Him. (John 5:18–23)

Jesus attempts to show these Jews that through the power of His Father He had been given the power to give eternal life. It was by virtue of that same great power that He, the Son of Man, would also be empowered to execute judgment on the world. Only the Son would be given power by the Father to give life and execute judgment.

It is not inconsequential that Jesus said He had power to execute judgment. The reason given was because He is the Son of Man. He possessed not only the power of deity but also the experiences of humanity. It is as a result of his humanity that He can be a truly faithful high priest and intercessor for all those of us who are the heirs of salvation. Because of His humanity He can be touched with all of the feelings of our infirmities. Therefore it was necessary and His desire as well to be made like His brethren in every way.

Therefore, in all things He had to be made like His brethren, that He might be a merciful and faithful High Priest in things pertaining to God, to make propitiation for the sins of the people. (Hebrews 2:17)

As the Son of Man, He was a fleshly creature of humanity. He was tempted in all of the ways we as humans suffer temptation. But none of His trials, temptations and afflictions resulted in sin.

For we do not have a High Priest who cannot sympathize with our weaknesses, but was in all points tempted as we are, yet without sin. (Hebrews 4:15)

The power of His divinity gave Him the power to suffer all of the trials of humanity but remain sinless and innocent before God. By the power of a sinless life He became the innocent Lamb of God, taking away the sins of the world. He only was worthy—and He only had the ability to execute righteous judgment on humanity.

Therefore I have believed and continue to believe the Spirit of God is God. God's Spirit is a primary characteristic or essence of His divinity in which to identify the power and only source of eternal life. In God's Spirit exists inherent eternal life, allowing Him only to be the giver and sustaining power of all life. By virtue of the power of His deity the life-giving power was also given to Jesus by His Father.

But those believing in Jesus would not have life in themselves or the power to execute judgment. These powers were only given to the Son, the heir of all things. Jesus made clear the source of eternal life is the Holy Spirit of God. He said whoever believes in Him, "out of his heart will flow rivers of living water." But this He spoke concerning the Spirit:

On the last day, that great day of the feast, Jesus stood and cried out, saying, "If anyone thirsts, let him come to Me and drink. He who believes in Me, as the Scripture has said, out of his heart will flow rivers of living water." But this He spoke concerning the Spirit, whom those believing in Him would receive; for the Holy Spirit was not yet given, because Jesus was not yet glorified. (John 7:38–39)

THE FATHER AND THE SON

The Holy Spirit was the Father of Jesus. It was God, the Holy Spirit, that overshadowed Mary at the conception of Jesus. Matthew says she was found with child of the Holy Spirit.

Now the birth of Jesus Christ was as follows: After His mother Mary was betrothed to Joseph, before they came together, she was found with child of the Holy Spirit. Then Joseph her husband, being a just man, and not wanting to make her a public example, was minded to put her away secretly. But while he thought about these things, behold, an angel of the Lord appeared to him in a dream, saying, "Joseph, son of David, do not be afraid to take to you Mary your wife, for that which is conceived in her is of the Holy Spirit. And she will bring forth a Son, and you shall call His name Jesus, for He will save His people from their sins. (Matt. 1:18–21)

There are reasons the scriptures point out the Father of Jesus was the Holy Spirit instead of "God the Father." The first reason is God was not "God the Father," in the sense of having His own begotten Son until the birth of Jesus. This Father–Son relationship began at the coming of Jesus into the world. Jesus was the combined product of the commingling of divinity with humanity—Almighty God and a Jewish virgin named Mary. I see no evidence at all in the Bible of the existence of Jesus as the Son of God before He was conceived and born. He was a product of the Holy Spirit (God) and Mary. That which became flesh (Jesus) was the Word (seed) of God. The Word was from the beginning. The Word was with God, but not as a separate person or being. The Word was God!

In Genesis the Bible begins by telling us that it was the Spirit of God that hovered over the waters at creation. That Spirit was the Holy Spirit of God.

In the beginning God created the heavens and the earth. The earth was without form, and void; and darkness was on the face of the deep. And the Spirit of God was hovering over the face of the waters. (Genesis 1:1)

To doubt that the Spirit of God at the creation was a different person or being than that which would become the Father of the Lord Jesus is without biblical proof in my view. I find no indication of this at all in the Bible. The same God who was the Creator of all things was also the Father of His begotten Son.

Two gospels, Luke and Matthew, give the account of the conception and birth of the Lord. In Luke's account, all of the things mentioned about Jesus coming into the world are talked about in a future tense. "He <u>will</u> be great." "He <u>will</u> be called the Son of the Highest." "The Lord God <u>will</u> give Him the throne of His Father David." "And He <u>will</u> reign over the house of Jacob forever, and of His kingdom there <u>will</u> be no end. All of these show the glory of the coming Son to be a future event.

Of course it is true that the eternal Word was from the beginning and without end, because the Word was with God and was God. However, the Bible simply does not indicate that the Word was with God as a separate person, but rather the Word was God prior to the birth of the Lord Jesus. It was the Word, which was with God and was God, that made possible the conception of Jesus. The Word became flesh through Mary. This was Jesus. This was the Son of God.

And the Word became flesh and dwelt among us, and we beheld His glory, the glory as of the only begotten of the Father, full of grace and truth. (John 1:14)

Next is the account of Luke testifying of the conception of the Lord Jesus. It was the action of the Holy Spirit coming upon Mary through the power of the Highest that caused the conception of God's Son.

Now in the sixth month the angel Gabriel was sent by God to a city of Galilee named Nazareth, to a virgin betrothed to a man whose name was Joseph, of the house of David. The virgin's name was Mary. And having come in, the angel said to her, "Rejoice, highly favored one, the Lord is with you; blessed are you among women!" But when she saw him, she was troubled at his saying, and considered *what manner of greeting this was. Then the angel said to her, "Do not be afraid, Mary, for you have found favor with God. And behold, you will conceive in your womb and bring forth a Son, and shall call His name Jesus. He will be great, and will be called the <u>Son of the Highest</u>; and the Lord God will give Him the throne of His father David. And He will reign over the house of Jacob forever, and of His kingdom there will be no end."*

Then Mary said to the angel, "How can this be, since I do not know a man?" And the angel answered and said to her, "<u>The Holy Spirit will come upon you, and the power of the Highest will overshadow you; therefore, also, that Holy One who is to be born will be called the Son of God</u>. (Luke 1:26–35)

Jesus was and is the only true child of God by virtue of being *begotten* of God. Christians become children of God only through and by *spiritual adoption*. Jesus was not naturally created, but was *begotten of God*. Before this He was not Jesus the Son, but was the *Word* of God that was to become flesh. By way of humanity, the Word became the fleshly Son of God, even though the Word had existed from the beginning. Even though we cannot fully comprehend reproductive deity (or fleshly reproduction either, for that matter), still we must accept the testimony of God as true. I see no reason to speculate beyond what is written.

It is only through faith in the redemptive work of the cross that anyone except Christ is given the right or the power to become a child of God, and this is only by adoption. Those who receive Jesus, however, are promised to become children of God. They are spiritually adopted into the family of God, and through a special process of regeneration will eventually become true children of God. Through Jesus, we are *given the right* to become children of God.

He (Jesus) was in the world, and the world was made through Him, and the world did not know Him. He came to His own (the Jews), and His own did not receive Him. <u>But as many as received Him, to them He gave the right to become</u>

children of God, to those who believe in His name: who were born, not of blood, nor of the will of the flesh, nor of the will of man, but of God. (John 1:10–13)

Since Jesus was the only begotten Son (or true offspring) of the Father, only He could claim God as His own true Father. Because of this Jesus became the sole inheritor of all things of the Father. The Bible tells us God has appointed Jesus heir of all things.

God, who at various times and in various ways spoke in time past to the fathers by the prophets, has in these last days spoken to us by His Son, whom He has appointed heir of all things, through whom also He made the worlds. (Heb. 1:1–2)

I was originally taught there was one God, unlimited in His power and might, and He fathered (or beget) a Son through humanity to become the redeemer of fallen sinful humanity. And still, to me, it's just that simple, but it has remained clouded by the continuing traditions of men. Now, I also believe, through this redemptive work of Christ, all of God's creation will eventually share in the glory. This is discussed more in depth later on.

JESUS: THE WORD OF GOD INCARNATE

With some fear of being redundant, I now want to continue to explore in more detail the subject of the incarnate Word. Many mysteries surround the deity of Christ. This section aims to review and explore some of this mystery. Some of the mystery is in connection with the scriptural fact that Jesus is the *incarnate* Word of God. The mystery of the pre-earthly existence of the Word, which became the fleshly existence of the Son of God, can partially be solved by understanding the meaning of two verses of scripture. Both were written by John, one being in the first chapter of the gospel of John, and the second in the first chapter of the first epistle of John. In the account in the gospel of John, he begins with the following words.

In the beginning was the Word, and the Word was with God, and the Word was God. (John 1:1)

It is important to realize that (1) The Word (Greek *logos*) is infinite and eternal. It was from the beginning, which is to say without beginning. (2) The Word was with God. The scriptures do not indicate that the Word (*logos*) was a separate being or person from God. It does not say that the Son was with the Father, but rather that the Word was with God. It simply declares that (3) The Word was God. This makes clear there was no distinction between the Word and God. The Word was God—not a god, but God.

To be incarnate means to be embodied in the flesh or in human form. Now listen to what John says as he continues in John, chapter 1.

And the Word became flesh and dwelt among us, and we beheld His glory, the glory as of the only begotten of the Father, full of grace and truth. (John 1:14)

His incarnation allowed Jesus to be referred to as both the Son of God and the Son of Man, born of both deity and humanity. Jesus would carry both titles during His earthly existence. However, the title the Lord carried from the beginning, which would eternally remain, was the Word. At one time He was neither the Son of God nor the Son of Man, only the Word with God. It was that (the Word) which eventually was made flesh. But it had existed from the beginning. And because of this we can say Jesus, as the Word of God, is the author and finisher of our faith. To receive Jesus is to receive the Word of God and to reject Him is to reject God's Word.

Looking unto Jesus, the author and finisher of our faith, who for the joy that was set before Him endured the cross, despising the shame, and has sat down at the right hand of the throne of God. (Hebrews 12:2)

This is important because otherwise the written Word of God has the tendency to become less than sufficient in matters dealing with eternal salvation. In other words, we cannot embrace Jesus and at the same time circumvent the scriptures. In the same way the worlds were framed by the power of the Word of God, even so Jesus' body was formed by that same power, the power of the Word! Jesus was the Son of God and the Son of Man. In this union of God and man He became the *incarnate* Word of God, becoming the author and finisher of our faith. "And the Word was made flesh." Everything said in the scriptures about Jesus can also be said about the Word of God in connection with eternal salvation.

Now I saw heaven opened, and behold, a white horse. And He who sat on him was called Faithful and True, and in righteousness He judges and makes war. His eyes were like a flame of fire, and on His head were many crowns. He had a name written that no one knew except Himself. He was clothed with a robe dipped in blood, and His name is called THE WORD of God. (Revelation 19:11–13)

So there is no doubt that in the beginning the Word existed with God and indeed was God, according to John's writing.

In the beginning was the Word, and the Word was with God, and the Word was God. (John 1:1)

In many places in scripture Jesus testified He was in some way with the Father before His fleshly birth. This is true because He came from God. But as noted previously, the Lord's pre-earthly existence was as the Word, later to become the incarnate Word, which was Jesus, the Son of God. He made the following and numerous other statements attesting to His pre-earthly existence.

And now, O Father, glorify Me together with Yourself, with the glory which I had with You before the world was. (John 17:5)

Most assuredly, I say to you, before Abraham was I AM. (John 8:58)

Notice the present tense of the verb *am* in the last verse just cited here—not just *was*, but rather *am*, showing the ever-present and eternal nature of the Word of God. The Word that became Jesus in His earthly existence, which was the express image of God, has existed from the beginning with God and as God.

The simple present tense is a timeless truth, something happening all the time, actions we do all the time. The present tense tells about activities we do again and again. We use the present progressive tense to talk about actions in progress at the moment of speaking (see Helping with Verbs, www.helpingwithverbs.com).

THE OMNIPRESENCE OF GOD

God is *omnipresent*. This simply means He is everywhere at the same time.

Where can I go from Your Spirit? Or where can I flee from Your presence? If I ascend into heaven, You are there; If I make my bed in hell, behold, You are there. If I take the wings of the morning, and dwell in the uttermost parts of the sea, even there Your hand shall lead me, and Your right hand shall hold me. (Psalms 139:7–10)

What then if you should see the Son of Man ascend where He was before? (John 6:62)

For I have come down from heaven, not to do My own will, but the will of Him who sent Me. (John 6:38)

Father, I desire that they also whom You gave Me may be with Me where I am, that they may behold My glory which You have given Me; for You loved Me before the foundation of the world. (John 17:24)

It is undeniable that it was at a specific time and place the Word became flesh as the only begotten Son of the Father.

But when the fullness of the time had come, God sent forth His Son, born of a woman, born under the law, to redeem those who were under the law, that we might receive the adoption as sons. (Galatians 4:4–5)

Some might argue that "God sent forth His Son" would mean Jesus existed as the Son of God in heaven. And this would make sense when we consider that God is *omniscient*, meaning that God knows everything, there-fore He knows the end from the beginning. But we live in time, and must consider events in the fullness of time rather than from a timeless view as God is able to do. John says in Revelation 13:8 that the Lamb (Jesus) was slain from the foundation of the world. With God all things are ever present. But we, the created, must calculate from the realm of time God has caused to be for us. Time is for our testing and enduring.

So about two thousand years ago, as we would calculate in our time-oriented system of endurance, God sent His Son into the world. He did this by causing the Word to become flesh.

And the Word became flesh and dwelt among us, and we beheld His glory, the glory as of the only begotten of the Father, full of grace and truth. (John 1:14)

The Greek word for *word* is *logos* as used in John 1:1. The definition of *logos* signifies much more than sounds or symbols having a communicable meaning. This we can see in the scripture just cited. The Word (*logos*) seems to convey the essence of the deity and creative power of the one true God of the universe. *Vine's Expository Dictionary* says it is (1) His distinct and super finite personality, (2) His relation in the Godhead, and (3) His creative power. The Word or *logos* is more than just another title for the Son of God, as some commentaries seem to conclude. *Logos*, in conveying the deity and creative power of the one true God, does so without any separation in personality or nature.

Therefore in summation: the Word existed before Jesus, the Son of God, was born in the flesh. But the Word did not become flesh or Jesus until His birth. Before His birth there was no fleshly Jesus, the only begotten Son of God, because of the nonexistence of His human side through Mary. However, before His birth and from the beginning, the Word, which would become flesh, existed. But before the birth of Jesus the Word was not the only begotten Son of God. The Word became the Son of God by being begotten, or conceived and born. Otherwise the birth of Jesus would not have had any effect on the Sonship of Jesus in regard to His relationship to the Father.

That which became flesh (Jesus) had existed from the beginning, not as a begotten Son of the Father, but as God Himself. He became a Son by being begotten of God. God became a Father by virtue of having begotten a Son. At a given point in time, designated by the Father, the Word became flesh. The statement that the Word *became flesh* indicates a change of substance or nature. Therefore the glorious transformation of the Word into human flesh was revealed by John's writing as "the only begotten of the Father, full of grace and truth."

MY INTRODUCTION TO TRINITY TEACHING

After being baptized into Christ in obedience to the gospel, I attended a church in another area of the country away from my childhood home. It was there I first remember hearing the doctrine of the Trinity. The idea seemed very strange to me at first. But with my limited knowledge I had neither the desire nor the courage to question it in the beginning. I, however, was never able to feel totally comfortable with a lot of the things I was hearing. For a while I accepted it—at least in part. It was not something the members of my congregation were required to accept in order to be in good standing in the church. This may have been the reason there was not a great deal of emphasis and teaching on this doctrine that was so prevalent among most denominational churches. Actually, I really don't know to what degree it was accepted or believed within the congregation. But I know it was accepted by some, if not most.

At that time, the thing I was hearing from this teaching seemed to be urging my mind to form a conceptualization of three gods in one. And the reason for this was because that was exactly what I was being taught! I wanted to believe it because it was what my church was teaching. And I especially didn't want to seem schismatic or rebellious to those I felt were spiritually superior to me in knowledge. But in my mind I could not grasp a view that taught three gods in any way, even though almost everybody seemed to agree these three beings or persons made up only one God.

I saw nothing in the Bible that came close, at least in my mind, to offering sufficient proof for the view I was listening to. Almost always the congregational teachers would sum up their remarks by saying there was really only one God. Very few religious issues have ever caused the degree of confusion in my mind as did this.

These three divine beings were purported to be the first, second and third persons in the Godhead. They were usually referred to as (1) God the Father, (2) God the Son and (3) God the Holy Spirit. Each of the three were said to be coequal and eternally coexisting. The idea of three beings, all with unlimited but coequal power, was one of the primary things that continued to bother me. In other words, I was confused about the concept of three separate deified persons all individually being called God, especially when each was said to be equally almighty in every way. My frustration only increased as I began studying more on my own.

In his sermon on the day of Pentecost Peter promised the gift of the Holy Spirit to obedient, penitent believers.

Now when they heard this, they were cut to the heart, and said to Peter and the rest of the apostles, "Men and brethren, what shall we do?" Then Peter said to them, "Repent, and let every one of you be baptized in the name of Jesus Christ for the remission of sins; and you shall receive the gift of the Holy Spirit. (Acts 2:37–38)

Even these two verses sent up red flags in my mind when examining the doctrine of a Holy Trinity. For example, is a spiritually reborn soul to believe the reception of the Holy Spirit would preclude God the Father being received into the heart or mind of the believer? And what about Jesus, He whom Trinitarians teach is God the Son? Was God the Father and Jesus not allowed into the heart of the believer at the point of the new birth? This one, the Holy Spirit, was promised to all those assembled at Jerusalem on the day of Pentecost, as well as to all future generations who would surrender their lives in faith to God through Jesus.

For the promise is to you and to your children, and to all who are afar off, as many as the Lord our God will call. (Acts 2:39)

The gift of God's Holy Spirit was vital to establish the congregation (church) of God on earth. The Spirit would lead and guide and enlighten the child of God for the remainder of her/his life. This is what Jesus had told His disciples about the Comforter, which He said was the Holy Spirit. Peter preached in Acts 2 that the prophet Joel had said that in the last days *God's Spirit would be poured out upon all flesh.* This meant without respect to race or nationality. The reception of God's Holy Spirit would give all of the disciples of Jesus the ability to know the things of God through the written word.

For what man knows the things of a man except the spirit of the man which is in him? Even so no one knows the things of God except the Spirit of God. (1 Cor. 2:11)

Jesus was the only truly begotten child of God. But all who would submit to God in obedience to the gospel of Christ would become children by adoption. This is made possible only through the reception of the Holy Spirit and being led by Him. It is called the *Spirit of adoption.*

For as many as are led by the Spirit of God, these are sons of God. For you did not receive the spirit of bondage again to fear, but you received the <u>Spirit of adoption</u> by whom we cry out, "Abba, Father." The Spirit Himself bears witness with our spirit that we are children of God. (Romans 8:15)

There is only one Holy Spirit. The one Holy Spirit is the Spirit of God the Father. Otherwise Paul's statement to the Ephesian church wouldn't make a lot of sense. There he says it is through Christ that all, both Jew and Gentile, have access to the Father by that one Spirit.

For through Him (Jesus) we both have access by one Spirit to the Father. (Eph. 2:18)

THE ORIGIN OF THE TRINITY TEACHING

The term trinity is not itself found in the Bible. It was first used by Tertullian at the close of the 2nd century, but received wide currency [common use in intellectual discussion] and formal elucidation [clarification] only in the 4th and 5th centuries. (New Bible Dictionary, 1996, "Trinity")

To fully understand the things of God in connection to His origin and nature is equivalent to fully understanding infinity. Few if any would ever claim to understand such a mystery. We can only ponder things revealed to us by God as regards deity. However, it is clear most things about deity are never revealed to us. One probable reason is because God has not equipped us with the intellectual tools needed to comprehend it. And without the wherewithal to understand, there is no need for revelation. But we do have the intellectual ability to understand the meaning of *one*, and because of this we can understand by God's revelation that there is only *one* God.

Hear, O Israel: The Lord our God, the Lord is <u>one</u>! (Deut. 6:4)

For since the beginning of the world men have not heard nor perceived by the ear, nor has the eye seen any God besides You, Who acts for the one who waits for Him. (Isa. 64:4)

[There is] one God and Father of all, who is above all, and through all, and in you all. (Eph. 4:6)

The ability to believe there is one God has been clouded by the teachings of the Trinity doctrine. If we say there is only one God, but at the same time we talk about, promote and practice a teaching that conveys three gods, we can never be fully convinced there really is only one God! The simple fact of the matter is that one means one. True, you might have three parts of something making up one something else. For example, you might have a body, soul and spirit (three things) making up one human being. But you won't ever have three human beings making up one person.

As previously stated, the word *trinity* does not appear in the scriptures. This word was never used until after the death of Christ. The scriptures are deathly silent in explicitly teaching the idea of three separate persons or beings that make up God. The King James Version of the Bible has 1 John 5:7 as saying, "For there are three that bear record in heaven, the Father, the Word, and the Holy Ghost: and these three are one." Most other versions omit this verse. This verse is one of the verses of scripture often used to validate the Trinity doctrine.

A verse of scripture that at first glance seems to give credence to faith in the Trinity doctrine is in Paul's second letter to the church at Corinth.

The grace of the <u>Lord Jesus Christ</u>, and the love of <u>God</u>, and the communion of the <u>Holy Spirit</u> be with you all. Amen. (2 Cor. 13:14)

In this verse the titles of Father, Son and Holy Spirit are individually listed. They are each given a particular spiritual attribute; with Jesus it is *grace*, with God it is *love*, and with the Holy Spirit it is *communion*. However, does this mean the attributes assigned to each of these three designations is unique to each? Not at all! Each designation or title of deity possesses all of them. The primary thing to understand is that each of the spiritual blessings is to be given to all the members of the body of Christ. In Hebrews 10:29 the Holy Spirit is referred to as "the Spirit of Grace." Romans 5:5 tells us that the "love of God has been poured out in our hearts by the Holy Spirit who was given to us." The word *communion* means a joint sharing or participation. Any spiritual sharing of blessings would come from God, who is the giver of every perfect gift.

Blessed be the <u>God</u> and Father of our Lord Jesus Christ, <u>who has blessed us with every spiritual blessing</u> in the heavenly places <u>in Christ</u>. (Ephesians 3:1)

But the *communion* or joint sharing of all blessings would also come from Jesus in that they are from God *in Christ*. All blessings originate with God, but He has given all power and authority in heaven and in earth to His Son.

Nothing can be attributed to the Father without glorifying His Son. And Jesus cannot be glorified without the Father. Ultimately the greatest of the blessings will be the blessing that allows God's redeemed to become joint heirs with His Son. Most of the scriptures used to give evidence for the doctrine of the Trinity fail greatly in doing so. Another verse that might seem to give evidence for the Trinity doctrine is in the great commission of Jesus in Matthew 28.

All authority has been given to Me [Jesus] in heaven and on earth. Go therefore and make disciples of all the nations, baptizing them in the name of the Father and of the Son and of the Holy Spirit. (Matthew 28:18–19)

Without belaboring this point, let's look a little closer at what is being said in these two verses. True and honest scriptural evidences are only valid when the scriptures are rightly divided by having been taken in context and in harmony with the rest of the Bible. Most of the Trinity arguments fail in this regard.

The argument for the Trinity is that each of the three persons of deity is named in Matthew 28. And it is true Jesus commanded baptism in the name of three, but three what? Is it three persons or beings? No, this is not what is taught here. To perform an action in the name of someone actually means to perform that action by the authority of that individual. This was what Peter told the audience when a man was healed on one occasion. Notice healing the man in the name of Jesus was the same as healing him by the authority of Jesus.

And when they had placed them in the center, they began to inquire; "by what power, or in what name, have you done this?" Then Peter, filled with the Holy Spirit, said to them, "Rulers and elders of the people, if we are on trial today for a benefit done to a sick man, as to how this man has been made well, let it be known to all of you, and to all the people of Israel, that by the name of Jesus Christ the Nazarene, whom you crucified, whom God raised from the dead, by this name this man stands here before you in good health." (Acts 4:7–10)

Peter was saying it was by the power or authority of Jesus this miracle was performed. But did this take the power of God or the power of God's Holy Spirit out of this action? Jesus said in Matthew 28 that "all authority" had been given to Him. So when he commanded baptism in the name of the Father, Son and Holy Spirit, and since He possessed all authority in heaven and on earth, He had been given power to do all things by the authority of Himself.

In the following two chapters I discuss at greater length the complete authority given to Jesus after His resurrection and glorification. He became King of Kings and Lord of Lords. His name or authority was to be exalted above every name.

And whatever you do in word or deed, do all in the name of the Lord Jesus, giving thanks to God the Father through Him. (Col. 3:17)

Therefore God also has highly exalted Him and given Him the name which is above every name, that at the name of Jesus every knee should bow, of those in heaven, and of those on earth, and of those under the earth, and that every tongue should confess that Jesus Christ is Lord, to the glory of God the Father. (Phil. 2:9–11)

It was at the name of Jesus that all those who took part in apprehending Him for trial drew back and fell to the ground. It was when the Lord said, "I am He."

CONCLUDING THOUGHT

I am persuaded that our purpose on the planet—no matter where or who we are—boils down to one thing. Our purpose in one word is to *glorify* our Creator. We were created by God for the purpose of glorifying Him, with an offer of immortality in return. We will glorify Him and live, or reject His glory and die.

Let us hear the conclusion of the whole matter: Fear God and keep His commandments, for this is man's all. (Ecclesiastes 12:13)

When we truly glorify our Creator our fear of Him will come out of reverence and awe, rather than a fear of punishment. We should never see Him as one who desires anything but good for us and for all of His creation as well. To see and understand our Creator from the inspired scriptures is to view and understand His love, mercy and compassion for all of His creation.

The scriptures teach that the way of a transgressor is hard. This is true. This is because of a lack of dependence on the power and presence of God. But Jesus said His yoke is easy and His burden is light. This is because of trusting in the power of the Creator.

Our Creator is our only source of everything necessary and good. Without Him there is nothing. All power, honor, glory and dominion issues from this source—the eternal one—the Great I Am!

CHAPTER 3
WHEN THE SON OF MAN COMES

When the Son of Man comes in His glory, and all the holy angels with Him, then He will sit on the throne of His glory. All the nations will be gathered before Him, and He will separate them one from another, as a shepherd divides his sheep from the goats. And He will set the sheep on His right hand, but the goats on the left. (Matthew 25:31–33)

I was brought up on a small farm in south central Missouri. Times were hard in the 1950s due to poor economic conditions in that part of the country, as well as severe drought conditions for several consecutive years. My father struggled to make a meager living by deploying all his farming skills against an uphill grind.

One of the things that helped our situation was Dad's ability to raise good corn crops even in the midst of the continued hot and rainless droughts of the 1950s. As most of our neighbors' corn crops seemed to fail when the rain stopped in the middle of the growing season, our corn still did relatively well in spite of the adverse conditions. It was not just the hot and arid situation that caused the diminished crop prospects. There were also insects, squirrels, raccoons and crows that were constant plagues. But even though all of these things had a negative effect on production, Dad's corn seemed to usually do better than on the adjoining farms.

I was always curious about why my dad did things the way he did. One day I asked him why he planted corn so much earlier than the other farmers in the community. He replied, "So it'll take root."

"What do you mean?" I asked him.

"When you plant early," he answered, "the top of the ground is cold and that causes the roots to go down deeper into the warmer soil. And having deeper roots causes the corn to be able to have moisture when the top of the ground gets hot and dry in the summer." What he said made a lot of sense to me even back then.

But getting the crop to harvest and in the barn was only part of the problem. There was still the problem with coons, corn weevils, mice and rats. It was a constant fight. Dad planted a type of open pollinated corn seed that had been passed on for several generations in the family. It was a white, soft-grained corn. It was excellent for making cornmeal. Because of its versatility he sold some of his corn on the market at a premium price. The rest was used for our family's consumption and for animal feed.

Each winter Dad would select the corn seed for the next year's planting. One day I watched him carefully selecting the ears to be used for seed. When choosing an ear he would first look at the length and diameter. Then he would shell off both ends of the ear, leaving only the best grains in the center of the cob. I kept asking why he did this or that and he would patiently tell me why. It was to ultimately have the best crop of corn possible.

As I grew older I began to use some of the lessons Dad had taught me about growing corn to other life situations. For example, the deeper something took root, the more apt it would be to survive. I was able to apply these principles many times in my life's journey, especially in my spiritual life. What he taught me was really all about making good judgments or decisions. Dad would often say, "Son, life will be a lot easier on you if you use good judgment."

UNTO THE LEAST OF THESE

In the spiritual realm we will have two judges making decisions about the quality of this temporal life, as well as judging our eternal destiny. The first is our own self. If we make decisions with sound judgment through the counsel of God's Word we can avoid a lot of hurtful problems. The best life decisions are made as we examine our own hearts and souls. Paul writes to the church about this in his first letter to the Corinthians.

For if we would judge ourselves, we would not be judged. But when we are judged, we are chastened by the Lord, that we may not be condemned with the world. (1 Cor. 11:31–32)

The last ultimately final, righteous and just judge is the Lord. His judgments are righteous, just and without error. His judgment is the final authority. His is the judgment of not just what we do, but also why we do what we do. He knows our motivation, even as we labor to know it ourselves. For this reason only He can judge righteously: only He fully knows us. His decisions are made with all the evidence necessary to render righteousness and justice in all of His decisions. He not only gives the final decision at the end of our lives but He will also make merciful judgments to help us as we live out our lives on earth. In this way He will allow for correction all along the way as we learn and as we surrender to His will.

Therefore I will save My flock, and they shall no longer be a prey; and I will judge between sheep and sheep. (Ezekiel 34:22)

Probably the phrase we would consider most synonymous with Judgment Day is "when the Lord comes." In a narrative given by Jesus and recorded in the gospel of Matthew, the Lord Jesus speaks both of judgment and of when He comes in the glory of the Father. And, as I think you will soon see, these events are actually one event spanning the Christian age. The description begins in Matthew 25:31 with the Son of Man coming in glory and sitting in judgment on His throne with all nations gathered before Him. This opening scene depicts the beginning of God's judgment on sin through Jesus. None of God's human creation will escape the judgment of His Son.

But why do you judge your brother? Or why do you show contempt for your brother? For we shall all stand before the judgment seat of Christ. (Romans 14:10)

For we must all appear before the judgment seat of Christ, that each one may receive the things done in the body, according to what he has done, whether good or bad. (2 Cor. 5:10)

As I previously noted, God's judgment on the world is sure. And God's judgment will be just. This judgment is based on who is qualified (not necessarily deserving) to be eternally saved. Those qualified to be saved will be those who have given an account of themselves through their faith in God. I will show by the scriptures that the Day of Judgment began more than two thousand years ago after Jesus was gloriously resurrected into immortality and elevated to become head over all things in connection to His church, which was and is His spiritual body.

Which He [the Father] worked in Christ when He raised Him from the dead and seated Him at His right hand in the heavenly places, far above all principality and power and might and dominion, and every name that is named, not only in this age but also in that which is to come. And He put all things under His feet, and gave Him to be head over all things to the church, which is His body, the fullness of Him who fills all in all. (Ephesians 1:20–23)

In Matthew's narrative of God's judgment, Jesus speaks of a great separation of people. The separation is really a result of the way the people have treated His Son, King Jesus. In this narrative some had rejected Him, thus rejecting God's will for their lives by rejecting the words of His Son.

For He [Jesus] received from God the Father honor and glory when such a voice came to Him from the Excellent Glory: "This is My beloved Son, in whom I am well pleased." (2 Peter 1:17)

The Lord pronounces a declaration of coming judgment on those who reject His words in the following verse.

He who rejects Me, and does not receive My words, has that which judges him—the word that I have spoken will judge him in the last day. (John 12:48)

In the scene of separation and judgment depicted in Matthew 25, the people had observed their fellow sojourners. They were hungry, thirsty, homeless, unclothed and in prison. Some had compassion on those who suffered from these things. Others did not. Jesus observed these merciful ones who lovingly attended to the needs of those who suffered. But many others had no mercy on these misfortunate souls. Jesus said those who had treated Him with compassion had done so by performing these deeds of love "unto the least of these." He refers to the least of these as His brethren and says by doing right by them they had done right by Him. The overriding principle here is love shown by a genuine concern for the least of these whom Jesus referred to as His brethren. This is a glaring illustration that the law of love is never at odds with the law of God.

If you really fulfill the royal law according to the Scripture, "You shall love your neighbor as yourself," you do well. (James 2:8)

For all the law is fulfilled in one word, even in this: "You shall love your neighbor as yourself." (Galatians 5:14)

The scene ends with the sentence of unending punishment for the wicked (those rejecting Him) and the gift of eternal life for the righteous (those accepting Him). But notice the execution of punishment does not come until the end of this Judgment Day story.

The general consensus of traditional thought is that this symbolic judgment story is to be fulfilled in its entirety only after the bodily resurrection of the dead. Judgment Day in the mind of the many Christians is only about when Jesus returns visibly to earth. In other words, it is the belief judgment will happen only after "all that are in the graves shall come forth" for the announcement of their final judgment (John 5:28).

Some scholars believe the Matthew 25 account details the judgment of all mankind. Others believe it pertains only to those who have lived in the Christian era. There is a variety of thought on who is or will be among those numbered in this Matthew 25 Judgment Day scene. I believe the scriptures, when rightly discerned, provide the answer to this question.

It seems very clear to me that this short narration represents the entirety of the Christian age, and that it begins with the institution of God's church (assembly/congregation) on earth and ends with the bodily resurrection of the dead for final judgment and reward. In this chapter and in the next chapter, entitled "In the Glory of the Father," my goal is to put forth scriptural evidence that Judgment Day has already begun.

I will attempt to show the Christian age was ushered into existence at the same time as the establishment of God's kingdom on earth. The purpose of the kingdom is to set up a court of righteous judgment for the eternal consequences or forgiveness of sin. It was to this time period and the events surrounding it that the prophets of God pointed as they spoke of the kingdom of God to come, declaring its purpose was to bring judgment and reward. The culmination of all things dealing with salvation and judgment of the world would take place only after the Father had put all things under the feet of His Son for this purpose. This complete power given to Jesus by the Father would begin to be executed with the establishment of His church on earth. Jesus instructed His disciples to pray God's kingdom would come to earth as it was already in existence in heaven.

In this manner, therefore, pray: Our Father in heaven, Hallowed be Your name. Your kingdom come. Your will be done on earth as it is in heaven. (Matthew 6:9–10)

The earthly kingdom would end at the resurrection of all of the dead when Jesus bodily returned to earth. After this, the Son would deliver the kingdom back to the Father.

Then comes the end, when He [Jesus] delivers the kingdom to God the Father, when He puts an end to all rule and all authority and power. For He must reign till He has put all enemies under His feet. The last enemy that will be destroyed is death. (1 Corinthians 15:24–26)

This point is elaborated on in the inspired letter to the Hebrews.

You have put all things in subjection under his feet. For in that He put all in subjection under him, He left nothing that is not put under him. But now we do not yet see all things put under him. But we see Jesus, who was made a little lower than the angels, for the suffering of death crowned with glory and honor, that He, by the grace of God, might <u>taste death</u> for everyone. (Hebrews 2:8–9)

By saying, "But now we do not yet see all things put under him," the writer indicates the work of salvation and judgment was not complete at that time, but rather was an ongoing work. Jesus first suffered and died to complete the meritorious sacrificial work. In this He tasted death for the whole world. He then was crowned King with all the honor and glory of the Father in order to begin the work of judgment. But in His work of judgment He would subdue all enemies of God—the last enemy would be death, which would be defeated in the end at the resurrection.

After completing His sacrificial work on the cross, and after the glorious exaltation by His Father, the sanctification process was made possible by that perfect sacrifice. And once made possible, that process would continue until the Lord comes back for His people who will then be resurrected into immortality. Jesus will then deliver up the kingdom to God the Father and once again subject Himself to the Father, that God may be all in all. Now read carefully the complete passage of 1 Corinthians 15:24–28.

Then comes the end, when He delivers the kingdom to God the Father, when He puts an end to all rule and all authority and power. For He must reign till He has put all enemies under His feet. The last enemy that will be destroyed is death. For "He has put all things under His feet." But when He says "all things are put under Him," it is evident that He who put all things under Him is excepted. Now when all things are made subject to Him [God], then the Son Himself will also be subject to Him [God] who put all things under Him, <u>that God may be all in all</u>. (1 Cor. 15:24–28)

THE CHURCH

Eternal judgment and reward began with the New Testament church of God at the beginning of our present Christian age. Even though the kingdom of God is everlasting, the reign of Christ over the kingdom on earth will be temporary. He "must reign <u>till</u> [or until] He has put all enemies under His feet." Then the kingdom will be delivered to the Father. The reign of Christ is for the purpose of salvation and judgment.

Therefore judgment or Judgment Day does not begin after the bodily resurrection of the dead as many believe, but rather it is finalized with the judgment of the wicked after the bodily resurrection and at the visible return of Jesus to earth. Rather than judgment beginning after the resurrection, the judgment process will be concluded at that time, having begun at the beginning of the church age.

Judgment truly began (past tense) at the house of God, according to the writing of the apostle Peter. The church (assembly or congregation) had already begun on earth with the preaching of the gospel to the Jews at Pentecost. Therefore the kingdom of God had already come to earth and was already in existence when Peter said, "For the time has come for judgment to begin at the house of God." Judgment Day had begun with those called by the gospel of Christ.

For the time has come for judgment to begin at the house of God; and if it begins with us first, what will be the end of those who do not obey the gospel of God?

The house of God on earth is the church of the living God. It is the members of the spiritual body of Christ. Paul writes the following to Timothy.

But if I am delayed, I write so that you may know how you ought to conduct yourself in the house of God, which is the church of the living God, the pillar and ground of the truth. (1 Timothy 3:15)

God's house on earth is not a building of materials erected by the hands of men. It is the assembly or congregation of God's people with the Holy Spirit of God living in their hearts. By the Spirit of God being in the hearts of His people, judgment could "begin at the house of God." The process of judgment has already begun!

Or do you not know that your body is the temple of the Holy Spirit who is in you, whom you have from God, and you are not your own? (1 Corinthians 6:19)

At the time of the apostolic letters to the churches the Lord Jesus had not bodily come back to earth, but He had come back invisibly in the Spirit as He had promised the original twelve disciples He would do.

If you love Me, keep My commandments. And I will pray the Father, and He will give you another Helper, that He may abide with you forever—the Spirit of truth, whom the world cannot receive, because it neither sees Him nor knows Him; but you know Him, for He dwells with you and will be in you. I will not leave you orphans; I will come to you. A little while longer and the world will see Me no more, but you will see Me. Because I live, you will live also. At that day you will know that I am in My Father, and you in Me, and I in you. (John 14:15–20)

Jesus told his disciples, "I will come to you." He obviously meant He would come in the Spirit, not bodily, as the *Spirit of truth*—as a *Comforter*—as a *Helper*. And Jesus did come in the Spirit on the day of Pentecost in about

AD 33. He came in all the glory and power of His Father to sit upon His throne of judgment. People representing all nations were gathered at Jerusalem on that day.

And there were dwelling in Jerusalem Jews, devout men, from every nation under heaven. (Acts 2:5)

Judgment Day began at the house of God. However, the judgment of all creation will be finalized only after the bodily resurrection of the dead at the Lord's visible return from heaven. The redemption of the body into immortality will finalize human salvation in Christ. Paul refers to this event as the revealing of the sons of God in his letter to the Romans. This is the event all creation is waiting for and expecting in order to be freed from the corruption brought on by the curse of sin.

For the earnest expectation of the creation eagerly waits for the revealing of the sons of God. (Romans 8:19)

All humanity having experienced sanctification by the blood of Christ during the Christian era will also experience the redemption of their bodies being resurrected into immortality. Those who are saved and those who lived before the Christian era—Abraham, Isaac, Jacob etc.—will be justified by faith in God with the blood of Christ flowing retroactively. The rest of the creation, with the exception of unredeemed humanity, will also be delivered from the bondage caused by man's sin and subsequent fall. The nonhuman innocent creation will then be restored back to the state that existed before sin came into the world, as Paul tells us in Romans 8. I discuss in more detail the restoration of the whole creation in another chapter.

Once again I might emphasize that the Day of Judgment began with the preaching of the gospel to the world after the resurrection and bodily glorification of Jesus into immortality. It will end with the bodily resurrection and glorification of all of the saints of God into immortality. The preaching of the gospel was foretold in the scriptures to begin at Jerusalem.

Now it shall come to pass in the latter days that the mountain of the Lord's house shall be established on the top of the mountains, and shall be exalted above the hills; and all nations shall flow to it. Many people shall come and say, "Come, and let us go up to the mountain of the Lord, to the house of the God of Jacob; He will teach us His ways, and we shall walk in His paths." For out of Zion shall go forth the law and the word of the Lord from Jerusalem. (Isaiah 2:2–3)

Luke speaks of the same event in the New Testament.

And that repentance and remission of sins should be preached in His name to all nations, beginning at Jerusalem. (Luke 24:47)

To better understand when judgment begins and ends, it is important to notice not only what the message contained—repentance and remission of sins—but also where it began—Jerusalem.

JUDGMENT DAY BEGINS

In his first general epistle to the church Peter addresses the issue of when judgment began. He shows it to be a present-day reality at the time of his writing. He also makes clear the beginning of judgment comes simultaneously with the acceptance or rejection of the gospel that is preached. Read once again what Peter writes.

For the time <u>has come</u> for judgment to begin at the house of God; and if it begins with us first, what will be the end of those who do not obey the gospel of God? Now if the righteous one is scarcely saved, where will the ungodly and the sinner appear? (1 Peter 4:17–18)

Judgment truly and literally begins at the house of God. Judgment begins with "us first," Peter says, speaking of those who had been spiritually separated (sanctified) out of the world by virtue of their surrender to Jesus as Savior through obedience to the gospel. The judgment of those sanctified takes place this side of the grave. Judgment of the lost will take place after the bodily resurrection.

Judgment is deciding. This is true of the one who is judged as well as the one who judges. The one who has been judged righteous is he who has surrendered his will to the will of God by submission to the lordship of Jesus. We in effect judge our own selves in this way. We must make the decision to surrender to God through faith in Jesus Christ and His blood.

Examine yourselves as to whether you are in the faith. Test yourselves. Do you not know yourselves, that Jesus Christ is in you—unless indeed you are disqualified? (2 Cor. 13:5)

Eternal or final judgment is a decision about who is faithful and who is not. This kind of judging is decided only by God, who knows the heart and motive of each individual. Righteousness that is sufficient to eternally save cannot be obtained by meritorious works. Salvation is not earned but is the gift of God's grace through Jesus. We must never forget this. We are saved by grace through faith in God, which gives us access to the atoning merits of the blood of Christ.

For it is by grace you have been saved, through faith—and this is not from yourselves, it is the gift of God— not by works, so that no one can boast. For we are God's handiwork, created in Christ Jesus to do good works, which God prepared in advance for us to do. (Eph. 2:8–10) (NIV)

Humanity has no inherent righteousness, as Paul plainly states.

And be found in Him [Christ], not having my own righteousness, which is from the law, but that which is through faith in Christ, the righteousness which is from God by faith. (Phil. 3:9)

Only faith that is willing to obey saves and creates righteousness. The New International Version (NIV) of the Bible refers to this process as obedience that comes from faith.

But now revealed and made known through the prophetic writings by the command of the eternal God, so that all the Gentiles might come to the obedience that comes from faith. (Romans 16:26) (NIV)

In other words, faith without works is dead! (James 2:20)

Was not Abraham our father justified by works when he offered Isaac his son on the altar? Do you see that faith was working together with his works, and by works faith was made perfect? (James 2:21)

Even though there is no inherent righteousness in any human, we can be counted as righteous because of the righteousness of Christ. This is God's promise to us when we submit to His righteousness by an obedient faith. The scriptures also refer to this plan of God's redemption as obeying the gospel. Responding by faith to the gospel message of God's love through Jesus will invoke God's power to save.

For I am not ashamed of the gospel of Christ, for it is the power of God to salvation for everyone who believes, for the Jew first and also for the Greek. For in it the righteousness of God is revealed from faith to faith; as it is written, "The just shall live by faith." (Romans 1:16–17)

Paul speaks of the fate of those who have heard and yet refuse obedience to God by not obeying the gospel (good news) of Christ.

When the Lord Jesus is revealed from heaven with His mighty angels in flaming fire taking vengeance on those who do not know God, and on those who do not obey the gospel of our Lord Jesus Christ … (2 Thessalonians 1:7–8)

After we make a choice as to whether we seek God, the final, eternal decision is made by the Supreme Judge. It is He who will separate those who choose life from those who reject mercy, and eventually there will be a pronouncement of eternal punishment or eternal life and reward after the resurrection.

Many people are confused about how judgment is to be carried out. One of the things causing confusion is that the average person thinks about Judgment Day only in terms of the pronouncement of a verdict of guilt or innocence. However, most of the time and effort consumed in judging humanity will not be in the pronouncement of a verdict. Rather it will be in sanctification, the process of separating the good from the bad during the Christian age. This will be accomplished by King Jesus while He sits on His throne of judgment. I talk about this more extensively in the next chapter.

At the last day, when all of the dead are bodily resurrected at the coming of Jesus, the separating process will have been completed. The judgment that began at the house of God will have been done. Those who have been sanctified by faith will be resurrected to immortality. They will then leave the earth to forevermore be with the Lord.

For the Lord Himself will descend from heaven with a shout, with the voice of an archangel, and with the trumpet of God. And the dead in Christ will rise first. Then we who are alive and remain shall be caught up together with them in the clouds to meet the Lord in the air. And thus we shall always be with the Lord. (1 Thessalonians 4:16–17)

Then, as previously stated, only the pronouncement of judgment and reward will remain. Therefore the process of judgment is not consummated in a twenty-four-hour day, but will take place throughout the entirety of the time Jesus sits on His throne of judgment. And He will sit on His throne throughout the entirety of His reign.

At the risk of being redundant let me once again emphasize this: only after the sanctification of the righteous (those saved by the blood of Christ) is accomplished will the Lord visibly come back to earth. This will be for execution of eternal judgment on the wicked and eternal life and reward for the righteous. Then Judgment Day (the reign of Christ) will end. Jesus, Lord and King, will then deliver the authority of the kingdom of God back to the Father. As I have previously noted, this fact is spelled out clearly in Paul's first letter to the Corinthian church as he gives details of the bodily resurrection of the righteous.

For as in Adam all die, so in Christ all will be made alive. But each in turn: Christ, the first fruits; then, when he comes, those who belong to him. Then the end will come, when he hands over the kingdom to God the Father after he has destroyed all dominion, authority and power. For he must reign until he has put all his enemies under his feet. The last enemy to be destroyed is death. For he "has put everything under his feet." Now when it says that "everything" has been put under him, it is clear that this does not include God himself, who put everything under Christ. When he has done this, then the Son himself will be made subject to him who put everything under him, so that God may be all in all. (1 Cor. 15:22–28)

Jesus' handing the kingdom back to God the Father will occur when the *end comes*. The end will come at the end of King Jesus' reign over God's kingdom. But for now, and until the time of the resurrection of the dead, the Father will put everything "under the feet" of the Son with the exception of Himself. Then after the resurrection of the dead, Jesus will deliver up the kingdom to the Father and subject Himself to the Father's authority. So Jesus has already come in His glory to begin judgment. He is now sitting on the judgment throne of His glory in the kingdom of God with all of the power of God the Father. Judgment Day is happening now!

When Jesus was on earth He sent out His disciples to declare the message of the kingdom to Israel. It was at this time that He made a profound statement that helps prove the kingdom and Jesus (invisibly) would come to earth shortly. He said these disciple evangelists who were sent out would not be able to go over all of the cities of Israel before the Son of Man would come.

When you are persecuted in one place, flee to another. Truly I tell you, you will not finish going through the towns of Israel before the Son of Man comes. (Matthew 10:23)

The following excerpt is from the noted John Gill. He comments on the phrase "before the Son of Man comes or till the son of man be come" (KJV), in Matthew 10:23, and he gives three possible explanations of what Jesus meant.

Till the son of man be come; which is not to be understood of his second coming to judgment, but either of his resurrection from the dead, when he was declared to be the Son of God, and when his glorification began; or of the pouring forth of the Spirit at the day of Pentecost, when his kingdom began more visibly to take place, and he was made, or manifested to be the Lord and Christ; or of his coming to take vengeance on his enemies, that would not have him to rule over them, and the persecutors of his ministers, at the destruction of Jerusalem. (John Gill's Exposition of the Bible, www. biblestudytools.com/commentaries/gills-exposition-of-the-bible/ matthew-10-23.html)

Here Gill gives several options; one being "of the pouring forth of the Spirit at the day of Pentecost, when his kingdom began more visibly to take place, and he was made, or manifested to be the Lord and Christ." I believe this to be in greater harmony with the rest of the scriptures, which I deal with more later on.

But Jesus obviously has not yet come back bodily. This will happen at the conclusion of His reign of salvation and judgment. Then he will come back to earth in the same manner as he left. This means as He visibly ascended into heaven, He will also visibly come back at the end of His reign.

After he said this, he was taken up before their very eyes, and a cloud hid him from their sight. They were looking intently up into the sky as he was going, when suddenly two men dressed in white stood beside them. "Men of Galilee," they said, "why do you stand here looking into the sky? This same Jesus, who has been taken from you into heaven, will come back in the same way you have seen him go into heaven." (Acts 1:9–11)

When Jesus comes again visibly, not just the saved but all will behold His glory and all will be fully aware of His presence.

Behold, He is coming with clouds, and every eye will see Him, even they who pierced Him. And all the tribes of the earth will mourn because of Him. Even so, Amen. (Revelation 1:7)

Jesus came in His Kingdom and in the Father's glory within the lifetime of His handpicked apostles. In speaking of His death He had told His disciples He would go away, but promised to return to them. Although He would one day return in His glorified body, He was not speaking of this in telling the disciples of His coming as the Comforter or Helper. Rather He was speaking of His return through the power of God's Holy Spirit. And He returned on the day of Pentecost, more than two thousand years ago, in all the power of the Holy Spirit of God. But even though He came to earth in the Spirit at that time, He continued to rule with all authority in heaven as well. All power in heaven and on earth had been given to Him, according to His own words in Matthew 28:18–20. Jesus spoke these words only moments before He ascended back into heaven.

Then Jesus came to them and said, "All authority in heaven and on earth has been given to me. Therefore go and make disciples of all nations, baptizing them in the name of the Father and of the Son and of the Holy Spirit, and teaching them to obey everything I have commanded you. And surely I am with you always, to the very end of the age." (NIV)

JUDGMENT DAY FORETOLD BY THE PROPHETS

The Christian age was the time to which the prophets had pointed for God's judgment of the world. From the resurrection of Christ to the bodily resurrection the kingdom of heaven would be established among men in this world. Both the prophet Daniel and the prophet Isaiah spoke of this great event as did many other Old Testament prophets. Daniel viewed the coming of God's kingdom in a vision of a great image of a man in which four successive world kingdoms are symbolized (Dan. 2). The first was the then present Babylonian kingdom. The next three would be the Persian, Grecian and the Roman Empires, as secular history also records. In speaking of the succession of the kings of the Roman Empire, Daniel says the following in connection with the eternal nature of God's spiritual kingdom.

In the time of those kings, the God of heaven will set up a kingdom that will never be destroyed, nor will it be left to another people. It will crush all those kingdoms and bring them to an end, but it will itself endure forever. (Daniel 2:44)

Daniel is clear in revealing that God would set up His kingdom in the days of these kings. When the kingdom of God has accomplished its purpose of salvation in this world through Jesus, all worldly kingdoms will have been subdued by it. Only God's kingdom will continue.

Isaiah views the coming of God's kingdom in the following way. He shows it as beginning at Jerusalem. He also speaks of it as a kingdom of peace in contrast to the kingdoms of the world. He points out that all nations shall flow to it, showing it to be made up of Gentiles as well as Jews.

The word that Isaiah the son of Amoz saw concerning Judah and Jerusalem. Now it shall come to pass in the latter days that the mountain of the Lord's house shall be established on the top of the mountains, and shall be exalted above the hills; and all nations shall flow to it.

Many people shall come and say, "Come, and let us go up to the mountain of the Lord, to the house of the God of Jacob; He will teach us His ways, And we shall walk in His paths." For out of Zion shall go forth the law and the word of the Lord from Jerusalem. He shall judge between the nations, and rebuke many people; they shall beat their swords into plowshares, and their spears into pruning hooks; nation shall not lift up sword against nation, neither shall they learn war anymore. (Isaiah 2:1–4)

Several key identifying points in this passage can aid in establishing the factual account of God's kingdom being established on earth. And with these key points in mind a much clearer idea of Judgment Day should emerge.

1. The first thing to notice is that the prophecy of Isaiah was dealing with Judah and Jerusalem. This prophecy was intended only for the

continuing nation of Judah before the Christian age, whose capital was at Jerusalem. Judah was the part of Israel that had continued to worship at Jerusalem after Israel was divided into two kingdoms. Judah would be the mother kingdom of the coming Messiah. Jacob had long ago, in conferring a blessing on his son Judah, testified to the continuance of Judah's role in bringing the scepter or kingship to Jesus the Messiah, referring to Him as Shiloh.

The scepter shall not depart from Judah, nor a lawgiver from between his feet, Until Shiloh comes; and to Him shall be the obedience of the people. (Gen. 49:10)

At the time of Isaiah, the nation of Israel had been divided into two nations. Up until the reign of Solomon, the son of King David, Israel had remained a united kingdom. However, after Solomon's reign, Solomon's son Rehoboam succeeded Solomon to the throne to rule over the kingdom of Israel. It was during Rehoboam's reign that Israel was divided. At that time ten tribes broke off, later to be called the northern kingdom of Israel, leaving only the tribes of Judah and Benjamin, which became known as the kingdom of Judah. Some of the Levites, who made up the priests, also remained with Judah.

The northern kingdom, thereafter called Israel, was established under the leadership of Jeroboam. The capitol city of Israel's northern kingdom was established at Samaria rather than Jerusalem. This left Rehoboam as the first king of Judah whose capitol was at Jerusalem (1 Kings 11–14). So the prophecy of Isaiah applied to the kingdom of Judah, which remained at Jerusalem, not the northern kingdom of Israel. The northern kingdom eventually assimilated into the Gentile nations.

2. Not only is it important to note the coming Messiah was prophesied to come from the tribe of Judah, but this kingdom would be superior in every way to all of the other kingdoms of the world. It was foretold

as being superior in power and longevity. Daniel says, "...the God of heaven will set up a kingdom that will never be destroyed.... It will crush all those kingdoms and bring them to an end, but it will itself endure forever" (Daniel 2:44)

3. Another great truth and identifying mark concerns the subjects of God's kingdom. This was making all citizens spiritual priests of the law, rather than the people being subjected to religious leaders who would interpret the law for them (1 Peter 2:9). God's people would no longer need interpreters of His will. They would have His will revealed through His word by His Spirit, which He promised to all (Acts 2:38–39). All would be priests, and all would be taught of God.

Many people shall come and say, "Come, and let us go up to the mountain of the Lord, To the house of the God of Jacob; <u>He will teach us</u> His ways, And we shall walk in His paths." (Isa. 2:3)

4. It is made perfectly clear in Jeremiah's prophecy that in God's kingdom through Christ each citizen would have a direct line of communication to God without the mediation of men.

"The days are coming," declares the LORD, "when I will make a new covenant with the people of Israel and with the people of Judah. It will not be like the covenant I made with their ancestors when I took them by the hand to lead them out of Egypt, because they broke my covenant, though I was a husband to them," declares the LORD. "This is the covenant I will make with the people of Israel after that time," declares the LORD. "I will put my law in their minds and write it on their hearts. I will be their God, and they will be my people. <u>No longer will they teach their neighbor, or say to one another, 'Know the LORD,' because they will all know me, from the least of them to the greatest</u>," declares the LORD. "For I will forgive their wickedness and will remember their sins no more." (Jeremiah 31:31–34)

5. Jerusalem was to be the place where the kingdom would be established and from where the law of God would go forth.

"For out of Zion shall go forth the law and the word of the Lord from Jerusalem." (Isa. 2–3)

6. God's kingdom would be a kingdom for the judgment of all the nations and all peoples of the world. This would fulfill God's promise to Abram to bless all peoples of the earth (Genesis 12:1–3). It would be a worldwide kingdom. It would be a kingdom that would ultimately bring everlasting peace to the world as declared by angels at the Lord's birth.

He shall judge between the nations, and rebuke many people; they shall beat their swords into plowshares, and their spears into pruning hooks; Nation shall not lift up sword against nation, neither will they learn war anymore.

MATTHEW 25

As we consider Matthew 25, beginning with verse 31 and continuing throughout the rest of the chapter, hopefully it will become obvious that this prophetic Judgment Day scene is a present and not just a future reality. The scriptures plainly teach the separation of the righteous from the unrighteous begins on Judgment Day and will continue during the entirety of the church age while the gospel is preached. During this period people are responding by accepting or rejecting it. This will continue until the bodily resurrection of the dead. After the bodily resurrection, judgment will be pronounced for punishment of the wicked and the righteous will be rewarded.

The previous passages of prophecy cited, along with many other prophetic messages, tell about the coming of God's kingdom to the world. All of these give context to the coming of Jesus as Savior of the world in the New Testament scriptures. In fact, the silver thread that runs throughout all bible prophecy is the coming of the Messiah in God's kingdom for judgment on planet earth.

Probably the most often used Judgment Day passage is Matthew 25. Now as we look closely at the words of Jesus and consider the complete text as recorded by Matthew, many of the truths about Judgment Day will be revealed.

When the Son of Man comes in His glory, and all the holy angels with Him, then He will sit on the throne of His glory. All the nations will be gathered before Him, and He will separate them one from another, as a shepherd divides his sheep from the goats. And He will set the sheep on His right hand, but the goats on the left. Then the King will say to those on His right hand, "Come, you blessed of My Father, inherit the kingdom prepared for you from the foundation of the world: for I was hungry and you gave me food; I was thirsty and you gave me drink; I was a stranger and you took me in; I was naked and you clothed me; I was sick and you visited me; I was in prison and you came to me." Then the righteous will answer Him, saying, "Lord, when did we see you hungry and feed you, or thirsty and give you drink? When did we see you a stranger and take you in or naked and clothe you? Or when did we see you sick, or in prison, and come to you?" And the King will answer and say to them, "Assuredly, I say to you, inasmuch as you did it to one of the least of these my brethren, you did it to me." Then He will also say to those on the left hand, "Depart from Me, you cursed, into the everlasting fire prepared for the devil and his angels: for I was hungry and you gave Me no food; I was thirsty and you gave Me no drink; I was a stranger and you did not take Me in, naked and you did not clothe Me, sick and in prison and you did not visit Me." Then they also will answer Him, saying, "Lord, when did we see You hungry or thirsty or a stranger or naked or sick or in prison, and did not minister to You?" Then He will answer them, saying, "Assuredly, I say to you, inasmuch as you did not do it to one of the least of these, you did not do it to Me." And these will go away into everlasting punishment, but the righteous into eternal life.

Jesus makes clear an identifying difference between the saved and lost will be in the disposition taken toward Him in His afflictions. "For I was hungry and you gave me food; I was thirsty and you gave me drink; I was a stranger and you took me in; I was naked and you clothed me; I was sick and you visited me; I was in prison and you came to me." When those on His right hand become confused as to when they ministered unto Him, He tells them it happened when they ministered unto "one of the least of these, my brethren." He said when they ministered unto His brethren it was equivalent to ministering unto Him. This is a profound statement. But it establishes unequivocally the greatest commandment, which is to love God and neighbor—on which commandment hangs all the law and prophets.

Jesus said to him, "'you shall love the Lord your God with all your heart, with all your soul, and with all your mind.' This is the first and great commandment. And the second is like it: 'You shall love your neighbor as yourself.' On these two commandments hang all the Law and the Prophets." (Matthew 22:37–40)

The disposition toward God and the love for humanity will eventually separate the saved from the unsaved. How is this? After taking a little thought, the point Jesus makes in Matthew 22 should be obvious. The difference between being saved or lost is a selfless, love-filled heart or its absence. This is the will (desire) of the Creator. This is why David was a man after God's own heart. This is why love is called the royal law. And on this hangs all the law and prophecies.

If you really fulfill the royal law according to the Scripture, "You shall love your neighbor as yourself," you do well; but if you show partiality, you commit sin, and are convicted by the law as transgressors. (James 2:8–9)

It's easy to feel the need to condense the requirements for salvation down to a set of rituals or a code of legal requirements. The mind has a natural tendency to seek a minimum-requirement religion by doing only what is absolutely necessary to earn God's favor. But love is not like this. Love does not stop with a minimum requirement. The Lord's requirement was not just a checklist of duties, but rather a love-filled life that will produce the works required to satisfy God's will through faith. As Christians, we don't do good works in order to be saved, but rather we are saved by grace (unearned favor) in order to do good works. This happens when our faith is working through love.

For in Christ Jesus neither circumcision nor uncircumcision avails anything, but faith working through love. (Galatians 5:6)

When the love of God is shed abroad in our hearts (Romans 5:5), by our obedience to the truth, it becomes a purifying agent for the sins of the soul.

Since you have purified your souls in obeying the truth through the Spirit in sincere love of the brethren, love one another fervently with a pure heart. (1 Peter 1:22)

The governing agent required to walk acceptably before God can be called a law. But it is not a meritorious legal system. James calls the law Jesus requires a "law of liberty." He also calls it "the royal law" of love and the law of the Spirit of life. It was by and through this law that our example was set by the Lord Jesus.

The law of liberty is not like the law Israel received from Moses, written on tablets of stone, but it is a promise of pardon from sin and a promise of eternal life through faith working by love. Jesus called it a more abundant life. To the Jewish Christians of the first century, this was a completely different way of thinking about law.

I [Jesus] have come that they may have life, and that they may have it more abundantly. (John 10:10)

The law of liberty is the requirements that flow out of love. It is called the law of liberty because everything that proceeds from a love-filled heart is by faith in God. We are spiritually motivated by a heart surrendered to God's will through love by faith. Love is the fulfilling of the law. There is no law against love.

But the fruit of the Spirit is love, joy, peace, longsuffering, kindness, goodness, faithfulness, gentleness, self-control. Against such there is no law. (Galatians 5:22–23)

James speaks of the law of liberty as he writes his letter to the early Christians.

But the one who looks into the perfect law, the law of liberty, and perseveres, being no hearer who forgets but a doer who acts, he will be blessed in his doing. (James 1:25)

The law of liberty is the perfect law. This perfect law of liberty could never have been made available to lost humanity without the redemptive work of Jesus. The whole creation was cursed and humanity was condemned under the law of sin and death. Death was inescapable without the divine justice of God being satisfied by an innocent blood sacrifice. James refers to the law of liberty, rather than the law of sin and death, in speaking of the royal law. Once again, the perfect law of liberty has been made available to sinful man only because of Jesus. In writing of this perfect law, James is really preaching the gospel (good news) of Jesus Christ. Obedience to the gospel of Christ is not just in performing rituals or legal requirements, but a grateful response to the message of God's love. Even though God's message of hope through Christ is called a law, it is not a law for the purpose of condemning, but rather for saving. It is a peace offering and pardon through the death of a Savior.

For God did not send His Son into the world to condemn the world, but that the world through Him might be saved. (John 3:17)

Paul called this system of serving God the "law of faith."

Where is boasting then? It is excluded. By what law? Of works? No, but by the law of faith. (Romans 3:27)

The law of liberty is a law where love is supreme. The law of liberty found in the kingdom of God's Son gives each citizen the opportunity to have his or her faith counted as righteousness.

Even the righteousness of God, through faith in Jesus Christ, to all and on all <u>*who believe*</u>*; for there is no difference. (Romans 3:22)*

Since there is one God who will justify the circumcised by faith and the uncircumcised through faith. (Romans 3:30)

Abraham became known as the father of faith because of his unwavering trust in God's promise. Even though Jesus had not been sacrificed during the time of Abraham, still it was this same system of faith that caused God to accept Abraham's works and account him righteous by faith. God has never changed in that righteousness and salvation come by grace through faith.

He (Abraham) did not waver at the promise of God through unbelief, but was strengthened in faith, giving glory to God, and being fully convinced that what He had promised He was also able to perform. And therefore "it was accounted to him for righteousness." Now it was not written for his sake alone that it was imputed to him, <u>*but also for us*</u>*. It shall be imputed to us who believe in Him who raised up Jesus our Lord from the dead, who was delivered up because of our offenses, and was raised because of our justification. (Romans 4:20–25)*

I might say one other thing in connection to the law of liberty. When James mentions the law of liberty, he also speaks of the sin of partiality shown by some in the church at that time. They were shown as being in violation of the command to love our neighbor as ourselves. I talk more extensively about partiality throughout this chapter, but first listen to the full context of the writing of James on the subject of partiality. Partiality is in direct opposition to the royal law. Only those who ascribe to keeping the royal law can have hope of living by the perfect law of liberty.

My brethren, do not hold the faith of our Lord Jesus Christ, the Lord of glory, with partiality. For if there should come into your assembly a man with gold rings, in fine apparel, and there should also come in a poor man in filthy clothes, and you pay attention to the one wearing the fine clothes and say to him, "You sit here in a good place," and say to the poor man, "You stand there," or, "Sit here at my foot-

stool," have you not shown partiality among yourselves, and become judges with evil thoughts? Listen, my beloved brethren: Has God not chosen the poor of this world to be rich in faith and heirs of the kingdom which He promised to those who love Him? But you have dishonored the poor man. Do not the rich oppress you and drag you into the courts? Do they not blaspheme that noble name by which you are called? If you really fulfill the royal law according to the Scripture, "You shall love your neighbor as yourself," you do well; but if you show partiality, you commit sin, and are convicted by the law as transgressors. (James 2:1–9)

James begins by saying, "My brethren, do not hold the faith of our Lord Jesus Christ, the Lord of glory, with partiality." He ends by saying, "But if you show partiality, you commit sin, and are convicted by the law as transgressors." The faith of (or in) our Lord Jesus Christ cannot be held onto when we are partial in our thoughts and actions. Our faith in Jesus is totally disabled with the absence of love. Love bears, believes, hopes and endures all things.

Love suffers long and is kind; love does not envy; love does not parade itself, is not puffed up; does not behave rudely, does not seek its own, is not provoked, thinks no evil; does not rejoice in iniquity, but rejoices in the truth; bears all things, believes all things, hopes all things, endures all things. (1 Corinthians 13:4–7)

To walk by faith is to recognize God's love toward us. It is understood by us—by receiving, believing and obeying the gospel message. Only in this way are we enabled to walk by faith. We walk by faith only when the realization of God's love is in our hearts. Paul tells us we all have sinned and are all condemned before God. Through the righteousness of Jesus, by His sinless life, God accepted the sacrifice of His death as an offering to pay for our sins, thus allowing us to be counted as righteous by faith.

For He made Him who knew no sin to be sin for us, that we might become the righteousness of God in Him. (2 Cor. 5:21)

Only Jesus was sinless, but He became sin for us.

Surely He has borne our griefs and carried our sorrows; yet we esteemed Him stricken, smitten by God, and afflicted. But He was wounded for our transgressions, He was bruised for our iniquities; the chastisement for our peace was upon Him, and by His stripes we are healed. All we like sheep have gone astray; we have turned, every one, to his own way; and the Lord has laid on Him the iniquity of us all. (Isaiah 53:4–6)

Only by embracing the righteousness in Christ can we be found guiltless from the curse of the law. We are guiltless not because we are sinless, but because of our trust in He who was. In Christ we can please God by living a life governed by selflessness and impartiality. These characteristics are not in the DNA of the unregenerate mind.

SPIRITUAL REGENERATION

Another word used in the Bible to describe the process of salvation through Christ is the word *regeneration*. Regeneration is a way to speak of the spiritual rebirth that comes through the generating power of God's Holy Spirit and the Word of God, which is the sword of the Spirit (James 1:18, 1 Peter 1:23, John 3:5–6, Hebrews 4:12).

For the word of God is living and powerful, and sharper than any two-edged sword, piercing even to the division of soul and spirit, and of joints and marrow, and is a discerner of the thoughts and intents of the heart. (Heb. 4:12)

But when the kindness and the love of God our Savior toward man appeared, not by works of righteousness which we have done, but according to His mercy He saved us, <u>through the washing of regeneration and renewing of the Holy Spirit</u>. (Titus 3:4–5)

Jesus speaks of regeneration not only as a process or method of obtaining salvation, but also as the time of judgment to come during His reign in God's kingdom.

So Jesus said to them, "Assuredly I say to you, that in the regeneration, when the Son of Man sits on the throne of His glory, you who have followed Me will also sit on twelve thrones, judging the twelve tribes of Israel." (Matt. 19:28)

Notice His reference to the time in which the Son of Man sits on His throne of glory. This time is referred to as the regeneration or the time in which judgment is happening. I never read the Bible a lot for myself before I became a Christian at the age of twenty. I heard a lot of people talk about the Bible. I also heard the Bible read a lot at church. I had a deep curiosity about God and spiritual matters and I truly believed the Bible was inspired by God. Nonetheless, I felt confident that almost all that had been handed down by my parents and my church was sound doctrine. I also felt I was not really qualified to study and interpret for myself—a mistake made by many. I figured that the wisest minds of the ages had already searched the scriptures and therefore the rest of us had been given the best interpretation of what was revealed therein. I no longer believe this.

I have now come to realize that the main reason for my lack of spiritual discernment was because I was in an *unregenerate* state, spiritually speaking. And this is the problem with many who only follow tradition and not God's counsel. I was spiritually afar off and alienated from the commonwealth of spiritual Israel.

That at that time you were without Christ, being aliens from the common-wealth of Israel and strangers from the covenants of promise, having no hope and without God in the world. (Ephesians 2:12)

In other words, I was not spiritually connected with God. I was in bondage to the desires of the flesh rather than led by the Spirit of God. In this state no one is even capable of "desiring the sincere milk of the Word" in order to grow and learn. We must be reborn and be a spiritual baby to desire spiritual milk. I could know I was powerless in regard to God's will, but I was unable to do anything about it in my alienated and unregenerate state. In other words, I was powerless and without hope because I was *without God in the world.*

The Word teaches we cannot know the things of God until God gives us the power of spiritual discernment. When we are given the ability to discern and spiritually understand we will then immediately desire to know, just as a newborn baby desires to nurse and receive its mother's milk. This can only happen as a result of a spiritual rebirth.

But the natural man does not receive the things of the Spirit of God, for they are foolishness to him; nor can he know them, because they are spiritually discerned. (1 Cor. 2:14) (KJV)

The apostle John tells us, "…because He who is in you is greater than he who is in the world" (1 John 4:4). After I was baptized into Christ I became a son rather than a stranger. And having then God's Spirit to lead me, everything began to change.

And because you are sons, God has sent forth the Spirit of His Son into your hearts, crying out, "Abba, Father!" (Galatians 4:6)

I began then to gradually realize that my relationship with the Father through His Son gave me as much as anyone the potential to receive God's counsel and know His will. This is often difficult to grasp when most of the Christian world looks to clergy for spiritual enlightenment. But the Bible clearly teaches all who are a part of the new covenant will be taught of God.

But this is the covenant that I will make with the house of Israel after those days, says the Lord: I will put My law in their minds, and write it on their hearts; and I will be their God, and they shall be My people. No more shall every man teach his neighbor, and every man his brother, saying, "Know the Lord," for they all shall know Me, from the least of them to the greatest of them, says the Lord. For I will forgive their iniquity, and their sin I will remember no more. (Jer. 31:33–34)

Without God's Word in us we cannot live by God's direction and counsel. Secondhand religion will not work! God's word is the sword (or cutting instrument) of the Spirit. It can pierce the heart. It is *a discerner of the thoughts and intents of the heart.* The same Spirit that quickens (makes alive) a believer also causes the Word abiding in us to be made alive. This living Word could also be called the Spirit of Christ or the Spirit of God. The Holy Spirit, the Spirit of God and the Spirit of Christ are the same Holy Spirit. There is only one Holy Spirit (Eph. 4:4).

For those who live according to the flesh set their minds on the things of the flesh, but those who live according to the Spirit, *the things of the Spirit. For to be carnally minded is death, but to be spiritually minded is life and peace. Because the carnal mind is enmity against God; for it is not subject to the law of God, nor indeed can be. So then, those who are in the flesh cannot please God. But you are not in the flesh but in the Spirit, if indeed the* Spirit of God *dwells in you. Now if anyone does not have the* Spirit of Christ, *he is not His. (Romans 8:5–9)*

As I continued in my Christian journey, I also became aware of what the apostle Peter said regarding God's word being necessary not only to discern God's will but to give us spiritual maturity as well.

Therefore, rid yourselves of all malice and all deceit, hypocrisy, envy, and slander of every kind. Like newborn babies, crave pure spiritual milk, so that by it you may grow up in your salvation. (1 Peter 2:1–2) (NIV)

Finally, my spirit was intensely craving to know God's will for my life. But this revelation was given only after I made my spiritual commitment to the lordship of Christ. But then, almost instantly, I really wanted to know what God's will was for my life. I was now a new spiritual creature in His kingdom. I wanted to know what part I was to play in His great scheme of redemption. I wanted to know about the past history of God dealing with the human race and all of creation. And I also wanted to know what He had revealed through His Word to show me what to expect for the future.

So I prayed for wisdom and His word instructed me. And I studied and meditated on God's will. I then, slowly but surely, began to learn and grow. At the time my progress seemed so very slow, but now as I look back over many years I realize it came faster than it seemed then. Certainly I learned at a far more rapid pace than I could possibly learn now in my older years. This is the reason it is important to seek our Creator in the days of our youth.

My wants and desires were changing. I also noticed things about the scriptures I had never noticed before. One was that even though all scripture is equally inspired, all scripture does not carry the same spiritual weight. The foundational commandments that proceed from love are weightier and more spiritually transformational. This is what Jesus wanted His disciples to understand when He spoke to the Jewish religious leaders about their omitting "weightier" matters of the law. *Justice, mercy and faith* are the foundational principles of the law of God, flowing directly from the love of God.

Woe to you, scribes and Pharisees, hypocrites! For you pay tithe of mint and anise and cummin, and have neglected the weightier matters of the law: justice and mercy and faith. These you ought to have done, without leaving the others undone. (Matt. 23:23) (KJV)

I began to learn new things about my traditional teachings. I learned these teachings can be a lot like a dear Christian brother in Christ once told me about money. He said, "Jerry, money is a wonderful servant." He then hesitated for a couple seconds and added, "But a very cruel master." Tradition rooted and grounded in God's word will serve us well. But when our traditions evolve into a sectarian and divisive mindset, we fail as a servant of God and become a servant of the traditions of men.

GOD DOES NOT SHOW FAVORITISM

The Word of God contains scriptures with great statements of promise. To me these passages of promise are the fundamental building blocks in the revelation of God's will for our life. In other words, our hope is built on promises. And these promises, generally speaking, are those explicit verses or passages that need no great study or interpretation. But even though these fundamental passages are simply and clearly set forth, they often are overlooked. For example, one of the first verses of this kind, which was eye-opening for me, is in the book of Acts. Listen to God's promise!

Then Peter began to speak: "I now realize how true it is that <u>God does not show favoritism</u>, but accepts from every nation the one who fears him and does what is right." (Acts 10:34–35) (NIV)

This verse was not only exciting for me in that it shed new light about the loving nature of my heavenly Father, but it also eliminated the possibility of eternal salvation being left to chance. It teaches God shows no favoritism toward anyone, but "<u>So</u> loved the world that He gave His only begotten Son." His offering of salvation was and is not a cold, one-size-fits-all plan. It was a "great" salvation, one not accidentally stumbled onto by some and missed by others. It was one made uniquely for every individual who entered by the same door—Jesus!

And like this passage, there are many other clearly stated great and precious scriptures of promise given as the Lord speaks to us through His word. Through the years as I became aware of these many promises I began to realize many previously held traditional beliefs were scripturally unfounded. And that is because I now see my heavenly Father in a different way.

For example, by understanding God has no favorites I have slowly come to realize Native Americans who lived on the North American continent thousands of years ago, by having feared God and by doing what they believed and knew to be right, could be accepted just as much as anyone else. Judgment is based on the disposition of the hearts of folks in what they have been enabled by God to do. There is no reason to think they would be treated differently by God than anyone else. The psalmist writes that the fear of the Lord is the beginning of wisdom. Listen as Paul writes to the Roman Christians, weighing in on this same thought.

For there is no partiality with God. For as many as have sinned without law will also perish without law, and as many as have sinned in the law will be judged by the law (for not the hearers of the law are just in the sight of God, but the doers of the law will be justified; for when Gentiles, who do not have the law, by nature do the things in the law, these, although not having the law, are a law to themselves, who show the work of the law written in their hearts, their conscience also bearing witness, and between themselves their thoughts accusing or else excusing them) in the day when God will judge the secrets of men by Jesus Christ according to my gospel. (Romans 2:11–16)

Scriptures like these, which I gradually became aware of early on in my Christian life, opened my mind to the greatness of the grace, love and mercy of the heavenly Father. They also made me realize dependency on traditional teaching can be spiritually dangerous. Another precious promise is found in Paul's letter to the Romans. He says all things work together for good to those who love God. I don't really have much of a clue how God does it—that is, to work everything out for good for those who love Him. But He says it and I believe it!

And we know that all things work together for good to those who love God, to those who are the called according to His purpose. (Romans 8:28)

And for those seeking glory, honor, and immortality, the great Creator grants eternal life, …eternal life to those who by patient continuance in doing good <u>seek</u> for glory, honor, and immortality. (Romans 2:7)

I cannot figure out how it all works. But I really don't need to know how the Lord does it. His ways are *past finding out*—but having said that, I believe with all my heart He does what He promises. And I believe it simply because I trust in His promises more than in myself and in my own human reasoning.

So now, with a more trusting faith, I can be fully assured everyone has equal worth in God's eyes. I'm not required to make judgment on anyone because of their nationality, color of skin, outward appearance, etc. This means any idea that might cast a shadow or bad reflection on God's impartiality is to be rejected. These beautiful passages showing God's impartiality are by no means the only foundational truths needing no special interpretation. I now realize sometimes it is less important to interpret the scriptures than to simply believe them.

I was able by simply trusting in this one single promise of God's impartiality (Romans 2:11–16) to be steered clear, over and over again, from many potential dangerous entanglements with tradition and erroneous doctrines of men. If we really believe God does not show partiality toward anyone, we can look at our fellow sojourners with more love and less judgment. And this is only one of many of God's promises to trust in order that our souls might be delivered from the deceptive snares of Satan. The principal point I would make is simply this—we must put our trust in the Word of God alone in all matters pertaining to salvation!

And that brings me back to the thought of "When the Son of Man comes in His glory" in Matthew 25. There are few things Jesus taught that give a more concise, but complete view of the judgment scene as does this account.

When the Son of Man comes in His glory, and all the holy angels with Him, then He will sit on the throne of His glory. (Matt.25:31)

CONCLUDING THOUGHT

When we take a close look at Matthew 25:31 depicting this scene of glory and judgment, we begin to understand many things about Judgment Day. There are some things in particular we will see as we focus on Matthew's account of Judgment Day in this passage. It will make it easier for us to understand when Judgment Day begins, the process that follows as it continues and how it will end. Most people have only followed traditional thinking in connection with what Judgment Day is all about. Traditional thinking has been almost completely connected with the thought that everything about Judgment Day would follow the bodily resurrection. My intention is to prove this theory wrong by the scriptures. I will not make this attempt by trying to justify or condemn any traditional church teaching; rather, my goal is to simply attempt to rightly divine the Word of God.

So we need to ask ourselves a couple of very important questions. Does the common traditional view of Judgment Day line up with the factual evidence produced by the scriptures when they are rightly divided? Or does our traditional thinking only fog up our spiritual vision, keeping the light of the scriptures from shining through? I ask you to temporarily close your mind to what is taught in the religious institutions and allow the Bible to become your only source of information for the present.

The fact that Jesus has already been given all power to judge and reward is very clearly borne out within the Spirit-breathed Word of God. He is now, at this present time, sitting on His throne in all the glory of the Father. And as He sits on His throne He exercises all of the power and authority given Him to judge and reward the world!

CHAPTER 4
IN HIS FATHER'S GLORY

One of the definitions of *glory* according to the *Merriam-Webster Dictionary* is a state of great gratification or exaltation. Sometimes as I think of glory it takes me back to one of my most cherished memories.

When I was growing up as a young boy our family was poor by most standards. But by working hard as a family unit we survived. My dad farmed with a team of horses before we finally got a small tractor. One of the workhorses we had back then was a mare named Maude. I was only about four years old when Dad began to let me come to the field to bring him water to drink. My purpose was simple—to bring him a container of water Mom had fixed for him, without dropping and breaking the jar. It was a half-gallon mason jar wrapped with Dad's winter jacket. I remember how big and heavy it seemed to me at the time.

When I got to the cornfield I would wait at the end of the row for Dad and Maude. And as Dad would come back down the row toward me I would hear him make a clicking noise with his tongue. This was done to control Maude's walking speed. There was also the occasional words "gee" or "haw," which was his way of telling Maude to move a little to the left or a little to the right in the row. But Maude seldom deviated in the least as she slowly walked forward in the row plowing the corn. She seemed to know exactly what Dad wanted from her, and she did it with grace and style. Many times I heard Dad praise Maude to Mom when his day of work with her was over.

Dad would then stop at the end of the row and I would hand him the water. This made me feel as though I was an important part of the operation. After he took his drink of water he would turn Maude around and then set me up on her back to ride as they worked until lunchtime.

It's difficult if not impossible to describe in human language how much I enjoyed this adventure! I really felt I was playing a major role with my dad and Maude as "we" plowed the corn. I would sit up close to her neck and hold on the horns of the harness hames while viewing a most beautiful world. I loved it all! I loved the thrill of riding on Maude's back, but mostly I loved the comfort and security of being with two of my favorite individuals in the whole world. I loved the scent of the soil being plowed. And when we came close to the rail fence along the back of the field, I looked on the beauty of the wildflowers along the fence, enjoying the scent of the honeysuckle as its fragrance would drift toward me and Maude. Even the smell of sweaty Maude made me feel good. It was like everything was just how it ought to be and the world was made just for me. I would sit up there, swaying with the rhythm of Maude's movements. It was glorious!

Experiences like these in my early life gave me my initial sense of certainty of the existence of a higher power. This initial faith was to be borne out and grow in later years as I read and studied the scriptures. My childhood ventures were natural experiences that began to form a definition of *glory* within my soul long before I ever used the word. Knowing I was loved—and viewing God's creation from the back of an old farm mare—would always help me. Actually, even then, these experiences were serving to form a foundation for my life. I was beginning to know something of the glory of the one true and living God!

We spend most of our lives looking at and thinking about things through our natural senses. In fact our natural lives are daily lived out by gathering evidence through our human senses in order to process thoughts and make decisions. If we are blessed to possess all of our sensory faculties, each day probably starts by opening our eyes to be awakened by the morning light. We then once again begin to sense the world around us. Every day begins by seeing, hearing, smelling, touching and tasting in order to receive vital information needed to survive and be sustained, as well as having the ability to enjoy or be warned. We begin this process at birth and it continues day after day as long as we live. This is our natural way of life. And this is the only life we will ever know as long as we are absent from a higher form of spiritual insight.

This natural (or non-spiritual) mind will continue to perceive only by and through its natural senses unless or until it is spiritually regenerated. I briefly touched on this in the second chapter. The natural sensory discerning ability is possessed in a great variety of specific ways in each created family or species. And even though the systems vary from one creature to another, they are given for the same purpose. This natural ability is the method of processing information God gives to all of His living creation. All of God's creation is equipped with sensory systems, giving His creatures the ability to do and be what the Lord desires of them.

Once again for emphasis: this is the only possible way *natural* man can gain knowledge and perception. It must come through the exercising of the natural human senses. I think Paul may have had something like this in mind when speaking to a group of people in Acts 17:28. He told them God was not far from each of them. He then said the following. "For in him we live and move and have our being."

PARTAKERS OF THE DIVINE NATURE

There is hope to elevate the *natural* mind above and beyond this natural realm. The natural human mind can be spiritually regenerated to discern beyond the ability of the human senses. In its unregenerate state the natural mind is only motivated by its physical or natural desires, whereas the regenerated mind can be motivated by spiritual or godlike desires. These motivations are generated by the Spirit of God through the discernment or counsel of His will or Word.

For those who live according to the flesh set their minds on the things of the flesh, but those who live according to the Spirit, the things of the Spirit. (Romans 8:5)

The effects of spiritual regeneration can occur only when our minds have been enabled to receive and know the things of the mind of Christ, which is to say, partaking in *divine nature*. This allows an escape from the corruptive influence of the fleshly or natural man.

But the natural man does not receive the things of the Spirit of God, for they are foolishness to him; nor can he know them, because they are spiritually discerned. But he who is spiritual judges all things, yet he himself is rightly judged by no one. For "who has known the mind of the Lord that he may instruct Him?" But we have the mind of Christ. *(1 Corinthians 2:14–16)*

Spiritual regeneration is a process that has a transformative effect on the perception of the mind. The process occurs by changing the motivational structure of the natural mind with Christlike desires. These are desires that are motivated only by love, creating a state of mind that seeks to do only the will of God. Ambitions motivated by love are pure and always go beyond the natural self-seeking fleshly ambitions. This change not only enables a transcending of fleshly impulses but also spiritually empowers the mind to quench or eliminate them. In short, the natural fleshly desires coming through the physical senses can never transform (change in form) the mind. The natural desires can only conform (act according to the law or rule) to the naturally built-in genetic programming present in the individual. If or when, however, the natural human mind is regenerated and enlightened by God's Holy Spirit, revealing God's will to that mind, the individual then becomes a "partaker of the divine nature."

By which have been given to us exceedingly great and precious promises, that through these you may be partakers of the <u>divine nature</u>, having escaped the corruption that is in the world through lust. (2 Peter 1:4)

The Spirit of God is the divine spiritual transmitter working in tandem with God's Word or will. Once it has been regenerated, the mind can operate on a higher plane that can then become enlightened to the truth of God's will. Only by God's Spirit, which dwells in His people, can we find the Spirit of truth. And, according to Jesus, by knowing the truth we can be made free.

The Spirit of truth, whom the world cannot receive, because it neither sees Him nor knows Him; but you know Him, for He dwells with you and will be in you. (John 14:17)

But when the Helper comes, whom I shall send to you from the Father, the Spirit of truth who proceeds from the Father, He will testify of Me. (John 15:26)

However, when He, the Spirit of truth, has come, He will guide you into all truth; for He will not speak on His own authority, but whatever He hears He will speak; and He will tell you things to come. (John 16:13)

So God's people can know the truth because of being enabled to operate with a higher and deeper source of information than is possible for the natural, unregenerate mind. This higher source of information is given through the *implanted word.*

Therefore lay aside all filthiness and overflow of wickedness, and receive with meekness the <u>implanted word</u>, which is able to save your souls. (James 1:21)

The implanted Word of God is in effect a divine counselor bringing God's will to a regenerated mind. It is very important to understand that the will of God is the <u>only</u> information the Spirit will bring to bear on the regenerated mind. This was the way of the pure mind of Christ as it guided his disciples by the Word of God through the revealing power of His Holy Spirit. This guidance is into the ways of His love and truth. Any and all other information brought to the mind is brought by the natural presence of the flesh. This is the struggle or war God's people fight continuously in the spiritual arena.

For though we walk in the flesh, we do not war according to the flesh. For the weapons of our warfare are not carnal but mighty in God for pulling down strongholds, casting down arguments and every high thing that exalts itself against the knowledge of God, bringing every thought into captivity to the obedience of Christ. (2 Cor. 10:3–5)

The spiritual regenerating process causes an individual to be reprogrammed by the Holy Spirit of God working through and acting upon the Word or will of God our Creator. In this special way each spiritual constituent becomes personally aware of God's will through God's power and presence in his or her life. And each is subsequently given the desire to seek after the will of the Father. By becoming enlightened to God's will the recipient becomes aware of his or her fleshly nature, which is in opposition to the will of God. He or she then can fight and conquer fleshly impulses *that war with the soul.* In a word, he or she can discern both good and evil. Peter shows the same Word of the Spirit that begets the children of God will also promote their spiritual growth and well-being.

Since you have purified your souls in obeying the truth through the Spirit in sincere love of the brethren, love one another fervently with a pure heart, having been born again, not of corruptible seed but incorruptible, through the word of God which lives and abides forever. (1 Peter 1:22–23)

Therefore, laying aside all malice, all deceit, hypocrisy, envy, and all evil speaking, as newborn babes, desire the pure milk of the word that you may grow thereby, if indeed you have tasted that the Lord is gracious. (1 Peter 2:1–3)

Once the believer has been made alive by the Spirit and has received the engrafted or implanted Word of God, a Christlike mind begins to develop. It is a mind given the ability to escape and rise above the limitations of the former fleshly nature. This is why the scriptures refer to this process as becoming a partaker of the *mind of Christ* and a partaker of the *divine nature*. The promise of God for all obedient believers to *receive the gift of the Holy Spirit* was given in the gospel message by Peter on the day of Pentecost. This is one of the precious promises Peter spoke of later in his second epistle. Trusting in His promises enables us to become *partakers of the divine nature.*

By which have been given to us exceedingly great and precious promises, that through these you may be <u>partakers of the divine nature</u>, having escaped the corruption that is in the world through lust. (2 Peter 1:4)

Paul makes clear to the church at Corinth that the enabling power of the Spirit allows the mind to make judgments from a spiritual perspective. This is the perception that has been symbolically drawn from living waters. It is indeed of the *mind of Christ.*

The person with the Spirit makes judgments about all things, but such a person is not subject to merely human judgments, for, "Who has known the mind of the Lord so as to instruct him?" But we have <u>the mind of Christ</u>. (1 Cor. 2:15–16) (NIV)

Once again, to the church at Corinth, Paul speaks plainly of the effect of the God's Holy Spirit on the mind of believers.

But as it is written: "Eye has not seen, nor ear heard, nor have entered into the heart of man the things which God has prepared for those who love Him." But God has revealed them to us through His Spirit. For the Spirit searches all things, yes the deep things of God. For what man knows the things of a man except the spirit of the man which is in him? Even so no one knows the things of God except the Spirit of God. Now we have received, not the spirit of the world, but the Spirit who is from God, that we might know the things that have been freely given to us by God. (1 Cor. 2:9–12)

After the natural mind has been regenerated, renewed and transformed through the power of this heavenly spiritual process, everything begins to change.

Therefore, if anyone is in Christ, he is a new creation; old things have passed away; behold, all things have become new. (2 Cor. 5:17)

In reality the things around us do not change, but the minds of individuals are changed with respect to how they view the things around them. This is the point at which the desires and motivational structure of the individual begin to change. He or she now seeks to please God rather than self. It all happens as a result of a changed relationship to God the Father, made possible by being led through the guidance of a divine receptor, which is the Holy Spirit of God.

Once this intimate relationship with God begins to occur, the newly reborn child of God can be motivated by love rather than fear. They are now (albeit by adoption) children of God.

For those who are led by the Spirit of God are the children of God. The Spirit you received does not make you slaves, so that you live in fear again; rather, the Spirit you received brought about your adoption to son-ship. And by him we cry, "Abba, Father." (Romans 8:14–15) (NIV)

The word <u>Abba</u> is an Aramaic word that would most closely be translated as "Daddy." It was a common term that young children would use to address their fathers. It signifies the close, intimate relationship of a father to his child, as well as the childlike trust that a young child puts in his "daddy." (From gotQuestions.org, www.gotquestions.org/Abba-Father.htm)

All of the transforming power of the Spirit comes only by way of the engrafted or implanted Word of God being welcomed into the heart of the believer. Listen once again.

Wherefore lay apart all filthiness and superfluity of naughtiness, and receive with meekness <u>the engrafted word</u>, which is able to save your souls. (James 1:21) (KJV)

The Word of God, which makes spiritual judgments and gives spiritual direction, is either accepted or rejected as the standard for one's life. When we reject the Word of God we cannot receive the things of the Spirit of God. And too the Word of God is the only standard for God's judgment on sin. During His personal ministry, Jesus made the following statement to His hearers.

He who rejects Me, and does not receive My words, has that which judges him—the word that I have spoken will judge him in the last day. (John 12:48)

So the spiritually regenerated mind stands in stark contrast to the carnal or unregenerate mind. In fact it stands in opposition, as an enemy to the natural or fleshly mind. The mind of a new spiritually created individual has been transformed to think differently. It desires no longer to put the greater emphasis on the seen, temporal things. Instead it begins a process of receiving and being guided by a spiritual compass toward the unseen, eternal things of God. Thus the new mind now receives things by and of the Living Word rather than through the natural impulses of a fleshly mind. Through this process the individual can be led by God's Spirit in order to continue receiving God's will. By knowing God's will he or she will learn how to think, speak and act to please God.

And do not be conformed to this world, but be transformed by the renewing of your mind, that you may prove what is that good and acceptable and perfect will of God. (Romans 12:2)

This spiritual way of life is only acquired by believing and trusting in the power of God through the word of His promises. Through this spiritual renewing process the newly regenerated mind is enabled not only to believe in God but also to walk (live a life) by faith rather than just by sight. It is not enough to just believe in God—we must believe God!

While we do not look at the things which are seen, but at the things which are not seen. For the things which are seen are temporary, but the things which are not seen are eternal. (2 Cor. 4:18)

We often refer to this spiritual perception as the eye of faith. Once again, we can understand by the scriptures that by trusting in God, through faith in His promises, we become perceptive to things that cannot be received through our natural senses. Now notice the impact of the following explicit scriptural fact.

However, as it is written: "What no eye has seen, what no ear has heard, and what no human mind has conceived the things God has prepared for those who love him." (1 Cor. 2:9) (NIV)

When I think of the awesomeness of the transformed life of a child of God, it takes my mind back to a lesson I gave at church a few years back, entitled "Metamorphosis." The lesson dealt with the similarities between the changed life of a Christian and a caterpillar being changed into a beautiful monarch butterfly. Following is a short excerpt from the lesson.

The Bible tells us that we must be in Christ to be a new creature or creation. Only in Christ is there hope of spiritual transformation. The monarch butterfly lays its eggs on a leaf. A tiny caterpillar is hatched. Its only desire is to eat. It first eats the eggshell, then the leaf on which it lies. By the end of the first day it has eaten more than its own weight. It eats and eats and does nothing else except to take short rests between meals.

But when the caterpillar is full grown it quits eating and attaches itself to a leaf. At this point the caterpillar must either submit to the process of *metamorphosis* or die. The caterpillar then makes a button of silk, which it uses to fasten its body to a leaf or a twig. Next, the caterpillar's skin comes off. In effect the caterpillar actually sacrifices itself and becomes dead to his old self in order to be in the place of transformation.

The same is true in the spiritual realm. We must put on or get in the place—the only place—where we can be transformed. We cannot become a new creation outside of Christ. But if anyone is in Christ they can become new creatures. The old things must pass away in order for the new things to begin. The Bible tells us, "We are all children of God by faith in Jesus Christ. For as many as have been baptized into Christ, have put on Christ" (Galatians 3:26–27).

THY KINGDOM COME

We are traditionally programmed to think the only reason Jesus came into the world was to bring salvation to fallen man. But there was another reason. The other reason was to bring about *the restoration of all things*, which is discussed in more detail in another chapter.

And that He may send Jesus Christ, who was preached to you before, whom heaven must receive until the times of <u>restoration of all things</u>, which God has spoken by the mouth of all His holy prophets since the world began. (Acts 3:20–21)

In the course of time many things had to come together and transpire in order for this end to be achieved. All of it would be accomplished through the power and authority of the incarnate Word—that was and is Jesus, the only begotten Son of God.

An important part of the mission of Jesus in this world was to choose and prepare certain men for the launching of the gospel message of salvation into all the world. After these special men were chosen, Jesus gradually taught them the mysteries of the kingdom of God before His death. It was only after the Lord's resurrection, by way of a baptismal (immersed) measure of the Holy Spirit, that the newly appointed apostles of Jesus were fully enlightened to the mysteries of His will. The teachings the disciples had previously heard from Jesus were brought back to their minds as the Lord has promised them before His death.

At a certain point in the Lord's personal ministry, the disciples asked Him to teach them to pray. This, at least at first glance, might seem like a strange request. The Lord's disciples undoubtedly had prayed with Jesus many times. But at one time or another in the life of every Christian this same need arises in the walk of faith. God's people are absolutely dependent on God for everything in life. How to pray is no exception.

Likewise the Spirit also helps in our weaknesses. For we do not know what we should pray for as we ought, but the Spirit Himself makes intercession for us with groanings which cannot be uttered. Now He who searches the hearts knows what the mind of the Spirit is, because He makes intercession for the saints according to the will of God. (Romans 8:26–27)

Jesus answered the disciples' request. His answer is given in Matthew's and Luke's gospels. The example of Jesus in how to pray is commonly referred to as the Lord's Prayer. The scope of this familiar model prayer is all encompassing. It taught the disciples to first give praise, reverence and honor to the Almighty Creator. They were to continue daily to ask Him for the necessities of life. This would ensure daily contact with God. They were to seek forgiveness by forgiving. And they were to beg to be led out of temptations and delivered from evil.

So He said to them, "When you pray, say: Our Father in heaven, hallowed be Your name. Your kingdom come. Your will be done. On earth as it is in heaven. Give us day by day our daily bread. And forgive us our sins, for we also forgive everyone who is indebted to us. And do not lead us into temptation, but deliver us from the evil one." (Luke 11:2–4)

In this prayer Jesus also had a very special request of God. The request concerned God's kingdom. The disciples were to beseech the Father to establish His kingdom on earth as it was in heaven.

And He said unto them, when ye pray, say, Our Father which art in heaven, Hallowed be thy name. <u>Thy kingdom come</u>, Thy will be done, as in heaven, so in earth. (Luke 11:2) (KJV)

The disciples, as well as most other Jews, believed according to the scriptures that God would establish His kingdom among His people, Israel. Therefore they probably were not surprised to hear Jesus requesting "Thy Kingdom come." But they were almost totally ignorant of the details regarding its establishment. They were looking for another kingdom of this world. They were looking for something like the temple of Solomon in Jerusalem with the Messiah reigning as king over a fleshly nation of Israel.

Jesus had stated, according to Matthew 16:27, that He would come in His Father's glory to reward each one according to their deeds. "For the Son of Man will come in the glory of His Father with His angels, and then He will reward each according to his works."

This too was not necessarily surprising to the disciples. This was consistent with the teachings of the Jews in regard to the blessings to be received when *Shiloh* or the Messiah would come in all of His power and splendor. But the disciples may have been somewhat surprised by what Jesus said in the next verse. It was then He told them the kingdom would soon come to earth, even within the lifetime of some of those with whom He spoke on that day! The idea that the kingdom came to earth way back then still seems somewhat surprising to many professing Christians today when they learn of it. However, Jesus said it and it happened just as He said.

For the Son of Man is going to come in his Father's glory with his angels, and then he will reward each person according to what they have done. "Truly I tell you, some who are standing here will not taste death before they see the Son of Man coming in his kingdom." (Matthew 16:27–28) (NIV)

The Lord's purpose in coming in all of the power of His Father's glory was to judge and reward. By putting together Matthew 16 and 25, the picture becomes clear. There would be the eventual pronouncement of eternal life and reward or of eternal death as shown in Matthew 25. However, execution of penalty or reward would be made only after judgment was made of guilt or innocence. In other words, judgment would not happen instantly at this spiritual coming of Jesus to establish His kingdom on earth. Rather it would begin when the Son of Man comes in the power of His Father's glory.

One of the greatest surprises of my personal studies was the day I finally reconciled the passages of Matthew 16 and 25 regarding the Lord coming in His kingdom. The reason it took me so long to do so was not because it is confusing or complicated, but because I had felt so comfortable with what the traditional Christian world believed. I now realize these two statements made by Jesus foretold the same event. But before this time I had viewed Matthew 25, beginning with verse 31, as discussing an event to happen only after the bodily resurrection of both the righteous and the unrighteous. Once again, this had not only been my view, but it seemed almost universal among those whom I had heard or read. Following religious tradition can sometimes be spiritually perilous.

But I finally realized these two passages were teaching the same event. Both were teaching the imminent coming of God's kingdom to earth. Upon realizing this, I began to think about other things. I began to examine other traditional ideas I previously had held. And from that time on I truly began to look afresh at the scriptures dealing with God's judgment of the world. Judgment Day and God's kingdom on earth then took on a different, clearer meaning. The chain-binding traditions were beginning to loosen their grip on me.

As Jesus spoke the words recorded in Matthew 16:28, He clearly states that some of those standing with Him would live to see the Son of Man (Jesus) coming in His kingdom. This event would be one of the most momentous events in all of history. For in coming in His kingdom He would sit on His judgment seat and begin His judgment of the world. In fact, this was the purpose of His coming. What is the purpose of a king while sitting on his judgment seat? Of course the purpose is to judge and reward.

Many fail to see this great truth taught by the reconciliation of these two passages of scripture. There are different reasons for failure to understand any truth, but with all due respect, it usually comes down to a complacent and traditional mindset. I once read something about the difficulty of changing a bad mindset. The writer believed fear was the determining factor in maintaining an unhealthy mindset. People are sometimes afraid to change their way of thinking, even when they know it to be unhealthy. They are afraid because of the way it will affect their friends and associates. And the easiest way not to change is to never entertain thoughts of the possibility of being wrong. But it is what we think with our minds that form the words that come out of our mouths. The writer said, "Be aware of what you say. The words that come out of your mouth go into your ears." Thoughts are put in our minds by traditional teaching. As a result, when the word of the teaching comes out of our mouths our ears hear it. Our faith in it is then reinforced in our minds because we believe what we say.

If we never allow ourselves to think we might be wrong we will never hear ourselves doubting our beliefs, but will continue only to hear others confirming the possible erroneous ideas we hold. In this way we never have to fear what our closest comrades think of us in connection to our beliefs. This is the way of the flesh, seeking the soothing reactions of complacency rather than seeking truth.

When we become spiritually complacent we begin to echo what others say around us without really thinking for ourselves. The *Merriam-Webster Dictionary* defines *complacent* as *satisfaction especially when accompanied by unawareness of actual dangers or deficiencies*. A complacent traditional mindset is one that can be satisfied with whatever information that might be given within the confines of family and friends or whatever group we associate.

As previously discussed, faith in the information we accept is always based on our faith in the individual or group source from whence it was received. The traditional mindset is lazy and usually content with an incomplete set of facts. Its conclusions are derived through dependency on traditional thought. This is often true even among the believing. Those who have been saved from past sins can still drift from an unconditional faith in Christ at conversion to eventually becoming entangled in doctrines and ideas formulated by others, especially a familiar religious sect. This was no doubt what caused Paul to warn the Galatian Christians by letter of the danger of having begun in the Spirit and then drifting back into a fleshly way of thinking.

Are you so foolish? Having begun in the Spirit, are you now being made perfect by the flesh? (Galatians 3:3)

It's really pretty easy to see why there is a misunderstanding about God's kingdom on the part of those who have never been born again. As I have discussed previously, they are without God's spiritual receiver and compass to give them guidance. But this should not be the case with those who have been spiritually transformed with renewed minds. Born-again believers have been given the wherewithal to be enlightened about the mysteries of the king-dom. In fact, this is exactly what the Lord told His disciples while He was with them on earth.

And He said, "to you it has been given to know the mysteries of the kingdom of God, but to the rest it is given in parables, that 'Seeing they may not see, and hearing they may not understand.'" (Luke 8:10)

By understanding what Jesus says in this verse we must conclude that many are not using the spiritual receiver and compass made available by the death of Jesus. For this reason they continually fail to learn of the things of God and His kingdom. Much of the current "Christian" teaching does not come from the word of God. It originates from unregenerate minds. Many current religious ideas today have evolved through many generations to finally become hardened into church doctrine.

Jesus told Nicodemus he would not be able to see or enter the kingdom of God unless he was born of water and of the Spirit. This is only one exam-ple of the Lord's words being ignored and subordinated to the whims of the doctrines of men.

Jesus replied, "Very truly I tell you, no one can see the kingdom of God unless they are born again." "How can someone be born when they are old?" Nicodemus asked. "Surely they cannot enter a second time into their mother's womb to be born!"

Jesus answered, "Very truly I tell you, <u>no one can enter the kingdom of God unless</u> <u>they are born of water and the Spirit</u>. That which is born of the flesh is flesh, and that which is born of the Spirit is spirit. Do not marvel that I said to you, 'You must be born again.'" (John 3:3–7) (NIV)

Those who have not been born again can only view the kingdom of God through the lens of the natural unregenerate mind. In other words, they have not experienced the renewal of their mind through faith in obedience to the gospel of Christ. They have never received the help of the Holy Spirit to enlighten them.

THE HELPER

Many things are recorded in the scriptures that will help us understand the coming of the kingdom. Parables Jesus taught are filled with clues in regard to the mysteries of the kingdom. Many of them began with phrases such as "The kingdom of Heaven is like …" John the Baptist laid out the general outline of the purpose and nature of the kingdom in his preaching. He also testified to the nearness of its coming by preaching, "Repent for the kingdom of God is at hand."

However, one of the most important things with which we should become acquainted in order to identify the coming of God's kingdom to earth is the event that preceded its institution. This event was the outpouring of the Holy Spirit on the Jewish day of Pentecost at Jerusalem about AD 33. The event marked the beginning of a new way God would make Himself known to the world through Jesus. It would be by His Holy Spirit, the power given to Jesus without measure.

For He whom God has sent speaks the words of God, for God does not give the Spirit by measure. (John 3:34)

The Father has given everything to the Son in order to redeem fallen humanity. All power in heaven and in earth has been given to Him, even all of the power of the Father's Holy Spirit.

God, who at various times and in various ways spoke in time past to the fathers by the prophets, has in these last days spoken to us by His Son, whom He has appointed heir of all things, through whom also He made the worlds; who being the brightness of His glory and the express image of His person, and upholding all things by the word of His power, when He had by Himself purged our sins, sat down at the right hand of the Majesty on high. (Hebrews 1:1–3)

Redemption of the souls of mankind was made possible through God's Son, who possessed His Father's Spirit without measure. Jesus brought God's kingdom to earth through the immeasurable power of the Spirit He had received of the Father. While on earth He was referred to as the Son of Man in order to identify His human earthly existence. After His resurrection and glorification Paul wrote to the Roman church that "He was declared to be the <u>Son of God with power</u> according to the Spirit of holiness, by the resurrection from the dead."

After His coronation as king over God's kingdom, Jesus assumed all power in heaven and on earth. God delivered all things to His Son regarding His kingdom on earth. God's kingdom on earth is the congregation or assembly of those who are being sanctified, usually referred to as the church.

And He put all things under His feet, and gave Him to be head over all things to the church. (Ephesians 1:22)

Jesus had told His disciples some of them would not die before He would come in His kingdom. This came to pass at Jerusalem more than two thousand years ago. But He did not come back bodily on the day of Pentecost, but *in His Father's glory*. He came in the power of the Holy Spirit without measure.

For the Son of Man will come in the glory of His Father with His angels, and then He will reward each according to his works. Assuredly, I say to you, there are some standing here who shall not taste death till they see the Son of Man coming in His kingdom. (Matthew 16:27–28)

That Jesus would come in His Father's power and glory was foretold by the Old Testament prophets in the Hebrew scriptures. Isaiah beautifully portrays the majestic glory and completeness of the rule of the Son, saying He would be called Mighty God and everlasting Father. The Child and Son was not the father but was called by His name because of the unlimited power and glory given by the Father.

For unto us a Child is born, unto us a Son is given; and the government will be upon His shoulder. And His name will be called Wonderful, Counselor, Mighty God, Everlasting Father, Prince of Peace. (Isaiah 9:6)

God's church on earth would not be built upon a foundation of earthly materials or fleshly motivation, but rather upon a foundation laid through faith in the name of Jesus Christ as the Son of God. This was the message Jesus gave to Simon Peter in Matthew 16.

When Jesus came into the region of Caesarea Philippi, He asked His disciples, saying, "Who do men say that I, the Son of Man, am?" So they said, "Some say John the Baptist, some Elijah, and others Jeremiah or one of the prophets." He said to them, "But who do you say that I am?" Simon Peter answered and said, "You are the Christ, the Son of the living God." Jesus answered and said to him, "Blessed are you, Simon Bar-Jonah, for flesh and blood has not revealed this to you, but My Father who is in heaven. And I also say to you that you are Peter, and on this rock I will build My church, and the gates of Hades shall not prevail against it. And I will give you the keys of the kingdom of heaven, and whatever you bind on earth will be bound in heaven, and whatever you loose on earth will be loosed in heaven." Then He commanded His disciples that they should tell no one that He was Jesus the Christ. (Matthew 16:13–20)

This message of faith would be initiated and facilitated by the outpouring of the Spirit of God into the hearts of those who would believe.

And it shall come to pass afterward That I will pour out My Spirit on all flesh; Your sons and your daughters shall prophesy, Your old men shall dream dreams, Your young men shall see visions. And also on My menservants and on My maidservants I will pour out My Spirit in those days. (Joel 2:28–29)

For I will pour out water on the thirsty land and streams on the dry ground; I will pour out My Spirit on your offspring and My blessing on your descendants. (Isa. 44:3)

Paul spoke of how the gospel was imparted by his own mouth and by implication by all of the apostles of Christ, by telling the Corinthian church about the work of the Spirit of God in the following way.

You show that you are a letter from Christ, the result of our ministry, written not with ink but with the Spirit of the living God, not on tablets of stone but on tablets of human hearts. (2 Corinthians 3:3)

Jesus had told his twelve disciples shortly before His death that He was going away. He was speaking of His death, resurrection and return to heaven. He continued by saying, "I will send another Comforter [or Helper], which is the Holy Spirit." He then said, "And <u>when I am come to you</u>." The fact is inescapable! Jesus was to come in the invisible form of the Holy Spirit. And that is exactly what happened.

We need to examine parts of three chapters in John, chapters 14, 15 and 16, to have a more complete meaning of the coming of the Comforter or Helper. He was to come with power after Jesus departed visibly from the disciples. I begin with John 14, with Jesus speaking.

He who does not love Me does not keep My words; and the word which you hear is not Mine but the Father's who sent Me. These things I have spoken to you while being present with you. But the Helper, the Holy Spirit, whom the Father will send in My name, He will teach you all things, and bring to your remembrance all things that I said to you. (John 14:24–26)

Although this may sound strange in view of traditional teaching, the fact is that before Jesus died He didn't possess the fullness of the Spirit of God. In other words, Jesus was not always perfect or almighty in power as the scriptures teach of the Father. Complete power had to be *given* to the Lord Jesus by His Father by virtue of His obedience to the Father's will.

"Why do you call me good?" Jesus answered. "No one is good—except God alone." (Mark 10:18) (NIV)

Yes, Jesus was sinless, but until His death and resurrection He did not perfectly attain that He was destined to become. As long as He was in the flesh He was tested through the flesh. Through His test of obedience to the Father He was perfected in every way. He grew. He learned and became perfect by completely surrendering to His Father's will. His last touch of perfection was through His resurrection into immortality. It was only after His glorification by way of His resurrection from death that He could say, "all power in heaven and earth is given unto Me." Before this, while in the flesh, Jesus learned to obey by suffering in the flesh, not unlike the disciples who would follow Him.

Son though he was, he _learned_ obedience from what he suffered. (Hebrews 5:8) (NIV)

So Jesus tells the disciples the words He spoke to them while present with them were actually the words of the Father. And then He tells them the Father would send the Helper or Holy Spirit after His departure. The Spirit would bring back to their remembrance all the things He had said to them while with them in the flesh. From this we can see the apostles were being transitioned from an outward teacher who was Jesus, to an inward teacher who was the Holy Spirit of God. This inward teacher was the *Helper* or *Comforter*, the Holy Spirit of God in His Son.

Jesus has come in His kingdom! He came within the lifetime of that present generation just as He promised. It was necessary for Him to come as the empowered king for the purpose of judging and rewarding the world. This is the message He taught in Matthew 16 and 25. His complete power was indelibly established in the hearts of His disciples after His resurrection and immediately before His ascension to heaven. At that time Jesus spoke these last words to them.

Then Jesus came to them and said, "All authority in heaven and on earth has been given to me. Therefore go and make disciples of all nations, baptizing them in the name of the Father and of the Son and of the Holy Spirit, and teaching them to obey everything I have commanded you. And surely I am with you always, to the very end of the age." (Matthew 28:18–20)

Once again this may also be surprising to some. Jesus has not always been empowered to judge and reward. Before He was given this power He had to finish the works His Father gave Him to do. He also spoke these words before His death.

But I have a greater witness than John's; for the works which the Father has given Me to finish—the very works that I do—bear witness of Me, that the Father has sent Me. (John 5:36)

Jesus gave His life for the sins of the world. And by way of a sinless life He conquered death through the power of His resurrection. It was at this point He had finished the works His Father gave Him to do. It was only after these things were accomplished that He was empowered by the Father to receive all authority in heaven and on earth. And by virtue of this complete power (the glory of the Father) He then became qualified to judge and reward.

By virtue of a sinless life and the power of resurrection from death to immortality, Jesus was qualified to come in His kingdom, judging and rewarding in all of the glory of the Father. Obviously He could come in His kingdom only after He became king. And he could only be empowered to judge and reward in His kingdom after He had received all power and authority. And this was made possible only after the victorious resurrection.

The apostle Paul beautifully narrates the extent to which the Father has empowered His Son to have the absolute fullness of authority and power in all matters pertaining to God's kingdom, which includes the power to judge and reward.

That the God of our Lord Jesus Christ, the Father of glory, may give to you the spirit of wisdom and revelation in the knowledge of Him, the eyes of your understanding being enlightened; that you may know what is the hope of His calling, what are the riches of the glory of His inheritance in the saints, and what is the exceeding greatness of His power toward us who believe, according to the working of His mighty power which He worked in Christ when He raised Him from the dead and seated Him at His right hand in the heavenly places, far above all principality and power and might and dominion, and every name that is named, not only in this age but also in that which is to come. And He put all things under His feet, and gave Him to be head over all things to the church, which is His body, the fullness of Him who fills all in all. (Ephesians 1:17–23)

Now let's review the facts we have gleaned from the scriptures up to this point. Jesus promised He would come in the glory of the Father. He was able to do this because he was exalted to the position of lord of all, crowned king of the kingdom of God in heaven and on earth. Only by having been given all authority in heaven and on earth was He empowered to become the eternal judge and reward giver. He came (by and in the Holy Spirit) to earth on the day Pentecost in about AD 33 as He had promised.

HE HAS APPOINTED A DAY

When the Day of Pentecost had fully come, they were all with one accord in one place. And suddenly there came a sound from heaven, as of a rushing mighty wind, and it filled the whole house where they were sitting. Then there appeared to them divided tongues, as of fire, and one sat upon each of them. And they were all filled with the Holy Spirit and began to speak with other tongues, as the Spirit gave them utterance. And there were dwelling in Jerusalem Jews, devout men, from every nation under heaven. (Acts 2:1–5)

This scripture fulfilled the words of Christ when he told His followers He would come in His kingdom before some of them died. Coming in the power of the Holy Spirit was the only way the Lord could have come in His kingdom within the disciple's lifetime. He promised after His ascension into heaven He would send back the Comforter or Helper, which was the Holy Spirit. The disciples witnessed His return when the Holy Spirit descended upon them on the day of Pentecost. Then they understood what He had meant by saying, "I will not leave you as orphans; I will come to you." They also understood how they could still be alive when He came in His kingdom.

Truly I tell you, some who are standing here will not taste death before they see the Son of Man coming in his kingdom. (Matthew 16:28)

And this He did. He came in His spiritual kingdom, bringing judgment and reward within the lifetime of those who stood with Him before His death. It also fulfilled the prophecy that "repentance and remission of sins should be preached in His name to all nations, beginning at Jerusalem." After His resurrection and before His ascension into heaven, Jesus began to enlighten His apostles to some of the mysteries of the kingdom.

When He had said this, He showed them His hands and His feet. But while they still did not believe for joy, and marveled, He said to them, "Have you any food here?" So they gave Him a piece of a broiled fish and some honeycomb. And He took it and ate in their presence. Then He said to them, "These are the words which I spoke to you while I was still with you, that all things must be fulfilled which were written in the Law of Moses and the Prophets and the Psalms concerning Me." And He opened their understanding, that they might comprehend the Scriptures. Then He said to them, "Thus it is written, and thus it was necessary for the Christ to suffer and to rise from the dead the third day, and that <u>repentance and remission of sins should be preached in His name to all nations, beginning at Jerusalem.</u>

And you are witnesses of these things. Behold, I send the Promise of My Father upon you; but tarry in the city of Jerusalem until you are endued with power from on high." And He led them out as far as Bethany, and He lifted up His hands and blessed them. (Luke 24:40–50)

These irrefutable events happened as Jesus had foretold, which also fulfilled many Old Testament prophecies. The particular day of Pentecost spoken of in Acts 2 was a tremendously exciting and eventful day, as well as one fulfilling much prophecy. On that particular day of Pentecost there were representatives from every nation, which fulfilled the words of Jesus in Matthew 25.

All the nations will be gathered before Him, and He will separate them one from another, as a shepherd divides his sheep from the goats. And He will set the sheep on His right hand, but the goats on the left. (Matt. 25:32–33)

But this Pentecost was of immeasurable consequence not only because of the gospel being preached in His name to all nations, beginning at Jerusalem, but also because it was the beginning of *Judgment Day* in this world. This Judgment Day was also the day of salvation for God's people to begin being sanctified on earth. This was the day God's people began to be separated out from the world. Judgment Day began on that day of Pentecost. It will end when Jesus comes back to earth at the resurrection. Paul speaks of this Judgment Day in his remarks on Mars Hill to the people of Athens.

Because He has appointed a _day_ on which He will judge the world in righteousness by the Man whom He has ordained. He has given assurance of this to all by raising Him from the dead. (Acts 17:31)

The criterion for salvation as given by Jesus in Matthew 25 can be reduced to one single cause. It was _the acceptance of Jesus_ for salvation! This acceptance of Jesus was conditioned on the acceptance of one another. We cannot accept Jesus without accepting one another. This truth has never changed. "Inasmuch as you have done it to one of the least of these my brethren, you have done it unto me. (Matthew 25:40). It may have been the knowledge of this truth that triggered the questions Paul put before the church at Rome.

But why do you judge your brother? Or why do you show contempt for your brother? For we shall all stand before the judgment seat of Christ. (Romans 14:10)

Matthew uses sheep and goats to symbolize the saved and the lost. Separating the sheep from the goats depicts the process used in judgment to set apart the righteous from the world. This process is the very work of sanctification. Separation of the good from the bad can come only by one who has the power to exercise righteous judgment. The things necessary to determine innocence or guilt are beyond the discerning power of mere man. The separation of God's people out of the world and into the kingdom of God began on this day of Pentecost. This process began only days after Jesus had ascended back into heaven. And this was the process Jesus spoke of in reference to the separation of the sheep from the goats in Matthew 25.

Other phrases used synonymously in connection with "Judgment Day" are "the end of the world" and "the end of the ages."

He then would have had to suffer often since the foundation of the world; but now, once at the end of the ages, He has appeared to put away sin by the sacrifice of Himself. (Hebrews 9:26)

Once again, the common thought is that judgment begins when Jesus visibly comes back to this world at the resurrection of the dead. This is actually when judgment is executed and finalized.

[Jesus is coming] in flaming fire taking vengeance on those who do not know God, and on those who do not obey the gospel of our Lord Jesus Christ. (2 Thess. 1:8)

The time of Jesus coming back to take vengeance on ungodliness is at the very end of the world, at the resurrection of the dead. However, it is not just the last age or dispensation of time, but the very end of the last age or Christian dispensation of time. Jesus will only judge as long as he is king, while he possesses all power and authority. Once again it is important to emphasize that Jesus was given this power only by virtue of his conquering death and resurrection. It was only through this means that He came "in the glory of the Father" to rule and reign over the kingdom of Heaven for the salvation of souls. He now reigns and exercises the power of the Father over the kingdom. When the reign is over, the rule is over, and the power (glory of His Father) will be once again relinquished back to the Father.

But Christ has indeed been raised from the dead, the first fruits of those who have fallen asleep. For since death came through a man, the resurrection of the dead comes also through a man. For as in Adam all die, so in Christ all will be made alive. But each in turn: Christ, the first fruits; then, when he comes, those who belong to him. Then the end will come, when he <u>*hands over the kingdom to God the Father*</u> *after he has destroyed all dominion, authority and power. For he must reign until he has put all his enemies under his feet. The last enemy to be destroyed is death. For he "has put everything under his feet." Now when it says that "everything" has been put under him, it is clear that this does not include God himself, who put everything under Christ. When he has done this, then the Son himself will be made subject to him who put everything under him, so that God may be all in all.* (1 Cor. 15:20–28)

The writer of Hebrews offers a different look at when the end of the world begins as he speaks of Christ's death.

For then must he often have suffered since the foundation of the world: but now once <u>*in the end of the world*</u> *hath he appeared to put away sin by the sacrifice of Himself.* (Heb. 9:26) (KJV)

Here Jesus is shown to have appeared to put away sin through His atoning death. This event, according to the writer, happened "in the end of the world." But this is not the same event as when He appears in "flaming fire to execute vengeance" on the sin that has not been put away. The sins of those who have been cleansed by the blood of Christ have already been put away during the time of the church. But the sins of those who have rejected Christ during this day of salvation will remain when Jesus returns at the resurrection. These are two events, but both happen at the end of the world in the final age or dispensation of time as God deals with the human race on earth.

Jesus began the process of putting away sin through His death and resurrection. By atonement and pardon, the righteous are sanctified (separated, set apart). Therefore the sins of believers are put away. This process begins at the beginning of Jesus' reign as king. He finishes the work of putting away sin at the end of His reign through His power as the supreme judge of those who are unsanctified. But the point is that both events are happening in "the end of the world," or in this last age or dispensation of time.

God has appointed this specific time period for judgment and reward, sometimes called a *day, To Day, the day of the Lord, the day of salvation, the day of judgment* and perhaps other terms. But they all have the same meaning in this respect: they refer to the time or age of the reign of Christ over the kingdom of God. Once again, Paul speaks to the idolatrous people of Athens and refers to the day the world will be judged in righteousness by Jesus, the man whom God has ordained.

Because He has appointed a day on which He will judge the world in righteousness by the Man whom He has ordained. He has given assurance of this to all by raising Him from the dead. (Acts 17:31)

The exhortation of promise from God to send Jesus into this world was sounded by the mouth of the prophet Isaiah long ago.

Thus says the Lord: "In an acceptable time I have heard You, and in the day of salvation I have helped You; I will preserve You and give You as a covenant to the people, To restore the earth, To cause them to inherit the desolate heritages. (Isaiah 49:8)

Isaiah 49:8 is clearly speaking of the coming of the Messiah in His kingdom for salvation and restoration. Paul echoed this same heavenly decree to the Corinthian disciples.

We then, as workers together with Him also plead with you not to receive the grace of God in vain. For He says: "In an acceptable time I have heard you, and in the day of salvation I have helped you." Behold, now is the accepted time; behold, now is the day of salvation. (2 Cor. 6:2)

We may not know the length of time for judgment in terms of human days or hours. But Matthew 25:31 does tell us when Judgment Day begins. It begins when "the Son of Man comes in His glory." Notice the following verse from the New International Version.

When the Son of Man comes in his glory, and all the angels with him, he will sit on his glorious throne.

The same time He comes in His glory will also be the time He will sit on the glorious throne. His coming and His sitting on the throne of His glory is obviously the same event. In fact, the time He begins to sit upon His throne of glory is prima facie evidence His judgment has begun. Since Jesus is Lord of Lords and King of Kings, it makes no sense that He could sit on His throne of glory without the power or authority to judge. His judgeship could not possibly begin before He sits on His throne because judging and rewarding are the purpose of His reign.

Once again, a lot of people are surprised to learn Jesus did not always have the power He has now. He has only been the King of Kings and Lord of Lords since the establishment of God's kingdom on earth. And as we have learned, He was exalted to the position of king over God's kingdom only after His sinless life and resurrection from the dead. The apostle Peter speaks of this exaltation in the first gospel message preached to the world on the day of Pentecost at Jerusalem.

Therefore being exalted to the right hand of God, and having received from the Father the promise of the Holy Spirit, He poured out this which you now see and hear. (Acts 2:33)

When the teachings of Matthew 16 are put together with those of Matthew 25 we have an even clearer view of what is meant. Matthew 16 becomes a much more interesting chapter when studied together with Matthew 25. This is because Matthew 16:27 says basically the same thing as Matthew 25:31. Comparing the two verses helps us see their similarities and differences.

For the Son of Man will come in the glory of His Father with His angels, and then He will reward each according to his works. (Matt.16:27)

When the Son of Man comes in His glory, and all the holy angels with Him, then He will sit on the throne of His glory. (Matt. 25:31)

The only way these two verses would not be talking about the same event would be for Jesus to have come at two different times, both times in His Father's glory, both times with His angels, both times sitting on His throne meting out rewards and punishments. But before we talk in detail about Matthew 16:27, let's review some of the things in the chapter leading up to it.

THE MESSAGE OF THE KINGDOM

In Matthew 16:13 Jesus begins to question his disciples as to what people were saying about Him. "Who do men say that I, the Son of Man, am?" They answered by telling Jesus people were saying he was John the Baptist or one of the Old Testament prophets. Jesus then put the question directly to them by asking in verse 15, "Who do you say that I am?" Simon Peter then gives an answer in verse 16 that would become the universal statement of faith on which eternal salvation is predicated. "You are the Christ, the Son of the living God."

Jesus calls Peter "blessed" for his confession of faith and then He makes a very profound statement. This statement is overlooked, perverted or minimized by most of religious orthodoxy today. The Lord tells Peter in verses 17 and 18 that it was upon this statement of his faith in Him (the acknowledgment of His deity) that He would build His church and that the gates of hades (death or the grave) would not prevail against it.

Jesus answered and said to him, "Blessed are you, Simon Bar-Jonah, for flesh and blood has not revealed this to you, but My Father who is in heaven. And I also say to you that you are Peter, and on this rock I will build my church, and the gates of Hades shall not prevail against it. (Matthew 16:17–18)

Jesus also tells Peter he will be given the keys of the kingdom with the authority to bind and loose things on earth. Obviously this was to be accomplished by establishing God's new covenant for the people on earth. In addition to this, He tells Peter the things bound or loosed on earth will be bound or loosed in heaven. In other words, Peter was to become the chief spokesman and door-opener of the kingdom of God on earth.

And I will give you the keys of the kingdom of heaven, and whatever you bind on earth will be bound in heaven, and whatever you loose on earth will be loosed in heaven. (Matt. 16:19)

The key would be in preaching God's good news of salvation through Jesus Christ. The prophets had foretold the coming of the kingdom and the message. Jesus talked to the disciples about this after His resurrection, immediately before His ascension back into heaven. The message would be repentance and remission of sins, the audience would be people from every nation, and the place the message was first to be preached would be Jerusalem.

Then He said to them, "O foolish ones, and slow of heart to believe in all that the prophets have spoken! Ought not the Christ to have suffered these things and to enter into His glory?" And beginning at Moses and all the Prophets, He expounded to them in all the Scriptures the things concerning Himself. (Luke 24:25–27)

Then He said to them, "These are the words which I spoke to you while I was still with you, that all things must be fulfilled which were written in the Law of Moses and the Prophets and the Psalms concerning Me." And He opened their understanding, that they might comprehend the Scriptures. Then He said to them, "Thus it is written, and thus it was necessary for the Christ to suffer and to rise from the dead the third day, and that repentance and remission of sins should be preached in His name to all nations, beginning at Jerusalem. And you are witnesses of these things. Behold, I send the Promise of My Father upon you; but tarry in the city of Jerusalem until you are endued with power from on high." And He led them out as far as Bethany, and He lifted up His hands and blessed them. Now it came to pass, while He blessed them, that He was parted from them and carried up into heaven. (Luke 24:44–51)

Sending the gospel into all the world was the message Jesus left with His immediate disciples before ascending back to the Father. Obedience to the gospel message involves the total surrender of self in an obedient response of faith in Christ as King of Kings and Lord of Lords. Jesus commanded that faith be shown by the outward response of water baptism in these final words in Mark 16:16, while still present with His disciples, before His ascension into heaven. Immersion in water would be the response commanded by the Lord for those who heard the message. This response would show both an outward and inward testimony of faith in Christ. Outwardly it would be a testimony of a truly living faith in God's grace through His Son. Jesus had left a departing message saying, "he that believes and is baptized shall be saved." To knowingly fail to comply with the last words of Jesus on earth would put professed believers in the same place as the demons that followed Satan's rebellion against God. Of course this would only apply to those who were given opportunity to hear the message and subsequently rejected it.

What does it profit, my brethren, if someone says he has faith but does not have works? Can faith save him? If a brother or sister is naked and destitute of daily food, and one of you says to them, "Depart in peace, be warmed and filled," but you do not give them the things which are needed for the body, what does it profit? Thus also faith by itself, if it does not have works, is dead. But someone will say, "You have faith, and I have works." Show me your faith without your works, and I will show you my faith by my works. You believe that there is one God. You do well. Even the demons believe—and tremble! But do you want to know, O foolish man, that faith without works is dead? (James 2:14–20)

Faithful works of outward obedience to God's commands are simply the response of a penitent, believing heart. Law does not give life and works of law without faith do not purge the conscience of sinful man. But willful disobedience to the command of God is rebellion and will result in His wrath.

Is the law then against the promises of God? Certainly not! For if there had been a law given which could have given life, truly righteousness would have been by the law.

So we should never think God's law and our obedience to it don't play a vital part in God's purpose toward salvation. The governing principles of law God gives to man is for the purpose of fulfilling His promises to the faithful. A law is kept for one of two purposes. Either it is kept to earn (merit) God's favor, or it is kept because of a grateful and love-filled heart. In essence, this is a heart that is grateful for what God has done for us through Jesus. Law doesn't give life, but a disobedient heart and a willful, rebellious spirit will not allow us to be justified by grace through faith. With the response by the sinner in submission to immersion in water, God promises to greatly spiritually reward this faith.

For you are all sons of God through faith in Christ Jesus. For as many of you as were baptized into Christ have put on Christ. (Galatians 3:26–27)

This obedience of faith from the heart will result in remission of sins and the reception of the Holy Spirit for every penitent believer as long as Christ is King, calling men and women to salvation. However, we must understand that it is the condition of the heart toward the will of God that causes the act of immersion in water to be of saving consequence. Baptism was never intended to be performed as a work to merit or earn salvation. It is an outward show of faith.

When the people heard this, they were cut to the heart and said to Peter and the other apostles, "Brothers, what shall we do?" Peter replied, "Repent and be baptized, every one of you, in the name of Jesus Christ for the forgiveness of your sins. And you will receive the gift of the Holy Spirit. The promise is for you and your children and for all who are far off—for all whom the Lord our God will call." (Acts 2:37–39) (NIV)

Inward obedience is the effect God's love and mercy have on the conscience of the believer. However, given the opportunity, this inward obedience is always reflected by outward works of righteousness. In the passage just cited, the effects of the gospel message Peter preached were obvious: "They were cut to the heart." Because they were cut to the heart, they responded to the command to repent and be baptized. Then, because they trusted in the power of Christ's death, their consciences were purged. Peter probably says it best in his first epistle.

For Christ also suffered once for sins, the just for the unjust, that He might bring us to God, being put to death in the flesh but made alive by the Spirit, by whom also He went and preached to the spirits in prison, who formerly were disobedient, when once the Divine longsuffering waited in the days of Noah, while the ark was being prepared, in which a few, that is, eight souls, were saved through water. There is also an antitype which now saves us—baptism [not the removal of the filth of the flesh, but the answer of a good conscience toward God], through the resurrection of Jesus Christ, who has gone into heaven and is at the right hand of God, angels and authorities and powers having been made subject to Him. (1 Peter 3:18–22)

LIVING STONES AND CHOSEN PEOPLE

Faithful obedience to the gospel message causes God to be able to create "living stones" from believers who can offer up "spiritual sacrifices." These living stones make up the congregation of God's people. This is how Jesus says He will build His Church. Peter speaks to the spiritual nature of the kingdom and its citizens in the pure language of the Spirit.

As you come to him, the living Stone—rejected by humans but chosen by God and precious to him— you also, like living stones, are being built into a spiritual house to be a holy priesthood, offering spiritual sacrifices acceptable to God through Jesus Christ. For in Scripture it says: "See, I lay a stone in Zion, a chosen and precious cornerstone, and the one who trusts in him will never be put to shame." Now to you who believe, this stone is precious. But to those who do not believe, "The stone the builders rejected has become the cornerstone," and, "A stone that causes people to stumble and a rock that makes them fall." They stumble because they disobey the message—which is also what they were destined for. But you are a chosen people, a royal priesthood, a holy nation, God's special possession, that you may declare the praises of him who called you out of darkness into his wonderful light. Once you were not a people, but now you are the people of God; once you had not received mercy, but now you have received mercy. (1 Peter 2:4–10) (NIV)

Once again I must emphasize the sum total of discipleship to Jesus Christ is in the total surrender of self. This is illustrated by Jesus in no uncertain terms as we continue on in Matthew 16:20–26.

Then He commanded His disciples that they should tell no one that He was Jesus the Christ. From that time Jesus began to show to His disciples that He must go to Jerusalem, and suffer many things from the elders and chief priests and scribes, and be killed, and be raised the third day. Then Peter took Him aside and began to rebuke Him, saying, "Far be it from You, Lord; this shall not happen to you!" But He turned and said to Peter, "Get behind Me, Satan! You are an offense to me, for you are not mindful of the things of God, but the things of men." Then

Jesus said to His disciples, "If anyone desires to come after me, let him deny himself, and take up his cross, and follow me. For whoever desires to save his life will lose it, but whoever loses his life for my sake will find it. For what profit is it to a man if he gains the whole world, and loses his own soul? Or what will a man give in exchange for his soul?"

Peter, at least momentarily, lost sight of the most important thing about discipleship. He forgot the disciple is not above his teacher. This was one of the great lessons Jesus, the master teacher, had taught Peter and His disciples. Peter in his rebuke of the Lord was showing he was not completely mindful of the things of God by forgetting the principle of denying self for the sake of discipleship.

A disciple is not above his teacher, nor a servant above his master. It is enough for a disciple that he be like his teacher, and a servant like his master. If they have called the master of the house Beelzebub, how much more will they call those of his household! (Matt. 10:24–25)

This brings us to Matthew 16:27.

For the Son of Man will come in the glory of His Father with His angels, and then He will reward each according to his works.

CONCLUDING THOUGHT

Matthew 16 up to this point reveals some of the particulars of the building of Jesus' congregation or assembly (church) here on earth. It also expresses the fundamental fact of discipleship, which is complete trust in Christ. It indicates that the sum total of discipleship is a denying of self with complete submission to God's will through faith in His Son. The chapter concludes by expressing the value of saving one's soul, the gaining of immortality and eternal life.

If we stopped at verse 27 and did not have the additional light of verse 28, much of the traditional teaching of Judgment Day found in Matthew 25 might remain as most people always believed it to be. In fact, without verse

28 the argument might be strengthened for the traditional view of Judgment Day beginning after the bodily resurrection rather than when Jesus begins His reign of salvation. However, the addition of verse 28 turns the traditional view on its head. Now let's read Matthew 16:27–28 together once more.

For the Son of Man is going to come in his Father's glory with his angels, and then he will reward each person according to what they have done. Truly I tell you, some who are standing here will not taste death before they see the Son of Man coming in his kingdom. (NIV)

CHAPTER 5

THE GOVERNMENT OF THE KINGDOM

I recall the first time I was informed of the benefits of government as a young boy. It was early on a frosty November morning. I remember Dad telling Mom he was going to town to pay his property taxes. He took down a cigar box from the top of a kitchen cabinet where he kept all of his important things pertaining to his figures and calculations about the home and farm. His important things consisted of a lead pencil, a small ledger, the family burial policies and Grandpa Richardson's pocketknife. The knife was a keepsake after Grandpa died. Dad would never carry the knife in his pocket for fear of losing it. So he kept it in the cigar box to sharpen the pencil.

From time to time during the year, Dad would accumulate a few extra dollars, which he saved in the cigar box. This was his way of having the money to pay his property taxes in the fall. When the bill came in the mail he almost always had the money saved. Having the money for taxes was very important to him. It almost seemed to make him happy to get the tax bill in the mail, especially when he had the money ready to pay the taxes. And he nearly always, if at all possible, paid them the very next day after he got his tax bill.

On that particular morning, as I heard Dad tell Mom he was going to town to pay his taxes, I became curious. "Why do you have to pay taxes?" I asked.

He sat down with me at the kitchen table and began to tell me the purpose of government and taxes. First he told me how thankful we should be to live in a country with the freedoms we have. Continuing on, he said, "We all pay taxes in order to have roads, schools and other things." He also told me we should always want to pay the taxes due because when we do we're doing our part. He said it was a way we could help each other. It was a short lesson, but it made a lot of sense to me. Later on I served Oregon County, Missouri, in the office of the Collector of Revenue for twenty-eight years. This was the same place where Dad paid his taxes.

NO AUTHORITY EXCEPT FROM GOD

Paul, in writing to the church at Rome, is unequivocal in his insistence that Christians should take their civic responsibilities seriously. One could expect those unconnected to ,God to balk at paying taxes and contributing to the overall well-being of their citizenry. This is because they serve the flesh rather than the Spirit. But those of us who profess discipleship to Christ should be different. We should not only feel a responsibility in this regard, but we should also want to be a part of God's plan in connection to a citizen's response to civil government.

Let every soul be subject to the governing authorities. For there is no authority except from God, and the authorities that exist are appointed by God. (Romans 13:1)

For because of this you also pay taxes, for they [civil servants] are God's ministers attending continually to this very thing. Render therefore to all their due: taxes to whom taxes are due, customs to whom customs, fear to whom fear, honor to whom honor. (Romans 13:6–7)

The governments of this world are set up or appointed by God. This does not mean all will be just and fair in every case. Neither does it mean all rulers will be God fearing. But the Lord knows what is best. And from time to time bad rulers and governments are set up to let the citizens know how thankful they should have been before the bad times arrived. This was the case with Israel over and over again.

The scriptures tell us God rules over the kingdoms and governments of men. In the book of Daniel we find the ancient story of Nebuchadnezzar, the great king of the Babylonian Empire. During Nebuchadnezzar's reign the children of Israel were in captivity at Babylon. Among them was Daniel. Though a captive in a foreign land and alienated from Jerusalem and Jewish places of worship, Daniel faithfully continued to serve and worship God in every way he could.

Because of his faithfulness to the Lord, Daniel was blessed with abilities above and beyond those of ordinary men. One of the supernatural abilities of Daniel was interpreting dreams. King Nebuchadnezzar heard of Daniel's power when he was troubled by a dream. He sent for Daniel, thinking he might be told the meaning of his dream.

But Nebuchadnezzar was a very vain and prideful individual. He had been lifted up with pride because of the perception of the great power he believed he possessed, which he thought could never be taken from him. The interpretation of the dream was this. The power of the great Babylonian king would be taken from him by the decree of heaven and the king would be humiliated almost beyond compare. However, the king rejected the inspired interpretation of the dream and the final sentence given to Nebuchadnezzar from Daniel was in the following words.

This decision is by the decree of the watchers, and the sentence by the word of the holy ones, in order that the living may know that the Most High rules in the kingdom of men, gives it to whomever He will, and sets over it the lowest of men. (Daniel 4:17)

For seven years this king of the greatest power on the planet at that time was cast out of his kingdom to become as an animal. He crawled on his belly. His hair grew like eagle feathers and his nails became as the claws of birds. It all happened on a day when the pride of Nebuchadnezzar was at its height. This is an example of the destructive power caused by fleshly ambition. Following are the words describing the event.

All this came upon King Nebuchadnezzar. At the end of the twelve months he was walking about the royal palace of Babylon. The king spoke, saying, "Is not this great Babylon, that I have built for a royal dwelling by my mighty power and for the honor of my majesty?" While the word was still in the king's mouth, a voice fell from heaven: "King Nebuchadnezzar, to you it is spoken: the kingdom has departed from you! And they shall drive you from men, and your dwelling shall be with the beasts of the field. They shall make you eat grass like oxen; and seven times shall pass over you, until you know that the Most High rules in the kingdom of men, and gives it to whomever He chooses." That very hour the word was fulfilled concerning Nebuchadnezzar; he was driven from men and ate grass like oxen; his body was wet with the dew of heaven till his hair had grown like eagles' feathers and his nails like birds' claws. (Daniel 4:28–33)

Nebuchadnezzar is only one example of a myriad of men throughout the ages who were brought to nothing because of pride. Among these was Pharaoh of Egypt as Moses led Israel out of Egypt, King Herod of the Jews as described in the gospels, and Alexander (called the great) and Hitler of Germany. The list goes on and on. They fell because of pride, while they failed to give glory to the God of heaven. And today the same thing happens every time anyone ignorantly supposes himself or herself to have power and fails to attribute that power to the Lord.

The United States of America, as a republic, has a democratic form of government. Democracy means and is defined as rule by the people. A republic is a government in which supreme power resides in a body of citizens entitled to vote and is exercised by elected officers and representatives responsible to them, governing according to law. Pure democracy would be a government directly ruled by a vote of the people, rather than the election of people to represent the interests of the people. Thus the government of the United States is a representative democratic republic.

However, the kingdoms of men or civil authorities derive their power from God, and from God only. The concept of God's power can be understood and espoused only by the spiritually transformed minds of the children of God. The source of all power being God only is accepted by faith and confirmed by His word. Once again, listen to the words of inspiration.

Let every soul be subject to the governing authorities. For there is no authority except from God, and the authorities that exist are appointed by God. Therefore whoever resists the authority resists the ordinance of God and those who resist will bring judgment on themselves. (Romans 13:1–2)

However, the mind of unregenerate humanity is blinded by a fleshly motivation to believe in the original or inherent power of humanity. But inherent power can only be truly attributed to God. Any power of the created universe, whether of angels, humans or subhuman creatures, is only allowed by God and can exist only through and by His power. He gives power and takes it away according to the immutable counsel of His own will. The only source of any power is in the Creator of all creation.

GOD'S KINGDOM AMONG MEN

God's kingdom is not a democracy like the United States. Nor is it a republic. It is a sovereign, autocratic monarchy. This means it is ruled by a king or monarch having sovereign power with no one else sharing power. God's kingdom is governed only by Jesus!

For to us a child is born, to us a son is given, and <u>the government will be on his shoulders</u>. And he will be called Wonderful Counselor, Mighty God, Everlasting Father, prince of Peace. (Isaiah 9:6)

This child and son would be Jesus, the anointed one, the only begotten Son of the Almighty God. Christ, as the Son of God, would be the king over His Father's kingdom, reigning to judge and reward. He is now enthroned, reigning today in the full capacity of supreme monarch. All power in heaven and earth has been given to Him in order to rule His Father's kingdom (see Matthew 28:18).

Some believe "the kingdom of God" is synonymous with "the church." And although the terms sometimes are used interchangeably, "the church" on earth does not nearly encompass the entirety of what God's kingdom, or the kingdom of heaven, consists of. The word *church* was used by English translators for the Greek word *ecclesia*. This word basically means those who were *called out* for some purpose. Therefore, the word *church* as used in the New Testament is simply an assembly or congregation of people called out for some purpose.

The kingdom of God consists of and includes much more than a called assembly or congregation of people. The kingdom of God did not begin in the church age. It existed in heaven before Jesus was brought into the world. It did not begin on earth with the death and the glorification of Jesus, but rather was brought down from heaven to exist on earth because of the death and the glorification of Jesus. The sacrificial life and death of God's Son made it possible for God to dwell in the hearts of His people by faith through His Spirit. The Spirit would reveal God's will to His people through the written word in the same way as it had brought the words of Jesus back to the minds of His apostles, beginning at Pentecost with the advent of God's Holy Spirit.

The church, or God's congregation or assembly, is now a part of the reign of God's kingdom under the rule of King Jesus.

Many of the inspired prophets of God spoke of a time when God's kingdom would be among men here on earth. In the model prayer Jesus taught His disciples, He told them to pray God's will would be done by God's kingdom coming to earth even as it was in heaven.

Your kingdom come, your will be done, on earth as it is in heaven. (Matthew 6:10) (NIV)

We have a glimpse of the fulfillment of the kingdom of God coming to earth when Jesus rode triumphantly into Jerusalem shortly before His death.

Rejoice greatly, Daughter Zion! Shout, Daughter Jerusalem! See, your king comes to you, righteous and victorious, lowly and riding on a donkey, on a colt, the foal of a donkey. (Zechariah 9:9)

NOT OF THIS WORLD

Even though God's people are a part of the kingdom, the kingdom of God is not of this world. God's people are in the world, but they are not of the world. In other words, it is not a temporal kingdom and governing entity that is to soon pass away. The kingdom of God is spiritual and eternal. It will remain forever. Jesus made the following statement to Pilate shortly before His death.

Jesus answered, "My kingdom is not of this world. If My kingdom were of this world, My servants would fight, so that I should not be delivered to the Jews; but now My kingdom is not from here." (John 18:36)

After Judas had betrayed Jesus with a kiss, the Jewish mob descended upon Him to arrest Him and deliver Him to the authorities. It was at this time that "one of those who was with Jesus" decided to take matters into his own hands in defense of his Lord. What follows is the narration of this event along with the rebuke Jesus gave this disciple by showing him carnal warfare is not a part of the warfare of the kingdom of God.

And while He was still speaking, behold, Judas, one of the twelve, with a great multitude with swords and clubs, came from the chief priests and elders of the people. Now His betrayer had given them a sign, saying, "Whomever I kiss, He is the One; seize Him." Immediately he went up to Jesus and said, "Greetings, Rabbi!" and kissed Him. But Jesus said to him, "Friend, why have you come?" Then they came and laid hands on Jesus and took Him. And suddenly, one of those who were with Jesus stretched out his hand and drew his sword, struck the servant of the high priest, and cut off his ear. But Jesus said to him, "Put your sword in its place, for all who take the sword will perish by the sword." (Matthew 26:47–52)

THE MYSTERIES OF THE KINGDOM

The Greek word for mystery, as used in the New Testament, is *musterion*. It is defined as follows: "a secret or "mystery through the idea of silence imposed by initiation into religious rites" (*Strong's Exhaustive Concordance of the Bible*, number 3466).

The New Testament uses the word *mystery* or *mysteries* about twenty-five times. It is used directly in reference to the mystery of God or Christ no fewer than eight times. It refers to God's will, the faith and the gospel in three places. In one place it refers to resurrection into immortality as Paul speaks about changing from mortal to immortal, and in another to the mystery of blindness in part that happened to Israel. It also talks of the spirit of iniquity or lawlessness. It refers to the fellowship of the mystery. Twice it speaks of the mystery being hidden from the foundation of the world or the beginning of the ages.

And to make all see what is the fellowship of the mystery, which from the beginning of the ages has been <u>hidden in God</u> who created all things through Jesus Christ. (Ephesians 3:9)

The mystery which has been <u>hidden from ages and from generations</u>, but now has been revealed to His saints. (Colossians 1:26)

Usually when the word *mystery* or *mysteries* is used in the New Testament it pertains to the kingdom of God. The things Jesus spoke to His disciples before His death came back to their minds after His death and resurrection. This was the beginning of the *mysteries* of God's kingdom being revealed. These things could only be discerned spiritually. They were hidden from the beginning. The apostles were the first to understand the mysteries.

But as it is written: "Eye has not seen, nor ear heard, nor have entered into the heart of man the things which God has prepared for those who love Him." But God has revealed them to us through His Spirit. For the Spirit searches all things, yes, the deep things of God. (1 Cor. 2:9–1)

Just as the prophets of the Old Testament were commissioned to communicate the will of God to Israel, the apostles of Christ were inspired to preach the gospel message to the world. In both cases the written word became the primary vehicle of communication. The mysteries of the kingdom continued to be revealed to the saved in Christ after the church was established. This first happened through miraculous impartations of the Spirit to the church. Later it happened through the writing of what is now referred to as the New Testament. Subsequently the Bible came to consist of the Old and New Testaments. The inspired Hebrew scriptures along with the gospels and letters of the New Testament writers became the authoritative communication for the church.

All Scripture is given by inspiration of God, and is profitable for doctrine, for reproof, for correction, for instruction in righteousness. (2 Timothy 3:16)

At the beginning of the church age each individual disciple was given what was needed for his or her part in God's kingdom on earth.

And God has appointed these in the church: first apostles, second prophets, third teachers, after that miracles, then gifts of healings, helps, administrations, varieties of tongues. (1 Cor. 12:28)

Placement as a member in the local congregation is not by accident or even of our choosing, for that matter. It is in effect a divine appointment. God makes the appointment for the congregation in order to ensure its spiritual health and maturity. Individual talents or abilities of each member, which may have previously been used to serve the devil, are converted to a labor of love by God's people. It's not really a consideration in how we choose to serve. Each member serves by utilizing his or her gifts. So the important thing is not so much how we serve but who we serve. It's a change from serving self to serving God. We either serve the creature or the Creator. All of our human abilities are put there by God to cause us to become vessels of honor. It only depends on how we choose to use them. These God-given abilities identify the purpose God has for us as members of the body of Christ. This is the determining factor in our placement in the church (body of Christ) that God is pleased to appoint us to.

For by one Spirit we were all baptized into one body—whether Jews or Greeks, whether slaves or free—and have all been made to drink into one Spirit. For in fact the body is not one member but many. If the foot should say, "Because I am not a hand, I am not of the body," is it therefore not of the body? And if the ear should say, "Because I am not an eye, I am not of the body," is it therefore not of the body? If the whole body were an eye, where would be the hearing? If the whole were hearing, where would be the smelling? But now God has set the members, each one of them, in the body just as He pleased. (1 Corinthians 12:13–18)

The first congregation of believers met in Jerusalem in about AD 33. This is the beginning location of the kingdom of God on earth. The scriptures had prophesied repentance and remission of sins was to be preached first at Jerusalem. And even though the church increased mightily in number from its inception, resistance to Christianity from the Jewish religious community began almost immediately. Righteous Stephen, who was appointed as one of the first Christian deacons, was murdered and became the first Christian martyr. This happened as a result of the self-righteous, tradition-keeping Jewish religious leaders. This was only the beginning of Christian persecution by the Jews. The persecution of Christians by the Jews was meant to stamp out talk of Christ, but in reality it helped spread the word by many in the church leaving Jerusalem and being scattered elsewhere.

At that time a great persecution arose against the church which was at Jerusalem; and they were all scattered throughout the regions of Judea and Samaria, except the apostles. And devout men carried Stephen to his burial, and made great lamentation over him. (Acts 8:1–2)

Communities of baptized believers continued to organize for worship and as working entities in order to spread the good news of God's grace wherever they went. The gospel had given these newly converted disciples the ability to seek God by being motivated to love. This was and is the difference between Christianity and all other religions that have ever existed on the planet. The early Christians knew law was not the way to bring the love of God to the hearts of humanity, but rather that the perception of God's love through Jesus was the only way to motivate hearts to love God and His counsel.

But whoever keeps His word, truly the love of God is perfected in him. By this we know that we are in Him. (1 John 2:5)

This was not the way of most Jews in their practice of the Jewish religion. As Stephen was about to be stoned to death, his words were tough, but applicable to the heart condition of the leaders of traditional Judaism at that time.

You stiff-necked and uncircumcised in heart and ears! You always resist the Holy Spirit; as your fathers did, so do you. Which of the prophets did your fathers not persecute? And they killed those who foretold the coming of the Just One, of whom you now have become the betrayers and murderers, who have received the law by the direction of angels and have not kept it. (Acts 7:51–53)

Yet Stephen, immersed in God's love, was able to forgive even these men who treated him with such disdain and violent hate. The final words of Stephen attest to the transformative effects of the love of God on human hearts.

And they stoned Stephen as he was calling on God and saying, "Lord Jesus, receive my spirit." Then he knelt down and cried out with a loud voice, "Lord, do not charge them with this sin." And when he had said this, he fell asleep. (Acts 7:59–60)

Adam and Eve were placed into the world fully grown. So were members of Christ's spiritual body at the beginning, through special gifts of the Spirit. Church officers were first set in congregations by divine appointment. Those receiving these appointments did not have to wait to mature spiritually through years of work and study. They were given miraculous gifts by the Spirit. Just as with the appointment of the apostles, there were also appointments of prophets, pastors or bishops, teachers and evangelists. They were placed in the body of Christ in a mature spiritual state of being.

Because of a change in government and law for God's people with the change of covenants, it was necessary to bring information directly and immediately to the church by miraculous spiritual gifts, as well as through inspired letters written to the churches. Paul wanted to let the early Christians know his epistles were inspired by the Spirit.

If anyone thinks himself to be a prophet or spiritual, let him acknowledge that the things which I write to you are the commandments of the Lord. (1 Corinthians 14:37)

The mysteries of the kingdom were passed on from the apostles to the church. These mysteries had been spoken by Jesus to His immediate disciples, but were not revealed until later, after He had been glorified by being raised from the dead.

These things I have spoken to you while being present with you. But the Helper, the Holy Spirit, whom the Father will send in My name, He will teach you all things, and bring to your remembrance all things that I said to you. John 14:25–26

It was only then that the mysteries of the kingdom were revealed to His apostles by the Holy Spirit. This is why Jesus was so insistent that some would know, but that some would not know and understand the mysteries of the kingdom.

And He said to them, "To you it has been given to know the mystery of the kingdom of God; but to those who are outside, all things come in parables." (Mark 4:11)

He answered and said to them, "Because it has been given to you to know the mysteries of the kingdom of heaven, but to them it has not been given." (Matthew 13:11)

And He said, "To you it has been given to know the mysteries of the kingdom of God, but to the rest it is given in parables, that 'Seeing they may not see, and hearing they may not understand.'" (Luke 8:10)

When Jesus came to earth it was not totally unexpected in the nation of Israel. In fact the Israelites were, for the most part, expecting the Messiah at that time. The Jews' ignorance was in how the kingdom would come and how it would look. They were thinking God's kingdom would be like Israel and other world governments, but God's kingdom would be superior in power. They were looking for the Messiah to deliver them from the Roman state by means of carnal weapons of war. Their idea of the kingdom coming was fleshly rather than eternal, spiritual and not of this world. They had not counted on the worldly kingdom to be discontinued and replaced with an entirely different system of government, one changed by a completely new covenant through Jesus. This is what prompted the apostle Paul to declare their ignorance and fleshly motivation about the Messiah and the kingdom.

Brethren, my heart's desire and prayer to God for Israel is that they might be saved. For I bear them record that they have a zeal of God, but not according to knowledge. For they being ignorant of God's righteousness, and going about to establish their own righteousness, have not submitted themselves unto the righteousness of God. For Christ is the end of the law for righteousness to every one that believeth. (Romans 10:1–4)

This was the change Jesus said would come: a spiritual kingdom. It was not of this world, as Jesus had made clear to His immediate disciples. The key to the mysteries of the kingdom was that it was spiritual, unlike the kingdoms of the world. Jesus had revealed this to His disciples while He was with them, but it was not revealed to others who did not have spiritual eyes and ears to understand. The mysteries of the kingdom are revealed by the Spirit only after spiritual regeneration.

So when the kingdom of God came into the world, it was not the kind of kingdom the Jews had longed for. They looked for a kingdom that would appeal to their fleshly pride and passion, one having nothing to do with motivating them to love God and their neighbors. And this is what a lot of Christians are waiting for today. They are still thinking about an elaborate temple and spectacular buildings of worship, regal robes and carnal warfare to establish the preeminence of God's people on earth. This is not the way righteousness is to be established in this world. And for this reason they are ignorant of God's righteousness, trying to establish their own righteousness rather than submitting to the righteousness of God through Jesus.

UNIVERSAL AND LOCAL GOVERNMENT

When we set out to follow the traditions of the early church found in the New Testament we won't stray far from God's plan for the church. And if we do stray by misunderstanding or misinterpreting the scriptures, we will probably be able to correct ourselves because we look for counsel to God's inspired Word rather than to men. Paul told the members of the church they should imitate him even as he imitated Christ.

Imitate me, just as I also imitate Christ. Now I praise you, brethren, that you remember me in all things and keep the traditions just as I delivered them to you. (1 Corinthians 11:1–2)

The church is both universal and local in nature. As a universal body it is spiritually without spot or blemish. It is sanctified and clean. It consists of only those who are pure in heart, those dedicated to pleasing God. No one has entered it without God's approval and those who fall back into an unfaithful state are cut off—only by the Lord. Jesus says it is only by His Father's desire that any can come to Him.

No one can come to Me unless the Father who sent Me draws him; and I will raise him up at the last day. (John 6:44)

Membership in the universal church only happens through divine passage. We cannot join the universal church; we are added to it by the Lord to become spiritual citizens in the kingdom of God. Membership rolls are not kept on earth, only in heaven. Death has no effect on membership in the universal church.

The local church is quite different. In it decisions are made by men who, it is hoped, are using the Bible for guidance. We should never think of the church as a governing entity that governs between the universal and local church. This system was not used in the New Testament church. Sectarian divisions throughout the history of the church have led to a denominational structure of government. This type of organization began with the Roman church elevating men to positions and creating offices in the church that never existed in first-century Christianity. Men assumed authority to mediate between God and His people. Jesus Christ is the only acceptable mediator between God and man.

For there is one God and one Mediator between God and men, the Man Christ Jesus. (1 Timothy 2:5)

But this is the exact effect modern denominationalism has had on the church: to take away the daily sacrifice of Christians and to hinder or disregard local church rule. They place men and man-made institutions between God and His people. Although the Bible sanctions qualified church officers who are scripturally appointed, this does not have to interfere with the individual priesthood of each believer. All Christians are priests in a spiritual sense. Decisions are made by elders and leaders in the local congregations, but with the conscience of the membership in mind. The apostle Peter was one of the appointed elders in the church at Jerusalem. His exhortation to his fellow elders of the local church puts the general duties of elders in perspective.

The elders who are among you I exhort, I who am a fellow elder and a witness of the sufferings of Christ, and also a partaker of the glory that will be revealed: Shepherd the flock of God which is among you, serving as overseers, not by compulsion but willingly, not for dishonest gain but eagerly; nor as being lords over those entrusted to you, but being examples to the flock; and when the Chief Shepherd appears, you will receive the crown of glory that does not fade away.

The idea of a denominational structure exercising authority over local communities (congregations) of believers was foreign to the early Christians. In the beginning local congregational autonomy was exercised by all local churches. Each church had its own elders and took care of its own affairs. Church leaders presiding over unscriptural sectarian or denominational alliances had no authority over local government. The early New Testament church did not accept this unscriptural form of government. All Christians are members of the universal church. In this sense there is only one church. It consists of all who have come to Jesus by being drawn by the Father.

No one can come to Me unless the Father who sent Me draws him; and I will raise him up at the last day. (John 6:44)

However, there are many churches, congregationally speaking. Each local church will be judged by Jesus personally, as with the seven churches of Asia spoken of in the book of Revelation. Only Jesus can remove the candlestick (meaning discipline or cut off) out of the churches. But there is no greater authority on earth to be exercised in the churches than that which is exercised locally.

CONCLUDING THOUGHT

It is very important to realize it is only by God's grace that we have an opportunity to come to Jesus. We have no power to make this happen on our own. Those who come to Christ are given to Him by the Father. Shortly before His death, while praying to the Father, Jesus said this very thing.

Now I am no longer in the world, but these are in the world, and I come to You. Holy Father, keep through Your name those whom You have given Me, that they may be one as We are. (John 17:11)

Only God the Father has the power to grant the right for anyone to come to His Son.

And He said, "Therefore I have said to you that no one can come to Me unless it has been granted to him by My Father." (John 6:65)

When we become citizens of the kingdom of heaven, the true record of our membership is recorded in heaven. This means only God has control over who is a member of the universal church. I believe this is what Paul had in mind when he writes these words to Timothy.

Nevertheless the solid foundation of God stands, having this seal: "The Lord knows those who are His." (2 Timothy 2:19)

Sectarian alliances and man-made religious organizations do not make the rules as to what constitutes membership in the universal body of Christ.

CHAPTER 6
WHAT IS JUDGMENT DAY?

HOW LONG IS A DAY?

Most of us probably don't give a lot of thought as to when Judgment Day will begin or how long it will take. I remember singing the old song "In the Morning of Joy" as a little boy at church. Even at a very young age I could visualize Jesus coming back early one morning to take all good people to heaven. And since this was Judgment *Day*, my thinking was, it should all be over by night-fall—right?

But, as far as I know, the Bible doesn't address this detail, and we really have no idea just how long Judgment Day will take. We have a tendency to fill in the blanks with our imaginations based on what we think we know by tradition. As I said, I never imagined it taking more than one day as we know time. Maybe it could be a twenty-four-hour period, or a part of a twenty-four-hour period, but this is something that cannot be proven by the Bible. And that's the way it is with so many things we assume the Bible tells us. We can conclude, however, that the time of the judgment of God is a *day*, either literally or figuratively, because most translations of the Bible actually use that term.

Because He has appointed a <u>day</u> on which He will judge the world in righteousness by the Man whom He has ordained. He has given assurance of this to all by raising Him from the dead. (Acts 17:31)

A *day* is most commonly defined as a twenty-four-hour period or the space of time from dawn until dark. The Jews counted a day from one sundown until the next, from about 6:00 PM until 6:00 PM. At creation God counted six days, beginning with the first day by saying, "the evening and the morning was the first day," and the second day, and so on. Usually we can tell how a day is reckoned or counted by the context. Strong gives all of these definitions for the word *day* in his concordance, but he also gives another. He says figuratively it can be a period (always defined more or less clearly by the context)—an age.

Clearly the scriptures sometimes refer to a day as a time period or an age. Peter says one day is as a thousand years with God and a thousand years as one day.

But do not forget this one thing, dear friends: With the Lord a day is like a thousand years, and a thousand years are like a day. (2 Peter 3:8)

Another thing to consider is that *Judgment Day* might not even be reckoned by a system of time as we know time. By the scriptures saying that with God a thousand years is like a day and a day is like a thousand years, we clearly see God is unaffected by time.

My opinion is that most things will drastically change for creation after Jesus visibly comes back to earth, when the complete transition from temporal and finite to eternal and infinite occurs. Time is only necessary—at least it appears this way to me—while God's creation is in a state of endurance, which is a proper way to describe time. As long as we are in our physical body we are in a state of endurance.

For we know that if our earthly house, this tent, is destroyed, we have a building from God, a house not made with hands, eternal in the heavens. For in this we groan, earnestly desiring to be clothed with our habitation which is from heaven. (2 Cor. 5:1–2)

However, when God's people are freed from the bondage of this temporal house we no longer suffer the pains of endurance. Everything about this earthly existence is about endurance. With a Christian, though, the enduring is worthwhile and profitable.

But he who endures to the end shall be saved. (Matt. 24:13)

Indeed we count them blessed who endure. You have heard of the perseverance of Job and seen the end intended by the Lord—that the Lord is very compassionate and merciful. (James 5:11)

But for the present we dwell in time and *Judgment Day* might be any length of time in human terms. Or it could be an indefinite period in time that might be figuratively referred to as a thousand years or as one day. These figures might indicate a very long or short time in human duration, but only as a timeless happening with God rather than a period of time.

JOSHUA'S DAY OF BATTLE

In all likelihood, Judgment Day is not a specific, one-day event in terms of time as we know it, but rather an unspecified duration to fit God's plan. It seems rather clear in the scriptures that God can and sometime does make adjustments to human endurance by the shortening or lengthening of time and duration. In speaking of the coming destruction of Jerusalem, which occurred in AD 70, Jesus says the days of this catastrophic siege would be shortened in order that lives would be spared. I take that to mean without divine intervention, the days would have been longer.

For then there will be great tribulation, such as has not been since the beginning of the world until this time, no, nor ever shall be. And unless those days were shortened, no flesh would be saved; but for the elect's sake those days will be shortened. (Matt. 24:21–22)

Another example is when God once lengthened a day in order to give Joshua's army an advantage over the enemies of Israel. In Joshua 10 we find the account of this unusual event wrought from the hand of the Almighty. In reading the following story of the long day of Joshua, we can easily see God is the Lord of time and not the other way around.

So Joshua ascended from Gilgal, he and all the people of war with him, and all the mighty men of valor. And the Lord said to Joshua, "Do not fear them, for I have delivered them into your hand; not a man of them shall stand before you." Joshua therefore came upon them suddenly, having marched all night from Gilgal. So the Lord routed them before Israel, killed them with a great slaughter at Gibeon, chased them along the road that goes to Beth Horon, and struck them down as far as Azekah and Makkedah. And it happened, as they fled before Israel and were on the descent of Beth Horon, that the Lord cast down large hailstones from heaven on them as far as Azekah, and they died. There were more who died from the hailstones than the children of Israel killed with the sword. Then Joshua spoke to the Lord in the day when the Lord delivered up the Amorites before the children of Israel, and he said in the sight of Israel: "Sun, stand still over Gibeon; And Moon, in the Valley of Aijalon." So the sun stood still, and the moon stopped till the people had revenge upon their enemies. Is this not written in the Book of Jasher? So the sun stood still in the midst of heaven, and did not hasten to go down for about a whole day. And there has been no day like that, before it or after it, that the Lord heeded the voice of a man; for the Lord fought for Israel. (Joshua 10:7–14)

Of course only those who depend on the infallible Word of God will give any credence to this account in the book of Joshua. But in addition to the biblical account, history seems to agree with this aberration regarding time as found within the pages of inspiration.

Historical writings about "a long day" appear in Chinese records from during the reign of Emperor Yeo, who lived about the same time as Joshua. In Egyptian recordings also mention the account of a long day. Mexican records document the sun standing still for an entire day in the same year Joshua defeated the Philistines. Note the following from an article written in the *Bible-Science Newsletter* about the long day in Joshua.

> There is apologetic value in ancient legends from various parts of the globe, however, including the following: "It is reported by historians that records of the Chinese during the reign of Emperor Yeo, who lived at the same time as Joshua, report 'a long day.' Also, Heroditus, a Greek historian, wrote that an account of 'a long day' appears in records of Egyptian priests. Others cite records of Mexicans of the sun standing still for an entire day in a year denoted as 'Seven Rabits,' which is the same year in which Joshua defeated the Philistines and conquered Palestine." (*Bible-Science Newsletter*, *Daily Reading Magazine*, Supplement, Vol. VIII, No. 5, May 1978, Caldwell, Idaho

RESERVED FOR FIRE

The scriptures use many terms to describe this present time of reckoning. It is called a "day" or "To Day" by the writer of Hebrews. It is referred to as the end of the world or the last days in other places. We are scripturally informed God will not rush things when the salvation of souls is at stake.

The Lord is not slack concerning His promise, as some count slackness, but is longsuffering toward us, not willing that any should perish but that all should come to repentance. (2 Peter 3:9)

We may have further insight as to the time period of God's judgment from one of the things Peter wrote to the early church. It is important to note, however, that the Bible does not always speak of the judgment of both good and evil in the same passage. In the following passage only the ungodly are under consideration.

But the heavens and the earth which are now preserved by the same word are reserved for fire until the Day of Judgment and perdition of ungodly men. But, beloved, do not forget this one thing, that with the Lord one day is as a thousand years, and a thousand years as one day. (2 Peter 3:8)

In this particular passage, the "Day of Judgment" is referred to as the day of "perdition" (destruction) of "ungodly men." The people mentioned here are lost souls who will be destroyed. In these verses the godly and saved are not included. This prophetic scene of judgment only speaks about the time when the ungodly are waiting for execution. The separation and retention are a part of the judgment process for the ungodly. The heavens and the earth are preserved (to continue unchanged) and are reserved (retained) for fire until the final destruction of ungodly men. This preservation and reservation of the heavens and the earth will continue until those who are unredeemed by the blood of Christ are destroyed by that same fiery destruction that will destroy the heavens and the earth and all that are in them. But this judgment does not include those things the writer of Hebrews alludes to in chapter 12 as the things that "cannot be shaken" (Hebrews 12:28)

Notice again that the heavens and the earth are preserved (will continue) until the "Day of Judgment" and "perdition" of "ungodly men." And the execution of judgment of the ungodly will not happen until Jesus comes back for the bodily resurrection of the dead. Peter seems to indicate this very thing as he speaks of the mercy the Lord has toward the righteous in this life. The fate of evildoers is reserved or retained for until after the bodily resurrection.

Then the Lord knows how to deliver the godly out of temptations and to reserve the unjust under punishment for the Day of Judgment. (2 Peter 2:9)

THE INVISIBLE KING

The separation of souls for judgment has continued to occur—the good from the bad—from the time Peter penned the words of 2 Peter 2:9. The *godly* are delivered from condemnation while the *unjust* are reserved under punishment for Judgment Day. This judgment that separates the godly from the unjust will continue until Jesus comes in flaming fire to execute judgment on sin. Although the judgment of the wicked will end in their final punishment, it begins with a decision of who is worthy to enter the kingdom of God. It is a judgment to be made by Jesus as He separates the saved from the unsaved, as we read in Matthew 25. This process began after the coronation of the Son of Man in the kingdom of God. The separation began with the fulfillment of the prophecy that "repentance and remission of sins" was to be preached in the name of Jesus to all nations, beginning in Jerusalem. There could be no judgment by this sanctification process without forgiveness or remission of sins. Listen to the words of the resurrected Lord Jesus.

Then He said to them, "These are the words which I spoke to you while I was still with you, that all things must be fulfilled which were written in the Law of Moses and the Prophets and the Psalms concerning Me." And He opened their understanding, that they might comprehend the Scriptures. Then He said to them, "Thus it is written, and thus it was necessary for the Christ to suffer and to rise from the dead the third day, and that repentance and remission of sins should be preached in His name to all nations, beginning at Jerusalem. And you are witnesses of these things." (Luke 24:44–48)

Jesus, as the Son of Man and as the Son of God, was crowned King of Kings and Lord of Lords. He was seated on the throne of God's judgment with all power and authority to rule in heaven and on earth. His reign began on the day of Pentecost in about AD 33. This was the prophetic fulfillment of the descent of the Holy Spirit of God from heaven as promised by Jesus. Remember Jesus has received an immeasurable portion of the Spirit.

But it did not happen with Jesus coming in a visible form, but rather in an invisible form, and with the immeasurable power of the Holy Spirit. He had talked to His immediate disciples about this very thing, as recorded in John's gospel. Jesus in His fleshly body was the temporary Comforter and Helper before He received the glory of the kingdom after His death. But He speaks of *another* Comforter or Helper to be sent to the disciples after His death. This Comforter or Helper would abide with His disciples forever. The comfort and help to His disciples would no longer be just a temporary assistance by the Son of Man in human form, but by His eternal abode with them as the Son of God through the power of the Holy Spirit of His Father.

And I will pray the Father, and He will give you another Helper, that He may abide with you forever—the Spirit of truth, whom the world cannot receive, because it neither sees Him nor knows Him; but you know Him, for He dwells with you and will be in you. I will not leave you orphans; I will come to you. (John 14:16–18)

Jesus would pray to the Father and His disciples would be given another Helper (Comforter [KJV]) to be with them forever. He says the world cannot receive the Comforter (Holy Spirit) because they cannot see or know Him. Then He says "But you [His disciples] know Him, because He dwells with you and is in you." Jesus continues to insist He will not leave them without help or comfortless and then concludes by saying, "I will come to you."

Jesus makes no distinction as far as being present with His disciples, whether bodily or through His invisible presence in the Holy Spirit. Either way, He would be present, helping and comforting them. So, hearing Jesus say, "I will come to you" in this conversation with His disciples before His death, it should not surprise us when Matthew speaks of Jesus coming to sit on His throne to judge, having reference to His coming in the Spirit in a non-visible form.

THE PROCESS OF SANCTIFICATION

It is very important to understand the difference between the judgment for the separation (those who are sanctified) and the judgment for the execution of sentence (those who are unsanctified). When one is judged innocent, there is no necessity for further judgment, only the declaration of exoneration. Those who have been made righteous by faith are spiritually separated (set apart or sanctified) from the unrighteous to wait for their final reward. The judgment process that separates the righteous from the unrighteous occurs before physical death and before the bodily resurrection. This will be the situation of those redeemed by the blood of Christ.

However, when one is judged guilty, because the blood of Christ has not been applied to his or her heart, a further decision is necessary to establish proper execution of judgment on unforgiven sin. This will be the situation of those who have not been redeemed by the blood of Christ after Jesus returns to earth. The wages of sin will be death for the unredeemed, but the gift of God will be eternal life for those *redeemed* (bought back) by the blood of Jesus. Therefore we may safely conclude that the righteous who have been *sanctified*, separated and set apart from the wicked shall not be subjected to a judgment for the purpose of punishment (sanctify, sanctification, *hagiasmos* [Greek] is used of [a] separation to God [1 Cor. 1:30; 2 Thess. 2:13; 1 Pet.1:2] and [b] the course of life befitting those so separated [1 Thess. 4:3, 4, 7; Rom. 6:19, 22; 1 Tim. 2:15; Heb.12:14] [*Vine's Expository Dictionary of New Testament Words*]).

The words of Jesus could be no plainer in connection to the waiving of judgment for condemnation of the righteous than in John 5:24. Here He assures us the believer will be separated from any judgment associated with guilt. The judgment will be waived or will pass over those who are sanctified by the blood of Christ.

Most assuredly, I say to you, he who hears My word and believes in Him who sent Me has everlasting life, and shall not come into judgment, but has passed from death into life. (Note: KJV uses *condemnation* rather than *judgment*.)

Final execution (or carrying out) of judgment will begin with the righteous. It will begin at the house of God.

For the time has come for judgment to begin at the house of God; and if it begins with us first, what will be the end of those who do not obey the gospel of God? (1 Peter 4:17)

However, in contrast with the unsaved after the resurrection, this judgment of God's people will not determine innocence or guilt. This will have already happened during the sanctification process occurring during this temporal life in the body. There will be immortality and reward for the faithful, in contrast to punishment and eternal death for the wicked. Notice once again, the fate of the righteous believer is sealed at physical death before the bodily resurrection at the second coming of the Lord, according to the words of Jesus.

Most assuredly, I say to you, he who hears My word and believes in Him who sent Me has everlasting life, and shall not come into judgment, but has passed from death into life. (John 5:24)

The righteous will have been pardoned by faith in the blood of Christ. On the other hand, the unrighteous will stand to be judged for their lawless deeds without the atoning merits of the blood of Christ. This is taught in many places by Jesus and the New Testament writers. However, it is important to understand that the pardon of those who are righteous, and who have passed from death into life, is conditional until after physical death. They have passed from death into life because of their trust in the death of Christ. They will remain spiritually alive as long as they maintain this trust. But if they go back into a state of unbelief, they cannot be saved without believing.

For without faith it is impossible to please God. (Heb. 11:6)

In this case, they have simply departed from the mercy and grace of God. The same path that brought them from death to life will lead them back into a state of spiritual death, separating them from the mercy of God. Once again listen to the words of Peter as he declares the destruction of the material evil world in the end.

But the heavens and the earth which are now preserved by the same word are reserved for fire until the Day of Judgment and perdition of ungodly men. But, beloved, do not forget this one thing, that with the Lord one day is as a thousand years, and a thousand years as one day. (2 Peter 3:8)

When Peter speaks of the preservation of the heavens and the earth for the coming fires of destruction, he is only talking about those things that are destructible. The things that cannot be destroyed are not included. The writer of Hebrews recalls when Moses received the law from the finger of God. It was at this time the children of Israel presented themselves before the holy mount from whence the law came. They were commanded not to touch the mountain under penalty of death. This was an awesome scene of reverence for God and His glory. But listen as the writer of Hebrews speaks in chapter 12. Here he compares this scene at Mount Sinai—the thunder, lightning, darkness, glory and power of God—with the time when Jesus returns to execute judgment on sin in this world. He also compares the things that will be shaken and destroyed with the things that are indestructible and cannot be shaken.

At that time his voice shook the earth, but now he has promised, "Once more I will shake not only the earth but also the heavens." The words "once more" indicate the removing of what can be shaken—that is, created things—so that what cannot be shaken may remain. Therefore, since we are receiving a kingdom that cannot be shaken, let us be thankful, and so worship God acceptably with reverence and awe, for our "God is a consuming fire." (Hebrews 12:26–29)

The things that are physical and material are the *created things*. They can and will be shaken and therefore removed. But this does not include the spiritually regenerated, new creatures in Christ. Redeemed humanity will have received its immortal bodies at this time. However, utter destruction is exactly what will happen to the entire created, physical universe. Only the new creation in Jesus Christ will stand unmoved and unshaken.

Therefore, if anyone is in Christ, he is a new creation; old things have passed away; behold, all things have become new. (2 Cor. 5:17)

This is the time of the revealing of the glory of the children of God Paul spoke of in Romans 8. It will be the time of the revealing of sanctified humanity. And it will be then that the rest of nonhuman creation will be delivered from the bondage of its corruption into the glorious liberty of the children of God.

But as we go back to 2 Peter 3:8, it's difficult to comprehend the magnitude of Peter's statement in connection to the preservation of the earth and heavens for destruction by fire without putting it into the context of the entire passage. Now listen as we look at the complete thought as Peter speaks about the second visible coming of the Lord Jesus. He speaks of doubters and scoffers as having *willfully* forgotten the previous destruction of the world by water. He then tells them the promise from God to destroy the world by water is from the same source as the promise to eventually destroy the world by fire.

Beloved, I now write to you this second epistle (in both of which I stir up your pure minds by way of reminder), that you may be mindful of the words which were spoken before by the holy prophets, and of the commandment of us, the apostles of the Lord and Savior, knowing this first: that scoffers will come in the last days, walking according to their own lusts, and saying, "Where is the promise of His coming? For since the fathers fell asleep, all things continue as they were from the beginning of creation." For this they willfully forget: that by the word of God the heavens were of old, and the earth standing out of water and in the water, by which the world that then existed perished, being flooded with water. But the heavens and the earth which are now preserved by the same word are reserved for fire until the Day of Judgment and perdition of ungodly men. But, beloved, do not forget this one thing, that <u>with the Lord one day is as a thousand years, and a thousand years as one day</u>. The Lord is not slack concerning His promise, as some count slackness, but is longsuffering toward us, not willing that any should perish but that all should come to repentance. But the day of the Lord will come as a thief in the night, in which the heavens will pass away with a great noise, and the elements will melt with fervent heat; both the earth and the works that are in it will be burned up. Therefore, since all these things will be dissolved, what manner of persons ought you to be in holy conduct and godliness, looking for and hastening the coming of the day of God, because of which the heavens will be dissolved, being on fire, and the elements will *melt with fervent heat? Nevertheless we, according to His promise, look for new heavens and a new earth in which righteousness dwells. (2 Peter 3:1–13)*

The one thing Peter asks his hearers to remember in his somewhat lengthy statement seems almost disconnected with the main thought of the passage. And this single verse is probably the least considered of the passage by most readers. But it is only reasonable to assume the writer deemed it vitally important. He says *do not forget this one thing*. It, therefore, was the most important thing in Peter's remarks regarding the judgment.

But, beloved, <u>do not forget this one thing</u>, that with the Lord one day is as a thousand years, and a thousand years as one day.

The only other place a reference is made to a thousand years in the New Testament scripture is in the book of Revelation. There it is connected to the reign of Christ and judgment. In Revelation 20:2–7 the writer speaks of those who live and reign with Christ for a thousand years. During this period Satan is bound. I discuss this in the next chapter.

CONCLUDING THOUGHT

Nothing is more dangerous to a would-be believer's mind than bondage to religious tradition. Few things are more subtle or as easy to believe. This has been one of the crown jewels of the devil's deception since the beginning of time. Throughout the Christian age, time and time again, allegiances to tradition have taken the place of fidelity to God's word.

The deception of Satan, the old serpent, continues just as it began in Eden. The only real test of life is the test of believing and trusting God rather than something or someone else. In the beginning Eve and Adam failed the test. Eve believed a snake rather than God. Adam trusted a human rather than God. In both cases they looked to the creature rather than their Creator for direction and counsel. It is an inherent fleshly weakness of humans to try to serve God by way of only the human senses.

But, as previously discussed, it seems right to follow the religious traditions we've been handed from childhood. These traditions come from those we have trusted. But Jesus said when the blind leads the blind, both will fall into the ditch. One of the greatest gifts we can give to those we love and trust is to point them toward the truth we find in the Word of God. The unadulterated counsel of God is the pearl of great price!

Again, the kingdom of heaven is like a merchant seeking beautiful pearls, who, when he had found one pearl of great price, went and sold all that he had and bought it. (Matt. 13:45–46)

CHAPTER 7

THEY LIVED AND REIGNED A THOUSAND YEARS

He laid hold of the dragon, that serpent of old, who is the Devil and Satan, and bound him for a thousand years; and he cast him into the bottomless pit, and shut him up, and set a seal on him, so that he should deceive the nations no more till the thousand years were finished. But after these things he must be released for a little while. And I saw thrones, and they sat on them, and judgment was committed to them. Then I saw the souls of those who had been beheaded for their witness to Jesus and for the word of God, who had not worshiped the beast or his image, and had not received his mark on their foreheads or on their hands. And they lived and reigned with Christ for a thousand years. But the rest of the dead did not live again until the thousand years were finished. This is the first resurrection. Blessed and holy is he who has part in the first resurrection. Over such the second death has no power, but they shall be priests of God and of Christ, and shall reign with Him a thousand years. Now when the thousand years have expired, Satan will be released from his prison. (Rev. 20:2–7)

As long as our spirit is housed in our physical body we are confined to the realm of the finite. In other words, we are bound to a system of temporary existence called time. The concept of infinity or eternity is basically foreign to our nature while we live in a physical, temporal state. Man was made for time and time was made for man. Time is a temporary reality rather than a constant eternal state. We will remain in bondage to time as long as we are in our temporal, fleshly body. However, God's people can rejoice knowing it is just a temporary state.

For we know that if our earthly house, this tent, is destroyed, we have a building from God, a house not made with hands, eternal in the heavens. (2 Corinthians 5:1)

When our spirit is freed from this earthly house of existence, we are no longer bound to the limitations of time. At that point our spirit is freed; we are then disconnected from all earthly ties ruled by the degrading influence of time. God clearly has designed the system we call time to be used by humanity for the present. Time has a special purpose in working His will to test the faithful endurance of His human creation.

In his letter to the Roman church Paul gives a glimpse of the collective "groaning" of humanity as well as the rest of creation. He compares our earthly existence with the future glorious redemption in Christ by saying it is not worthy to be compared. It is not just humanity that has been affected by the sin of Adam, but all the creation of God.

For I consider that the sufferings of this present time are <u>not worthy to be compared</u> with the glory which shall be revealed in us. For the earnest expectation of the creation eagerly waits for the revealing of the sons of God. For the creation was subjected to futility, not willingly, but because of Him who subjected it in hope; because the creation itself also will be delivered from the bondage of corruption into the glorious liberty of the children of God. For we know that the whole creation groans and labors with birth pangs together until now. Not only that, but we also *who have the first-fruits of the Spirit, even we ourselves groan within ourselves, eagerly waiting for the adoption, the redemption of our body. (Romans 8:18–23)*

It was through the curse of the sin of one man, Adam, that all creation was subjected to the pains of dying and death. And it was through the sacrifice and gift of one man, the Lord Jesus, by which many would be delivered from this bondage and death.

But the gift is not like the trespass. For if the many died by the trespass of the one man, how much more did God's grace and the gift that came by the grace of the one man, Jesus Christ, overflow to the many! (Romans 5:15) (NIV)

Unlike creation, God dwells in an eternal and infinite existence. He is unaffected by this system of duration we call time. Our system of time and endurance has no power over the Eternal One. Human knowledge of the celestial realm is almost nothing. However, what we can know about eternity, the timeless realm, will only come through our knowledge of God and His Word.

Now to the King eternal, immortal, invisible, the only God, be honor and glory for ever and ever. Amen. (1 Tim. 1:17)

Once again, where God dwells there are no effects by the system of duration called time. It is this temporal existence that brings deterioration, decay and eventual death to the created. We need to understand God's eternal existence stands in stark contrast to the effects time has on His creation and on all that endure and dwell in it. The Creator of time is unaffected by it and dwells in a very different existence. The Creator has only devised this system for His created beings by which they undergo testing and enduring.

But he who <u>endures</u> to the end shall be saved. (Jesus) (Matt. 24:13)

If we <u>endure</u>, we will also reign with him. If we disown him, he will also disown us. (2 Timothy 2:12) (NIV)

In the New Testament the word *endure* sometimes means simply to continue or abide. But in the verses just cited the Greek word for endure is *hupomeno,* meaning to abide under, to bear up courageously (under suffering.) This definition accounts for the groaning of all creation affected by time.

Once we understand time as being only for a temporary purpose for the created and not for the Creator, it makes more sense why God chooses sometimes not to codify and define events by the rules of measurement used in our time system. For example, David said a thousand years in the sight of God was like yesterday or a single day.

For a thousand years in Your sight are like yesterday when it is past, And like a watch in the night. (Psalms 90:14)

Again, in the letter to the Roman church, Paul writes extensively about God's relationship with the patriarch Abraham. The story of this relationship gives us a glimpse into the infinite and timeless realm of the Creator. Abraham is commonly referred to as the father of the faithful. Abraham's faith did not come from what he could see and know, but from his trust in Him who sees and knows all things without the hindering effects of time.

In Romans 4 Paul addresses the eternal power and foreknowledge of the Almighty. In verse 17 he points out two characteristics of God that show the awesomeness of the power of the Eternal One. It was because Abraham embraced this knowledge of God's greatness that a full assurance of faith was generated within his heart.

The first characteristic of God mentioned in Romans 4 considers the inherent power of a life-giving Creator. Abraham believed God's power was without limit, even to give the power of life to the dead. This faith was predicated upon Abraham's faith in God's complete power of foreknowledge. The second characteristic is directly related to infinite foreknowledge—God's ability to foretell things existing before they actually exist in time, not just knowing things will happen in the future, but believing with God all things are present. This can be believed but never understood while existing in time. Notice carefully what is said in this verse.

As it is written, "I have made you a father of many nations." He is our father in the sight of God, in whom he believed—the God who gives life to the dead and calls into being things that were not. (Romans 4:17) (NIV)

The New King James renders Romans 4:17 in the following way.

As it is written, "I have made you a father of many nations") in the presence of Him whom he believed—God, who gives life to the dead and calls those things which do not exist as though they did.

As a child I listened to an old church song with amazement. Only after I became a child of God did its meaning slowly become clearer in my mind. It was entitled "Hold to God's Unchanging Hand."

Time is filled with swift transition; naught of earth unmoved can stand.

Build your hopes on things eternal, hold to God's unchanging hand.

When your journey is completed, if to God you have been true,

Fair and bright the home in glory, your enraptured soul will view.

The unchangeable nature of God, at least in part, is due to freedom from the effects of time. Ability is diminished in direct proportion to the effects and limitations of time. Jesus declared all things are possible with God. The Lord does not wait for the passing of time in order to know and do what needs to be done for the good of His creation. He operates in the timeless present, always dwelling in the here and now.

In regard to God's ability to give life to the dead, the most probable explanation would be connected with Abraham's great test when he offered up his son Isaac as a sacrifice to God in compliance with the Lord's command. The scriptures record that Abraham trusted God to the extent that he was fully confident the Lord was able to raise Isaac up from the dead.

Concluding that God was able to raise him up, even from the dead, from which he also received him in a figurative sense. (Hebrews 11:19)

The second characteristic, which is to call those things that do not exist as though they did, is no doubt connected to God's declaration to Abraham: "I have made you a father of many nations." At the time Abraham received these words from the Lord no nations had descended from him. In fact, God spoke these words to Abraham at a time when he only had one son by whom this promise could be fulfilled. This son was Isaac, his only son of promise, whom the Lord had commanded Abraham to kill as a sacrifice. Although God stopped Abraham from slaying his son, the scriptures tell us the faithful servant believed God was able to raise him from the dead.

The story of Abraham's relationship with God, as illustrated by the writer of Romans, teaches our system of duration called time has never had an effect on God's ability to foreknow and carry out His will. At a specific point in time God could say to Abraham, "I have made you a father of many nations." But the fact is that this had not yet happened, at least not by our time system. It would happen hundreds of years later. But with God, even though it is beyond our human comprehension, it had happened! And it could happen because God was and is not restricted by the effects of time.

So using the irrefutable logic that God's system of reckoning is infinitely superior to man's, it is not unreasonable to conclude that one day is as a thousand years with the Lord, and a thousand years is as one day. This would mean any sacred event could begin and conclude within an indefinite period of duration not fixed in exact human time as we would understand it.

For example, God can refer to the time allotted for the salvation of human souls as "the day of salvation." And this phrase, without any exact consideration of time (in other words, not bound by natural restrictions), would be a true statement. It would simply be an indefinite period of endurance known only to the eternal God. The Lord also calls other indefinite periods of duration or time by terms denoting an unspecified amount of duration. *The Day of Judgment, the day of the Lord,* and *the hour of His judgment* all are examples of God's way of communicating indefinite periods of time. These terms all represent the period(s) of time He has allotted to separate the righteous from the unrighteous and to judge and reward.

I have previously shown in Matthew 25 that the separation of the good from the bad happens throughout the reign of Christ as He sits on His throne over God's kingdom. This is also the period when Satan will be bound, preventing him from no longer deceiving the nations until the symbolic thousand years are finished.

SYMBOLS IN PROPHECY

Now let's consider somewhat more closely the prophecy in Revelation 20 regarding the thousand-year reign. The book of Revelation contains, along with other biblical prophecy, highly figurative and symbolic language. This means much of prophecy is not written in a common literal style, but with the aid of symbolic language. Note the following definition of symbolism.

> Symbolism occurs when a noun which has meaning in itself is used to represent something entirely different. One example of symbolism would be to use an image of the American flag to represent patriotism and a love for one's country. (Online version of *Your Dictionary*)

This defines exactly what happens in many of the prophecies of the scriptures. For example, in Daniel 2 the prophet had a vision of a great image. Beginning with the head of the image, successive kingdoms were represented on down to the feet. The head of the image represented the then-existent Babylonian Empire. According to our definition of symbolism, the head had a meaning in itself, but the head of the figurative image was used to represent something entirely different.

Many of the prophecies of Revelation contain highly figurative symbols representing something different than the meaning of the noun (person, place or thing) mentioned. This is the case with the thousand-year reign of Christ. Only when we understand Jesus came in the Spirit to establish His spiritual kingdom in this world can we build a framework of reference to make this case. This truth is borne out by several scriptures I have previously discussed, including Matthew 16 and 25.

SATAN BOUND FOR A THOUSAND YEARS

Then I saw an angel coming down from heaven, having the key to the bottomless pit and a great chain in his hand. He laid hold of the dragon, that serpent of old, who is the Devil and Satan, and bound him for a thousand years; and he cast him into the bottomless pit, and shut him up, and set a seal on him, so that he should deceive the nations no more till the thousand years were finished. But after these things he must be released for a little while. (Revelation 20:1–3)

It's easy to minimize the thousand-year binding of the devil in this chapter by allowing the thousand-year reign of Christ to take an overshadowing position in the text. But these two events must be studied together in order to receive the proper meaning of both, as they are dependent on each other. Satan is bound for a thousand years, and at the same time Jesus is reigning over the kingdom of God. In order to understand the significance of Satan being bound for a thousand years we need to know how the event is connected with the reign of Christ for a thousand years.

Many doctrinal assumptions have been formulated, some valid and some invalid, about this symbolic thousand-year reign in prophecy. But there is one thing of which we can be certain: this is when Satan will lose his most destructive power over the hearts and minds of the human race. He is to be bound from deceiving the nations during this time. We might compare this thousand-year binding of Satan with the Lord binding him in order to prevent him from taking the life of Job long ago. Although he was allowed to inflict many other tribulations on God's servant Job, he was bound from taking his life. Matthew Henry makes the following comment on these first three verses of Revelation 20. He speaks of the restraints laid on Satan as a power to keep the devil from deceiving mankind.

Here is a vision, showing by a figure the restraints laid on Satan himself. Christ, with Almighty power, will keep the devil from deceiving mankind as he has hitherto done. He never wants power and instruments to break the power of Satan. Christ shuts by his power, and seals by his authority. (*Matthew Henry Commentary on the whole Bible [Concise]*)

The purpose of the confinement of the devil, the accuser of the brethren, is stated clearly in Revelation 20:3. Satan was bound in order that he would be powerless to *deceive the nations* from that time forth. However, he would regain his power over the nations when he would be loosed for a little while after the thousand years expired.

And he cast him into the bottomless pit, and shut him up, and set a seal on him, so that he should deceive the nations no more till the thousand years were finished. But after these things he must be released for a little while.

Nothing shown here indicates Satan will be rendered completely powerless by his imprisonment. We understand by the Word of God that he possesses great power, and we observe the effects of that power daily on the souls of men. But during the reign of Christ he is to become powerless only in this one respect; to *no longer deceive the nations*. But what does this mean?

As a general rule the phrase "the nations," as used in the scriptures, refers to the Gentile world. Once, after Jesus had healed many, he warned the people not to make His power known. Jesus declared this to be for the purpose of fulfilling the scriptures concerning the salvation he would bring to the Gentile world. The following passage is from the NKJV, but most versions render the word *Gentiles* used here as "the nations."

Yet He warned them not to make Him known, that it might be fulfilled which was spoken by Isaiah the prophet, saying: "Behold! My Servant whom I have chosen, My Beloved in whom My soul is well pleased! I will put My Spirit upon

Him, and He will declare justice to the <u>Gentiles</u>. He will not quarrel nor cry out, nor will anyone hear His voice in the streets. A bruised reed He will not break, and smoking flax He will not quench, till He sends forth justice to victory; and in His name <u>Gentiles</u> will trust." (Matthew 12:15–21)

In all probability "the nations" in which Satan was bound has reference to the Gentile nations. Spiritually bound, Satan was prevented from deceiving these nations for the duration of the reign of salvation on earth. The "nations" were the people who were not a part of the original promise God made to Abraham, a promise fulfilled through his son Isaac. In other words, the Gentiles were the non-Jewish world.

But in what way were the Gentiles kept from being deceived? This could not mean a complete halt to Satan's deception on the whole world. As a matter of fact, in Revelation 12, the devil and his angels are cast out of heaven, and he is charged with "deceiving the whole world." Of course one might argue that the casting of Satan out from heaven may have been before or after the thousand-year period of his being bound. But the point is simply this: the devil has never been without power to deceive since the original deception in Eden. It is, however, clear in this instance: he is bound in that he <u>cannot deceive the nations</u> again in some way until the completion of the thousand-year reign of Christ.

So the great dragon was cast out, that serpent of old, called the Devil and Satan, who deceives the whole world; he was cast to the earth, and his angels were cast out with him. (Revelation 12:9)

I can think of nothing more vital for God to withhold from Satan's deception on humanity than the gospel of Christ. The gospel, that *pearl of great price,* is indispensable in bringing the news of Jesus—God's grace and glory—to the world. This may have been especially true for the Gentile world. After the glorious resurrection of the Lord, God's communication for salvation was broadcast into every nation, not just Israel.

John beheld in his revelation vision the gospel ready to be sent to the earth for every nation, kindred, tongue and people. This sending of the gospel launched the period of salvation and judgment on earth under the kingship of the Lord Jesus. Notice that it speaks of *the hour of His judgment* beginning at the exact same time as the gospel comes to the people on earth.

Then I saw another angel flying in the midst of heaven, having the everlasting gospel to preach to those who dwell on the earth—to every nation, tribe, tongue, and people—saying with a loud voice, "Fear God and give glory to Him, for the hour of His judgment has come; and worship Him who made heaven and earth, the sea and springs of water." (Revelation 14:6–7)

In His earthly ministry Jesus did many things to alleviate human suffering. But His crowning work was not in alleviating the suffering of the body, but alleviating the effects of sin on the soul. When John the Baptist was in prison, he inquired of Jesus' disciples as to the authenticity of Jesus. Jesus then sent word back to John. With the following words the Lord put to rest the fears of John.

The blind see and the lame walk; the lepers are cleansed and the deaf hear; the dead are raised up and the poor have the gospel preached to them. (Matthew 11:5)

Those who were poor in this world's goods did hear the gospel message preached. The gospel was preached, beginning in Jerusalem, just as the prophets foretold. But it was not just those who were materially destitute who heard the saving message of Jesus. The gospel was preached to governors and kings in the first century of the Christian era. But whether kings or paupers, it was only received by those humbled by the love and mercy of God. It was those who became *poor in spirit* who responded to the message, those who had an attitude of mercy toward *the least of these*, just as the Lord Jesus said in Matthew 25.

Blessed are the poor in spirit, for theirs is the kingdom of heaven. (Jesus) (Matthew 5:3)

The preaching of the gospel to the world was the foremost thing Jesus had on His mind before He ascended back into heaven.

Then Jesus came to them and said, "All authority in heaven and on earth has been given to me. Therefore go and make disciples of all nations, baptizing them in the name of the Father and of the Son and of the Holy Spirit, and teaching them to obey everything I have commanded you. And surely I am with you always, to the very end of the age." (Matthew 28:18–20) (NIV)

He said to them, "Go into all the world and preach the gospel to all creation. Whoever believes and is baptized will be saved, but whoever does not believe will be condemned. (Mark 16:15–16) (NIV)

The important fact is that Satan was bound in that he could not prevent the gospel from being preached to the Gentiles. He was prevented from deceiving the nations until the thousand-year reign of Christ was over. This was accomplished by the power of God and His Christ, in creating an avenue whereby the message of the saving gospel could have free course throughout the world. Satan was bound in this way for the duration of the spiritual reign of Christ in His kingdom. The thousand years represented the *day of salvation*, as well as the *hour of His judgment*, separating the good from the bad.

THE REIGN OF ALL BELIEVERS

And I saw thrones, and they sat on them, and judgment was committed to them. Then I saw the souls of those who had been beheaded for their witness to Jesus and for the word of God, who had not worshiped the beast or his image, and had not received his mark on their foreheads or on their hands. And they lived and reigned with Christ for a thousand years. (Rev. 20:4)

There are strongly held traditional doctrines within the Christian community concerning the thousand-year reign spoken of in the book of Revelation. This is especially true within the Protestant denominations, probably more so than in the Catholic Church. And though views vary in detail, the basic tenets are similar.

Protestants commonly believe the thousand-year reign is a literal time period when at least some of the righteous ones will reign with King Jesus. Although there are differences in the details, most believe Christ will return to earth and establish a material earthly kingdom. Once again remember what Jesus said in Matthew 16. He said some of those with whom He spoke would not *taste of death* before He came in His kingdom, meaning it would be within their lifetimes.

In viewing the situation portrayed in the above text in verse 4, the first scene presented to the mind suggests royalty and power among those who are first mentioned and reigning. *And I saw thrones, and they sat upon them, and judgment was committed to them.* It is a view of enthroned individuals who have been given the authority to judge in some way. Ruling or reigning with the power to judge is probably the most identifying characteristic of a king. Although these were portrayed as kings sitting on thrones, they were subject to the King of Kings while reigning together with Him. In Matthew 16 Jesus had told His disciples some of them would not die before the Son of Man would come in His glory. Earlier in the same chapter the Lord had committed authority to Peter to make judgment in connection with things pertaining to God's kingdom on earth. This declaration by Jesus aligns with what He said to His disciples at the Passover supper on the night of His betrayal preceding His death.

But you are those who have continued with Me in My trials. And I bestow upon you a kingdom, just as My Father bestowed one upon Me, that you may eat and drink at My table in My kingdom, and sit on thrones judging the twelve tribes of Israel." (Luke 22:28–30)

Jesus said Simon Peter was to receive the "keys of the kingdom." In receiving the keys of the kingdom Peter would be given a great amount of authority to sit on a throne of judgment within the kingdom.

He said to them, "But who do you say that I am?" Simon Peter answered and said, "You are the Christ, the Son of the living God." Jesus answered and said to him, "Blessed are you, Simon Bar-Jonah, for flesh and blood has not revealed this to you, but My Father who is in heaven. And I also say to you that you are Peter, and on this rock I will build My church, and the gates of Hades shall not prevail against it. And I will give you the keys of the kingdom of heaven, and whatever you bind on earth will be bound in heaven, and whatever you loose on earth will be loosed in heaven." (Matthew 16:15–19)

To the vast majority of people professing Christianity, the idea that all Christians would in any way be kings is ridiculous, like the idea of all being priests. And of course this would be true if the passage was to be interpreted in literal, nonsymbolic language, rather than in a symbolic spiritual way. But it makes perfect spiritual sense according to the teaching of the scriptures. In fact John opens Revelation by referring to God's people as "a kingdom and priests."

And from Jesus Christ, who is the faithful witness, the firstborn from the dead, and the ruler of the kings of the earth. To him who loves us and has freed us from our sins by his blood, and has made us to be <u>a kingdom and priests</u> to serve his God and Father—to him be glory and power for ever and ever! Amen. (Revelation 1:5–6)

Jesus was called the Lamb of God who would take away the sins of the world. Jesus and the New Testament writers spoke of God's people in the Christian age as being royalty many times and in many ways. Peter called the followers of Christ a royal priesthood.

But you are a chosen people, <u>a royal priesthood</u>, a holy nation, God's special possession, that you may declare the praises of him who called you out of darkness into his wonderful light. (1 Peter 2:9) (NIV)

Jesus said His spiritually adopted children are given a kingdom from their Father.

Do not be afraid, little flock, for your Father has been pleased to give you the kingdom. (Luke 12:32) (NIV)

As I have repeatedly pointed out, the kingdom of God is not an earthly kingdom. It is a spiritual kingdom whose foundation is Jesus Christ, and every spiritual stone laid upon the foundation is only through faith in Christ.

For no one can lay any foundation other than the one already laid, which is Jesus Christ. (1 Cor. 3:11) (NIV)

You also, as living stones, are being built up a spiritual house, a holy priesthood, to offer up spiritual sacrifices acceptable to God through Jesus Christ. (1 Peter 2:5)

God's kingdom is not now located in Jerusalem; neither does it exist in any earthly geographic location. The kingdom of God is within the hearts of His people. In the gospel of Luke, the Lord made this perfectly clear. But even so, many of the traditional doctrines of men seek an earthly kingdom of God to be established on earth at a future date.

Now when He was asked by the Pharisees when the kingdom of God would come, He answered them and said, "The kingdom of God does not come with observation; nor will they say, 'See here!' or 'See there!' For indeed, the kingdom of God is within you." (Luke 17:20–21)

When John saw kings in his vision sitting upon thrones and being given the power to judge, he was not observing a special class of Christian saints. He was seeing all those redeemed in Christ. Those beheaded for the witness of Jesus and for the Word of God were some of those who were sitting on thrones and participating in the reign of Jesus. Even though some were killed for allegiance to Jesus, this does not imply all of those reigning had been physical martyrs. The martyrs were only some of those reigning. Others were those who had not worshipped the symbolic beast and its image. But all were God's blood-bought people who had come out of their own great tribulation and had experienced their own suffering for the cause of Christ. These were those who had been faithful unto death. Paul did not have just the martyrs or any particular class of the Lord's disciples in mind as he wrote the following words to Timothy.

If we suffer, we shall also reign with him: if we deny him, he also will deny us: (2 Timothy 2:12)

In Revelation 5, John also saw a scene showing the Lamb of God as the only one worthy to open the seals of a scroll. Here he speaks of people from every tribe, language, people and nation, saying they were made to be a kingdom and priests and would reign on the earth.

And they sang a new song, saying: "You are worthy to take the scroll and to open its seals, because you were slain, and with your blood you purchased for God persons from every tribe and language and people and nation. You have made them to be a kingdom and priests to serve our God, and they will reign on the earth." (Revelation 5:9–10)

CONCLUDING THOUGHT

It matters how and why a person studies the Bible. Within its spiritually illuminating contents, the pages of inspiration will only be revealed to the spiritually regenerated mind. There is a reason for this. The carnal mind is motivated by something other than the approval of God. The carnal mind has no tools (power) to tap into the mind of Christ. In order to receive the approval of God, we must first be approved of God. This approval can only be realized when we surrender to God's will and care enough to study and meditate on God's word—in a word, to seek His will because we seek His approval. Remember what the apostle Paul told the young evangelist Timothy.

Be diligent to present yourself approved to God, a worker who does not need to be ashamed, rightly dividing the word of truth. (2 Timothy 2:15)

And in order to prove what is acceptable to God, there must first be a transformed mind by way of spiritual regeneration.

And do not be conformed to this world, but be transformed by the renewing of your mind, that you may prove what is that good and acceptable and perfect will of God. (Romans 12:2)

A transformed mind had its motivational structure changed by tapping into the spiritually transmitting *mind of Christ*. This comes only by way of the sword of the Spirit, which is the Word of God. After all, Jesus was the Word made flesh.

Therefore, God's word must be studied out of a desire to receive God's will. Its revelation will not be received as long as the motive is to only further substantiate our doctrinal preconceptions. It will never come by way of seeking to perpetuate our prideful traditions. These kinds of motivations are fleshly and carnal. They will never receive the things of the Spirit.

Because the carnal mind is enmity against God; for it is not subject to the law of God, nor indeed can be. (Romans 8:7)

CHAPTER 8
THE FIRST RESURRECTION

And I saw thrones, and they sat on them, and judgment was committed to them. Then I saw the souls of those who had been beheaded for their witness to Jesus and for the word of God, who had not worshiped the beast or his image, and had not received his mark on their foreheads or on their hands. And they lived and reigned with Christ for a thousand years. But the rest of the dead did not live again until the thousand years were finished. This is the first resurrection. Blessed and holy is he who has part in the first resurrection. Over such the second death has no power, but they shall be priests of God and of Christ, and shall reign with Him a thousand years. (Revelation 20:5–6)

SYMBOLIC LANGUAGE

Although there are varying ideas about the first resurrection, as with the thousand-year reign, we can sure of this one thing: either the first resurrection is a bodily resurrection or it is not. I believe the latter. When we take a hard look at the sacred record it is difficult not to see the first resurrection as a spiritual rather than a bodily resurrection. It depicts the saved individual being arisen to live spiritually. It is symbolized by sharing spiritually in the death, burial and resurrection of Jesus Christ. Only when we conclude it is symbolic do the pieces of the puzzle begin to fit together.

Most of the book of Revelation is not meant to be taken literally. The very first verse of Revelation tells us this. John writes that the prophecies of the book were "signified" by His angel to His servant John. *The Merriam-Webster Dictionary* defines *signify* as follows: "to make a sign or signal." Therefore we must conclude that when the book of Revelation is studied it should be looked at as a revelation of symbols rather than taken as literal language.

The Revelation of Jesus Christ, which God gave Him to show His servants— things which must shortly take place. And He sent and signified it by His angel to His servant John. (Rev. 1:1)

SYMBOLISM: Symbolism is the use of symbols to signify ideas and qualities by giving them symbolic meanings that are different from their literal sense. Symbolism can take different forms. Generally, it is an object representing another to give it an entirely different meaning that is much deeper and more significant. Sometimes, however, an action, an event or a word spoken by someone may have a symbolic value. For instance, "smile" is a symbol of friendship. Similarly, the action of someone smiling at you may stand as a symbol of the feeling of affection which that person has for you. Symbols do shift their meanings depending on the context they are used in. "A chain," for example, may stand for "union" as well as "imprisonment." Thus, symbolic meaning of an object or an action is understood by when, where and how it is used. It also depends on who reads them. (© 2017 Literary Devices)

Several things need to be taken into consideration in order to have confidence in a correct view regarding the first resurrection. One thing to consider is the fact that some of the Bible is written figuratively as previously mentioned, rather than in literal language. Most of the New Testament writing is literal with a few exceptions, the book of Revelation being the main exception. But with the book of Revelation figurative or symbolic writing is the rule and not the exception. Within the New Testament, only in the book of Revelation is the phrase "the first resurrection" used to refer to spiritual regeneration, even though similar language is sometimes employed elsewhere.

We should never expect a strictly literal meaning in a prophetic text when symbols or figures are clearly used in the context. A little common sense can go a long way to determine if something is symbolic and figurative. And once it is determined not to be a literal statement, we need to look elsewhere in the scriptures for clues that will help us interpret the figurative words and symbolic messages used to reveal God's will.

It is always wise to thoroughly search the scriptures before coming to a conclusion about any subject. And it is especially important to pull all pertinent scriptural information together and rightly divide it when dealing with symbolism. For example, in studying about the first resurrection, we should check all scriptures for the word *resurrection*, as well as any other words or phrases meaning the same: words like *risen, raised up* etc. This will require time and patience, but it will pay spiritual dividends in the end.

Next we should carefully consider the text. The text is the immediate main body of thought surrounding the verse or word under consideration. The text should always be examined very closely by making sure words are correctly defined and clearly understood. Equally important is a consideration of the context (the body of thought surrounding the text). After thoroughly evaluating the context, similar words and thoughts found in the context should be researched throughout the Bible. When dealing with symbolism a careful study should be undertaken by a thorough search within the book of Revelation relating to the subject, as well as looking at other Bible prophecy.

Last is perhaps the greatest key to finding the truth within a passage of scripture. We need to prayerfully clear our mind of any and all presupposition and prejudice. In other words, we must lay aside the pride of our religious tradition and upbringing. We can't afford to allow ourselves to be deceived by Satan. The powerful influence of tradition is one of the devil's most important tools.

He answered and said to them, "Why do you also transgress the commandment of God because of your tradition?" (Matthew 15:3)

The bottom line in gleaning the truth is in the understanding of this simple fact. We are not really looking for truth until we are ready to turn loose of tradition for the cause of Christ, no matter how precious a particular traditional idea is to us!

The term *first resurrection* clearly has a variety of meanings within the confines of sectarian walls in the Christian community. These different interpretations have spawned traditions of thought that have gradually evolved into religious doctrines over the past two thousand years. And, as already mentioned, in order to find truth we must seek to use rightly divided scripture as evidence without allowing traditional preconception to cloud the mind. When we continue to allow our mind to dwell on what we have accepted by traditional teaching, we will feel it less necessary to study the scriptures in depth for ourselves.

Now listen to the pure, albeit symbolic language of the Spirit speaking about the first resurrection.

The rest of the dead did not come to life until the thousand years were ended. (Rev. 20:5) (NIV)

From this verse we can derive the following bits of truth. First, those who do not take part in the first resurrection ("the rest of the dead") will not come to life, or will not be resurrected, until after the symbolic thousand-year reign of Christ. This means that in some sense all of the dead will not be resurrected simultaneously. Some will come to life before the thousand-year reign, and some will be resurrected after the reign. Both of these two distinct resurrections are spoken of by the Lord in John 5. Here, without using the phrase "the first resurrection," Jesus talks to his disciples about when the first resurrection will happen.

Most assuredly, I say to you, he who hears My word and believes in Him who sent Me has everlasting life, and shall not come into judgment, but has passed from death into life. Most assuredly, I say to you, the hour is coming, and now is, when the dead will hear the voice of the Son of God; and those who hear will live. For as the Father has life in Himself, so He has granted the Son to have life in Himself, and has given Him authority to execute judgment also, because He is the Son of Man. (John 5:24–27)

It is during the period of Christ's reign (the church age or Christian dispensation of time) when Jesus, together with those taking part in the first resurrection, begins the celebration of the reign of salvation and judgment. The reign will continue as long as the symbolic "day of salvation" or the time of separation (sanctification) of God's people from out of the world continues on earth. Here are four undeniable facts.

1. Jesus could begin this reign only after He was crowned king. His Kingship and reign began on the day of Pentecost and will end after death is no more at the resurrection. *Then the end will come, when he [Jesus] hands over the kingdom to God the Father after he has destroyed all dominion, authority and power. For <u>he must reign until he has put all his enemies under his feet. The last enemy to be destroyed is death</u>. For he "has put everything under his feet." Now when it says that "everything" has been put under him, it is clear that this does not include God himself, who put everything under Christ. When he has done this, then the Son himself will be made subject to him who put everything under him, so that God may be all in all. (1 Cor. 15:24–28) (NIV)*

Contrary to some popular thinking, the reign of Christ is not eternal but temporary. The kingdom of God is eternal, but the reign of Christ is for a fixed period known only to God. During the reign Jesus will have all power in heaven and on earth. After this time Jesus will deliver the kingdom back to God the Father and be subject to Him who put everything under Him during the reign. So, as we see again in the scripture just cited, after the bodily resurrection Jesus will surrender His rule and authority over the kingdom back to the Father.

Then comes the end, when He delivers the kingdom to God the Father, when He puts an end to all rule and all authority and power. (1 Corinthians 15:24) (NKJV)

Then the end will come, when he hands over the kingdom to God the Father after he has destroyed all dominion, authority and power. (NIV)

This verse, taken from the NKJV and NIV Bibles, shows Jesus will deliver or hand over the kingdom to God the Father after having destroyed all other dominion, authority and power. Jesus' reign is only for the period of the church age—from the day of Pentecost in AD 33 until the resurrection of the dead at his visible coming. The victory over death, the last enemy, will mark the end of the Lord's reign.

For the perishable must clothe itself with the imperishable and the mortal with immortality. When the perishable has been clothed with the imperishable, and the mortal with immortality, then the saying that is written will come true: "Death has been swallowed up in victory." (1 Cor.15:53–54)

2. Jesus could be crowned King only after His resurrection. Only after His death conquering resurrection was He qualified to receive all power and authority from the Father. Paul makes this fact clear in his letter to the Roman church.

And declared to be the Son of God with power according to the Spirit of holiness, by the resurrection from the dead. (Romans 1:4)

3. Jesus could only become King and begin His reign after He had been given all power in heaven and on earth to judge and reward by God the Father. The future coming of Christ, with all power to judge and reward in the Kingdom of Heaven, is beautifully foretold by the prophet Isaiah.

The people who walked in darkness have seen a great light; those who dwelt in the land of the shadow of death, upon them a light has shined. You have multiplied the nation and increased its joy; they rejoice before You according to the joy of harvest, as men rejoice when they divide the spoil. For You have broken the yoke of his burden and the staff of his shoulder, the rod of his oppressor, as in the day of Midian. For every warrior's sandal from the noisy battle, and garments rolled in blood, will be used for burning and fuel of fire. For unto us a Child is born, unto us a Son is given; and the government will be upon His shoulder. And His name will be called Wonderful, Counselor, Mighty God, Everlasting Father, Prince of Peace. Of the increase of His government and peace there will be no end, upon the throne of David and over His kingdom, to order it and establish it with judgment and justice from that time forward, even forever. The zeal of the Lord of hosts will perform this. (Isaiah 9:2–7)

4. Jesus, according to His own words, would come in His kingdom in the glory of the Father within the lifetime of some of His followers.

In waiting for the promise of the descending of the Holy Spirit, the apostles had been instructed by Jesus to go and wait at Jerusalem for the Holy Spirit to empower them.

Behold, I send the Promise of My Father upon you; but tarry in the city of Jerusalem until you are endued with power from on high. (Luke 24:40) (NIV)

So, in obedience to the Lord's command, the apostles waited at Jerusalem for the descent of the Holy Spirit. On that day of Pentecost multitudes had gathered at Jerusalem from all over the known world. Those who gathered were mostly Jews who had come from "every nation under heaven" to celebrate the Jewish Passover and related ceremonies. On that day, at about nine o'clock in the morning, the Holy Spirit descended from heaven upon and within the disciples of Jesus exactly as Jesus had earlier promised.

When the day of Pentecost came, they were all together in one place. Suddenly a sound like the blowing of a violent wind came from heaven and filled the whole house where they were sitting. They saw what seemed to be tongues of fire that separated and came to rest on each of them. And they were all filled with the Holy Spirit and began to speak with other tongues, as the Spirit gave them utterance. (Acts 2:1–4) (NIV)

Thus begins the fulfillment of Jesus' promise to build His church according to His words to Peter (Matt. 16:18). This was the establishment of God's kingdom on earth as the prophets had foretold (Dan. 2:44, Isa. 2:1–4). This began the reign of salvation. All those, throughout the Christian age, who would be spiritually elevated to walk in newness of life would be spiritually resurrected to take part in this first resurrection. Paul, in speaking to the Roman Christians, reminds them of their spiritual resurrection to walk in newness of life with Christ.

Therefore we were buried with Him through baptism into death, that just as Christ was raised from the dead by the glory of the Father, even so we also should walk in newness of life. (Romans 6:4)

It all began with the miraculous work of the Holy Spirit operating on Peter and the apostles of Christ. The Spirit revived their remembrance to the things Jesus had said to them while living in His fleshly body before His death.

But the Helper, the Holy Spirit, whom the Father will send in My name, He will teach you all things, and bring to your remembrance all things that I said to you. (John 14:26)

The following scripture is the essence of what Peter tells the hearers gathered at Jerusalem on the Day of Pentecost.

God has raised this Jesus to life, and we are all witnesses of it. Exalted to the right hand of God, he has received from the Father the promised Holy Spirit and has poured out what you now see and hear. (Acts 2:32–33) (NIV)

Now we will look once again at the complete text in Revelation 20, as John sees those who are worthy to be in the first resurrection.

LIVING AND REIGNING WITH CHRIST

I saw thrones on which were seated those who had been given authority to judge. And I saw the souls of those who had been beheaded because of their testimony about Jesus and because of the word of God. They had not worshiped the beast or its image and had not received its mark on their foreheads or their hands. They came to life and reigned with Christ a thousand years. [The rest of the dead did not come to life until the thousand years were ended.] This is the first resurrection. Blessed and holy are those who <u>share in</u> the first resurrection. The second death has no power over them, but they will be priests of God and of Christ and will reign with him for a thousand years. (Rev 20:4–6) (NIV)

The first resurrection was to be "shared in" by those who spiritually come to life and reign with Christ. The writer declares, "This is the first resurrection." Those who share in it are called "blessed and holy." In this statement they are identified as those who were separated out (sanctified, blessed and made holy) from a world of sin and ungodliness.

Another identifying mark of those who share in the first resurrection is that "the second death has no power over them." Those who are sanctified by the blood of Christ are not subject to the second death. Just as the death angel passed over the houses of the children of Israel in Egyptian bondage, death passes over all those who are sanctified by the blood of Jesus. Death, which is the wages of sin, is only present in an individual when imputed sin is present in his or her life.

For the wages of sin is death, but the gift of God is eternal life in Christ Jesus our Lord. (Rom. 6:23)

Blessed are those whose lawless deeds are forgiven, and whose sins are covered; Blessed is the man to whom the Lord shall not impute sin. (Romans 4:7–8)

Nowhere does Revelation 20:4–6 indicate the first resurrection is a bodily resurrection. The passage speaks of souls rather than bodies. But it is a resurrection shared in by those who come to life spiritually and reign with the Lord Jesus by virtue of identifying with Him in His death, burial and resurrection. Paul revisits the account of the conversion of the Christians at Rome in his letter to them. They, through faith in Jesus, had repented and were immersed in water. This was also the command of Peter to sinners on the day of Pentecost (Acts 2:38). These actions were taken in obedience to God's will and were symbolic of the death, burial and resurrection of the Lord Jesus Christ.

Or do you not know that as many of us as were baptized into Christ Jesus were baptized into His death? Therefore we were buried with Him through baptism into death, that just as Christ was raised from the dead by the glory of the Father, even so we also should walk in newness of life. For if we have been united together in the likeness of His death, certainly we also shall be in the likeness of His resurrection, knowing this, that our old man was crucified with Him, that the body of sin might be done away with, that we should no longer be slaves of sin. For he who has died has been freed from sin. Now if we died with Christ, we believe that we shall also live with Him, knowing that Christ, having been raised from the dead, dies no more. Death no longer has dominion over Him. For the death that He died, He died to sin once for all; but the life that He lives, He lives to God. Likewise you also, reckon yourselves to be dead indeed to sin, but alive to God in Christ Jesus our Lord. (Romans 6:3–11)

Paul refers to the message of the death, burial and resurrection of Christ as the gospel (good news). The receiving, standing in it and being saved by it was to be the faithful response of those hearing it preached.

Now, brothers and sisters, I want to remind you of the gospel I preached to you, which you received and on which you have taken your stand. By this gospel you are saved, if you hold firmly to the word I preached to you. Otherwise, you have believed in vain. For what I received I passed on to you as of first importance: that Christ died for our sins according to the Scriptures, that he was buried, that he was raised on the third day according to the Scriptures. (1 Corinthians 15:1–4) (NIV)

Paul also called the gospel a "form of doctrine" delivered to those obedient to its command. The doctrine of salvation in Christ was in the message of His death, burial and resurrection. A form of the doctrine was the symbolic death, burial and spiritual resurrection of the believer by faith, repentance and immersion in water.

Do you not know that to whom you present yourselves slaves to obey, you are that one's slaves whom you obey, whether of sin leading to death, or of obedience leading to righteousness? But God be thanked that though you were slaves of sin, yet you obeyed from the heart that <u>form of doctrine</u> to which you were delivered. And having been set free from sin, you became slaves of righteousness. (Romans 6:16–18)

Romans 6 begins with the following words:

What shall we say then? Shall we continue in sin that grace may abound? Certainly not! How shall we who died to sin live any longer in it? Or do you not know that as many of us as were baptized into Christ Jesus were baptized into His death? (Romans 6:1–3)

It is of great significance that those sharing in the first resurrection are *blessed and holy*. They are not blessed and holy only because they share in it, but they share in it because they are blessed and holy by having united with Christ through His death, burial and resurrection. Those who are *blessed and holy* are those who are forgiven. Nothing else will bring happiness or a blessed state. Nothing else will bring holiness or a pure state. They have been forgiven because they have had hearts predisposed to righteousness through faith in

Jesus. The blessedness Jesus spoke of in the Sermon on the Mount shows this to be true. This is the reason Paul speaks the words of David regarding the state of blessedness and the pardon of sin.

Blessed are those whose lawless deeds are forgiven, and whose sins are covered; blessed is the man to whom the Lord shall not impute sin. (Rom. 4:7–8)

Those who share in the first resurrection are not only blessed, but they are holy as well. All Christians are figuratively spoken of as a holy temple. When Peter preached the first gospel sermon on the day of Pentecost telling the hearers to "repent and be immersed" they were promised forgiveness of their sins upon obedience to that command. They were also given another promise, which was that they would receive the gift of the Holy Spirit. This amounted to the reception of God within them, revealing His will to them through the Word. Their bodies would be the abode of God just as Jesus had said.

Jesus answered and said unto him, If a man love me, he will keep my words: and my Father will love him, and we will come unto him, and make our abode with him. (John 14:23)

God's people are the holy temple of God.

If anyone defiles the temple of God, God will destroy him. For the temple of God is holy, which temple you are. (1 Cor. 3:17)

Another characteristic of those who share in the first resurrection is that the second death has no power over them. The second death is the final and complete death of the wicked, occurring as a result of punishment. The everlasting destruction of the wicked is the consequence of being separated from the presence and power of Almighty God.

But the cowardly, unbelieving, abominable, murderers, sexually immoral, sorcerers, idolaters, and all liars shall have their part in the lake which burns with fire and brimstone, which is the second death. (Revelation 21:8)

These shall be punished with everlasting destruction from the <u>presence</u> of the Lord and from the glory of His <u>power</u>. (2 Thess. 1:9)

Before Jesus raised Lazarus back to life an interesting conversation took place between Jesus and Martha, the sister of Lazarus. In this exchange, Jesus gives us a salvation 101 lesson about life and death. Martha, knowing her brother had been physically dead for four days, was sorrowful because Jesus had not come to be with the family before he died. Martha told Jesus Lazarus would not have died had the Lord been there. Martha, believing the Lord could still raise Lazarus from the dead, said to Jesus, "But even now I know that whatever you ask of God, God will give you" (John 11:22).

Following is the remainder of this conversation between Jesus and Martha. I believe this to be a key passage of scripture in understanding the mystery of the first resurrection of Revelation.

Jesus said to her, "Your brother will rise again." Martha said to Him, "I know that he will rise again in the resurrection at the last day." Jesus said to her, "I am the resurrection and the life. He who believes in Me, though he may die, he shall live. And whoever lives and believes in Me shall never die. Do you believe this?" She said to Him, "Yes, Lord, I believe that You are the Christ, the Son of God, who is to come into the world." (John 11:23–27)

Martha was a true believer in a bodily resurrection. In Judaism the sect of the Pharisees believed in a bodily resurrection of the dead, whereas the sect of the Sadducees opposed the doctrine. Therefore Martha was not surprised when Jesus said Lazarus would rise again. But the resurrection at the end of the world was not what she had in mind. She obviously believed Jesus could raise him again now!

As happened many times in His teaching, Jesus here uses a temporal, physical situation to teach an eternal, spiritual truth. "I am the resurrection and the life." This statement beginning with "I am" presents Jesus as the here-and-now source and substance of the resurrection from the dead. "I am the resurrection and the life" shows life from the dead in a spiritual sense. It speaks of the eternal life that can abide in the soul while it is still living in the physical body. This eternal life is the result of a spiritual resurrection, not a bodily resurrection—not just a coming alive now but also remaining alive now, nevermore to die. Jesus was and is the fountainhead of eternal life. And he now speaks to Martha of a resurrection of the soul unto eternal life while still abiding in the body. This does not refer to the glorified, immortal body in the hereafter, but to the soul of the spiritually resurrected inner man.

Therefore, the first resurrection is one of the inward self. It is a resurrection of the inner spiritual man without the physical body being presently affected. Paul makes this point clear in his letter to the Ephesian church.

And you He made alive, who were dead in trespasses and sins, in which you once walked according to the course of this world, according to the prince of the power of the air, the spirit who now works in the sons of disobedience, among whom also we all once conducted ourselves in the lusts of our flesh, fulfilling the desires of the flesh and of the mind, and were by nature children of wrath, just as the others. (Ephesians 2:1–3)

The body will not be redeemed until the general bodily resurrection when the Lord visibly comes back to earth. Both the inward (spirit or soul) and outward (body) must be redeemed by the blood of Christ, but the present mortal body is only a temporal house for the spirit. The spirit/soul is the real self of an individual. In the epistle written by James we are told that the body without the spirit is dead.

For as the body without the spirit is dead, so faith without works is dead also. (James 2:26)

Peter tells us redemption comes from the blood of Christ, not from corruptible things. This is true whether it is the redemption of body or spirit. However, the redemption of the real self, which is the inner man or spirit, comes first. The redemption of the body will happen at the bodily resurrection when the Lord visibly comes back to earth.

Knowing that you were not redeemed with corruptible things, like silver or gold, from your aimless conduct received by tradition from your fathers, but with the precious blood of Christ, as of a lamb without blemish and without spot. (1 Peter 1:18–19)

Those who have been spiritually resurrected with Christ are affected by a disposition or nature of the higher calling, a heavenly nature. They are seeking those things above, the things of the reigning and immortal King Jesus.

If ye then be risen with Christ, seek those things which are above, where Christ sitteth on the right hand of God. (Col. 3:1) (KJV)

Paul spoke to the churches at both Corinth and Ephesus about the resurrected and ongoing spiritual life of those belonging to Christ.

Therefore we do not lose heart. Even though our outward man is perishing, yet the inward man is being renewed day by day. (2 Corinthians 4:16)

That He would grant you, according to the riches of His glory, to be strengthened with might through His Spirit in the inner man. (Ephesians 3:16)

The spiritually regenerated inward man has life beyond physical life and existence, but has yet to obtain the redemption of the body—which is the final or complete process to immortality.

Now may the God of peace Himself sanctify you completely; and may your whole spirit, soul, and body be preserved blameless at the coming of our Lord Jesus Christ. (1 Thessalonians 5:23)

But the inside must become spiritually alive before the body can be redeemed. The life of the pardoned inner man occurs only through a spiritual regenerating process by faith in the Son of God.

He who believes in Me, though he may die, he shall live. And whoever lives and believes in Me shall never die.

CONCLUDING THOUGHT

In the book of Revelation, notice the scene of the souls, not bodies, of martyrs waiting for fellow servants to join them. These are redeemed, disembodied souls whose bodies are yet to be redeemed. *When he opened the fifth seal, I saw under the altar the souls of those who had been slain because of the word of God and the testimony they had maintained. They called out in a loud voice, "How long, Sovereign Lord, holy and true, until you judge the inhabitants of the earth and avenge our blood?" Then each of them was given a white robe, and they were told to wait a little longer, until the full number of their fellow servants, their brothers and sisters, were killed just as they had been. (Revelation 6:9–11) (NIV)*

CHAPTER 9
A VIEW OF ETERNAL PUNISHMENT

TRADITIONS GOOD AND BAD

As I have said before, in beginning my Christian journey as a young adult, I was mostly a product of my traditional religious upbringing. I never considered that the vast consensus of the Christian world could be wrong about traditional teachings as fundamental as heaven and hell. At that time I had not studied the Bible much for myself and I had never felt a great need to study things already agreed upon among all those I knew. I was comfortable to accept what was handed down to me.

Tradition has a lulling effect on the mind. And complacency, which usually follows, is the product of a traditional mindset. Sometimes we know—way deep down in our souls—when something has entered our religious mind that was not put there by the truth of God's Word. But the acceptance of tradition seems a lot safer to our natural human minds than does the rejection of it. We are more comfortable when our minds are allowed to slumber in the convenience of a secondhand religion than when we risk rocking the boat of our established religious traditions and practices.

Traditions are often wonderful and even productive. This may or may not be true with family traditions, but it is always true with the traditions that are established and grounded in the light of God's counsel. The traditions or ordinances of the New Testament church became a primary source of truth, unity and inspiration for the early Christians. However, these were the traditions or ordinances inspired by the Spirit of God. Scripture tells us the early church continued in the traditions or ordinances given by the inspired apostles of the Lord.

And with many other words he testified and exhorted them, saying, "Be saved from this perverse generation." Then those who gladly received his word were baptized; and that day about three thousand souls were added to them. And they continued steadfastly in the apostles' doctrine and fellowship, in the breaking of bread, and in prayers. (Acts 2:40–42)

The divinely inspired apostolic traditions were written down and passed on to successive generations of Christians. In contrast, the traditions handed down by our parents are treasured largely because of their sentimental value to us, even though some of them may serve us well. Our goal should be to receive divine instructions inspired by God's Spirit. Our minds need to be rooted in a desire for God's counsel. It will be this kind of mind that will forsake any and all human traditions for information from God! Jesus warned of the perils connected with receiving human traditions at the expense of ignoring God's counsel. Listen as He speaks to the teachers and keepers of Jewish law.

So the Pharisees and teachers of the law asked Jesus, "Why don't your disciples live according to the tradition of the elders instead of eating their food with defiled hands?" He replied "Isaiah was right when he prophesied about you hypocrites; as it is written: 'These people honor me with their lips, but their hearts are far from me. They worship me in vain; their teachings are merely human rules.' You have

let go of the commands of God and are holding on to human traditions." And he
continued, "You have a fine way of setting aside the commands of God in order to
observe your own traditions! For Moses said, 'Honor your father and mother,' and,
'Anyone who curses their father or mother is to be put to death.' But you say that
if anyone declares that what might have been used to help their father or mother
is Corban [that is, devoted to God]—then you no longer let them do anything for
their father or mother. Thus you nullify the word of God by your tradition that you
have handed down. And you do many things like that." (Mark 7:5–13) (NIV)

UNREDEEMED HUMANITY

Without doubt the Bible teaches punishment for unredeemed humanity.
It tells us what the ultimate punishment will be, also without doubt. It will
be death—not eternal life in misery as many believe. Judgment or accounting for the sins of those who are redeemed will take place on this side of the
grave. They will be sanctified and forgiven through the redemptive work of
Jesus. They will then be resurrected to immortality at the coming of Jesus,
caught up in the air to forever be with the Lord. The only judgment left for
the righteous is the reward for their good works as they enter into the joy of
their Lord. These works have been built on the spiritual foundation of faith
in Christ. Even though their works may not be perfect, their hearts have been
cleansed and the direction of their minds is sure. Their lives have been established by faith in Jesus. Their faith will be subjected to fiery trials to test all
their works. In the hereafter they will be rewarded for every work that is by
faith. The Day mentioned in what follows is Judgment Day, the day of judgment and salvation for the redeemed.

For no other foundation can anyone lay than that which is laid, which is Jesus
Christ. Now if anyone builds on this foundation with gold, silver, precious stones,
wood, hay, straw, each one's work will become clear; for the Day will declare it,
because it will be revealed by fire; and the fire will test each one's work, of what sort

211

it is. If anyone's work which he has built on it endures, he will receive a reward. (1 Corinthians 3:11–14)

The reward for the works of those who are sanctified is not to be confused with everlasting life, which is a gift due to their submission to Christ.

On the other hand, judgment for the unredeemed will be pronounced and executed only after the bodily resurrection. Up until now most of the concern of this writing has been in connection with the eternal destiny of the redeemed in Christ. I now want to consider what the scriptures teach as to the eternal fate of those who will remain unredeemed.

Even though much of the book of Revelation is written in symbolic language and therefore is highly figurative, some of it must be taken literally in order for it to find harmony with the rest of the scriptures. In Revelation 20 John deals extensively with God's judgment on the unredeemed sins of humanity. This chapter tells of the loosening of Satan from his thousand years of being bound to prevent him from deceiving the nations (Gentiles) during this period.

Now when the thousand years have expired, Satan will be released from his prison and will go out to deceive the nations which are in the four corners of the earth, Gog and Magog, to gather them together to battle, whose number is as the sand of the sea. (Revelation 20:7–8)

As has been previously shown this binding of Satan does not mean he is powerless, but only that he cannot deceive the nations of the Gentiles from having access to the gospel of Christ. When the thousand years are fulfilled he is once again loosed to have power to do the very thing in which he was bound to prevent—that is, to deceive the nations.

The loosening of Satan will obviously be for only a short time before the bodily resurrection. In all likelihood the book of Revelation was written shortly before the end of the first century. In chapter 12 John foretells that

Satan and his angels will be cast out of heaven, down to the earth, at some time subsequent to John's writing.

And war broke out in heaven: Michael and his angels fought with the dragon; and the dragon and his angels fought, but they did not prevail, nor was a place found for them in heaven any longer. So the great dragon was cast out, that serpent of old, called the Devil and Satan, who deceives the whole world; he was cast to the earth, and his angels were cast out with him. (Revelation 12:7–9)

Evidently, previous to the time he was cast out of heaven, and during the time of Job, when Satan communicated with God about Job, Satan had access to both heaven and earth.

Now there was a day when the sons of God came to present themselves before the Lord, and Satan also came among them. And the Lord said to Satan, "From where do you come?" So Satan answered the Lord and said, "From going to and fro on the earth, and from walking back and forth on it." (Job 1:6–7)

This shows that during the days of Job Satan inhabited both heaven and earth. But at a future date Satan would be cast out of heaven, having only the earth to inhabit. And when Satan is cast out of heaven, we are told, all the hosts of heaven will rejoice. But it is certainly not a good thing for the inhabitants on the earth.

Then I heard a loud voice saying in heaven, "Now salvation, and strength, and the kingdom of our God, and the power of His Christ have come, for the accuser of our brethren, who accused them before our God day and night, has been cast down. And they overcame him by the blood of the Lamb and by the word of their testimony, and they did not love their lives to the death. Therefore rejoice, O heavens, and you who dwell in them! Woe to the inhabitants of the earth and the sea! For the devil has come down to you, having great wrath, because he knows that he has a short time." (Revelation 12:10–12)

Satan is cast out of heaven to the earth. He is very angry because he knows time is running out for him. I do not claim to have put together all of the pieces of the end-time puzzle. But some things can be ascertained with minimum effort. One important thing, in my opinion, is to understand something about the sequential events of the end time. By understanding something about the order in which things happen, we will be able to fill in a lot of other things that are revealed.

1.   There will be a bodily resurrection of both redeemed and unredeemed humanity. Jesus says, "do not marvel at this; for the hour is coming in which all who are in the graves will hear His voice and come forth—those who have done good, to the resurrection of life, and those who have done evil, to the resurrection of condemnation" (John 5:28–29).

2.   There will be a judgment of both redeemed and unredeemed humanity. However, the judgment of the righteous will not be for the purpose of determining guilt or innocence. These will have already passed from eternal death into everlasting life before physical death, and will have already been sanctified by having been redeemed by the blood of Jesus. Jesus tells us, "Most assuredly, I say to you, he who hears My word and believes in Him who sent Me has everlasting life, and shall not come into judgment, but has passed from death into life" (John 5:24).

3.   The judgment of the redeemed begins with those who are sanctified in this world (during the church age) before the bodily resurrection. Peter says, "For the time has come [is now] for judgment to begin at the house of God; and if it begins with us first, what will be the end of those who do not obey the gospel of God?" (1 Peter 4:17).

4.   Those who are unredeemed will be judged by the law of God after their bodily resurrection. Their sins have been unaccounted for in this life, unlike the sins of the saved, which will have been purged by

the blood of Christ. Paul declares, "Some men's sins are open beforehand, going before to judgment; and some men they follow after" (1 Tim. 5:24).

When Satan is loosed from his symbolic thousand-year imprisonment, his power may be at its greatest since the beginning of human history. Listen to the narration of John as he speaks of the devil being bound and loosed. When he is released, it will be only for a little while.

Then I saw an angel coming down from heaven, having the key to the bottomless pit and a great chain in his hand. He laid hold of the dragon, that serpent of old, who is the Devil and Satan, and bound him for a thousand years; and he cast him into the bottomless pit, and shut him up, and set a seal on him, so that he should deceive the nations no more till the thousand years were finished. But after these things he must be released for a little while. (Revelation 20:1–3)

Chapter 20 goes on to talk about the symbolic thousand-year reign of Christ and of the first resurrection, as I have previously discussed. The first resurrection is the spiritual resurrection of those redeemed by the blood of Christ during the church age. In verse 7 the "little while" of Satan's wrath begins on those living in the world at the end of time.

Now when the thousand years have expired, Satan will be released from his prison and will go out to deceive the nations which are in the four corners of the earth, Gog and Magog, to gather them together to battle, whose number is as the sand of the sea. (Revelation 20:7–8)

At this time Satan, the father of lies, is unleashed on the world. He is now ready to wage a spiritual battle—his last—on the saints of God. His wrath against God is great *because he knows he has a short time.* But the battle is short-lived.

They went up on the breadth of the earth and surrounded the camp of the saints and the beloved city. And fire came down from God out of heaven and devoured them. (Revelation 20:8)

This is likely the fire accompanying Jesus when He returns to earth. His return has a dual purpose. He will come to receive His own—those who have surrendered to the will of God through the benefits of His death and resurrection—but also to take vengeance on those who do not know God and do not obey the gospel.

And to give you who are troubled rest with us when the Lord Jesus is revealed from heaven with His mighty angels, in flaming fire taking vengeance on those who do not know God, and on those who do not obey the gospel of our Lord Jesus Christ. (2 Thessalonians 1:7–8)

The camp of the saints is the group or assembly of blood-bought citizens of the kingdom of God left on the earth when Satan is loosed. They are the minority. Jesus once asked, "Nevertheless, when the Son of Man comes, will He really find faith on the earth?" (Luke 18:8).

The Bible strongly indicates that before the second visible return of Jesus to earth the harvest of souls who have answered the gospel's call will have been completed. This would mean the vast majority of humanity left physically alive on the planet will remain in an impenitent state. Even before Jesus returns, generally speaking, the day of salvation is over. The door to eternal bliss will have been closed, just as it was for the five foolish virgins who did not have sufficient oil for their lamps at a wedding.

And at midnight a cry was heard: "Behold, the bridegroom is coming; go out to meet him!" Then all those virgins arose and trimmed their lamps. And the foolish said to the wise, "Give us some of your oil, for our lamps are going out." But the wise answered, saying, "No, lest there should not be enough for us and you; but go rather to those who sell, and buy for yourselves." And while they went to buy, the bridegroom came, and those who were ready went in with him to the wedding; and the door was shut. (Matthew 25:6–10)

At that time the thousand-year reign of the Lord will be over. Satan will have been released on the world in wrath and fury for a short time. The gospel will have been preached to the Jews at the beginning of the Christian age, but Israel will have largely rejected it. The Jews will then be generally cut off from the spiritual tree (although God can graft them in again) and the nations of the Gentiles will have been grafted in.

Listen now as the apostle Paul explains to the Roman Christians the situation that will occur in the Christian age in reference to the salvation and condemnation of both Jews and Gentiles. Remember, at the time this letter was written, the Jews had basically rejected faith in salvation through Christ. Paul explains only a remnant had remained faithful to Jesus.

Just as it is written: "God has given them [the Jews] a spirit of stupor, eyes that they should not see and ears that they should not hear, to this very day." And David says: "Let their table become a snare and a trap, a stumbling block and recompense to them. Let their eyes be darkened, so that they do not see, and bow down their back always." I say then, have they stumbled that they should fall? Certainly not! But through their fall, to provoke them to jealousy, salvation has come to the Gentiles. Now if their fall is riches for the world, and their failure riches for the Gentiles, how much more their fullness! For I speak to you Gentiles; inasmuch as I am an apostle to the Gentiles, I magnify my ministry, if by any means I may provoke to jealousy those who are my flesh and save some of them. For if their being cast away is the reconciling of the world, what will their acceptance be but life from the dead? For if the first-fruit is holy, the lump is also holy; and if the root is holy, so are the branches. And if some of the branches were broken off, and you, being a wild olive tree, were grafted in among them, and with them became a partaker of the root and fatness of the olive tree, do not boast against the branches. But if you do boast, remember that you do not support the root, but the root supports you. You will say then, "Branches were broken off that I might be grafted in." Well said. Because of unbelief they were broken off, and you stand by faith. Do not be haughty, but fear. For if God did not spare the natural branches, He may not spare you either. Therefore consider the goodness and severity of God: on those who fell, severity; but toward you, goodness, if you continue in His goodness. Otherwise you also will be cut off. And they also, if they do not continue in unbelief, will be grafted in, for God is able to graft them in again. For if you were cut out of the olive tree which is wild by nature, and were grafted contrary to nature into a cultivated olive tree, how much more will these, who are natural branches, be grafted into their own olive tree? For I do not desire, brethren, that you should be ignorant of this mystery, lest you should be wise in your own opinion, that blindness in part has happened to Israel until the fullness of the Gentiles has come in. (Romans 11:8–25)

The Bible indicates that before the Jews can be grafted in again the Gentile church will first fail in faith, not unlike the spiritual fall of the Jews, and as a result will finally come to the fullness of its harvest. Notice Paul says the spiritual blindness of Israel was *in part*, but this blindness would continue only until the fullness of the Gentiles had come. Jesus seems to say basically the same thing in Luke's gospel.

And Jerusalem will be trampled by Gentiles until the times of the Gentiles are fulfilled. (Luke 21:24)

In Revelation 20 all of these happenings seem to have already occurred. The camp of the saints may mainly consist of Israel when the Jews are grafted in again. No matter what the situation is with Jews and Gentiles, Satan seems clearly to have gained the upper hand at this juncture, but his false hope is only temporary—he will not survive the battle. He gathers his forces from all over the world and encompasses the camp of the saints. He has only a short time, *a little season*, to attempt his deceptive and destructive work, and because of the magnificent power of God Almighty he miserably fails! Before he can unleash his first assault, fire comes down out of heaven and devours them. "Them" are Satan's worldwide forces of impenitent humanity that he has gathered from the four corners of the earth. The whole world is in his army with the exception of the camp of the saints. "Them" also does not include Satan.

They went up on the breadth of the earth and surrounded the camp of the saints and the beloved city. And fire came down from God out of heaven and devoured them. (Revelation 20:9)

So the physical bodies of those Satan gathers from the four corners of the earth, those who will blindly follow his deception, are devoured. But this is not their final judgment or punishment. Here the unredeemed suffer only physical death by the fire coming down from heaven and devouring them. This will obviously happen to thwart the tactics of the evil one. Unredeemed humanity will be bodily resurrected when the Lord Jesus comes back as its judge. It will stand before the Great White Throne of God and will be condemned by the Word of the Lord, then be cast into the lake of fire and destroyed. This destruction is called the second death. It will destroy not only the body, but the soul as well. This will occur only after God's just verdict is pronounced. The deceived humans will first be devoured, while still in their physical bodies, by the fire that comes down from heaven. After Jesus returns they will be resurrected and eternally judged. But Satan the deceiver is not devoured by the fire coming down out of heaven, but rather cast alive into the lake of fire prepared for him and his fallen angels.

The devil, who deceived them, was cast into the lake of fire and brimstone where the beast and the false prophet are. And they will be tormented day and night forever and ever. (Revelation 20:10)

THE GREAT WHITE THRONE JUDGMENT

Then I saw a great white throne and Him who sat on it, from whose face the earth and the heaven fled away. And there was found no place for them. (Revelation 20:11)

And now we come to the final judgment of fallen humanity, the Great White Throne judgment. The throne and the Judge appear and the final heavenly court proceeding for earth's judgment can begin. So great and so ominous is the scene that from the face of the eternal Judge of all creation all of the material universe, both on earth and in heaven, has fled. The sin-cursed, material universe, temporarily rooted in the destructive realm of time and matter, no longer has a place in the hereafter, in the celestial realm of God. Henceforth nothing will attempt to enter this heavenly Jerusalem which is not borne of love and cleansed by the blood of Christ.

And I saw the dead, small and great, standing before God, and books were opened. And another book was opened, which is the Book of Life. And the dead were judged according to their works, by the things which were written in the books. (Revelation 20:12)

As the judgment begins only the dead now stand before God. The living have already been judged and absolved. The Great White Throne judgment is the judgment that has passed over those saved by the blood of Christ, much like the angel of death passed over the houses of the children of Israel when the lamb's blood was applied on the door. This is the judgment of which Jesus said believers would take no part in it.

He who hears My word and believes in Him who sent Me has everlasting life, and shall not come into judgment, but has passed from death into life. (John 5:24)

The prophetic words of Jesus about judgment now ring very clear. Once again, this is the judgment that will pass over those believing in Him. He made clear eternal life begins in this life for believers in speaking to Martha as He was about to raise her brother Lazarus back to life.

Jesus said to her, "I am the resurrection and the life. He who believes in Me, though he may die, he shall live. And whoever lives and believes in Me shall never die. Do you believe this?" (John 11:25–26)

Those trusting in the redemptive work of Jesus, though their spirits may be separated from their bodies in physical death, will continue to live on, never dying. God's Holy Spirit will have borne witness with their spirit that they are children of God. The power of the Spirit of adoption delivers believers from the spirit of fleshly bondage into the inheritance only true children can receive in the kingdom of the Son of His love.

For you did not receive the spirit of bondage again to fear, but you received the Spirit of adoption by whom we cry out, "Abba, Father." (Romans 8:15)

He has delivered us from the power of darkness and conveyed us into the kingdom of the Son of His love. (Colossians 1:13)

Upon physical death, the believing children of promise are sealed by the Holy Spirit of promise.

In Him you also trusted, after you heard the word of truth, the gospel of your salvation; in whom also, having believed, you were sealed with the Holy Spirit of promise. (Ephesians 1:13)

The Holy Spirit of God, which has made the righteous spiritually alive in their earthly existence through the death and resurrection of Jesus, will continue to make them alive forever.

And what is the exceeding greatness of His power toward us who believe, according to the working of His mighty power which He worked in Christ when He raised Him from the dead and seated Him at His right hand in the heavenly places. (Ephesians 1:19–20)

And you He made alive, who were dead in trespasses and sins. (Ephesians 2:1)

It is in this life that the believer's spirit (inner man) is made spiritually alive; eternal life abides within him and will continue as long as he believes.

These things I have written to you who believe in the name of the Son of God, that you may know that you have eternal life, and that you may continue to believe in the name of the Son of God. (1 John 5:13)

The believer arises from the watery grave of baptism *to walk in newness of life.* The body has not changed; it is still in the grip of mortality. It remains in a deteriorating state, growing old and dying. But he who believes and remains faithful to God will receive an *earnest* (down payment) of the Holy Spirit with eternal life abiding in him or her. This is the Spirit of adoption as children of God. As long as God's Spirit remains in us we cannot die.

And because you are sons, God has sent forth the Spirit of His Son into your hearts, crying out, "Abba, Father!" (Galatians 4:6)

At the bodily resurrection the process of salvation will be completed for believers. At that time, even as the Holy Spirit has given eternal life to the individual spirits of believers, it will also change their vile bodies from mortal to immortal.

But if the Spirit of Him who raised Jesus from the dead dwells in you, He who raised Christ from the dead will also give life to your mortal bodies through His Spirit who dwells in you. (Romans 8:11)

So, once again, in the verses that follow we see the dead standing before God.

And I saw the dead, small and great, standing before God, and books were opened. And another book was opened, which is the Book of Life. And the dead were judged according to their works, by the things which were written in the books. The sea gave up the dead who were in it, and Death and Hades delivered up the dead who were in them. And they were judged, each one according to his works. (Revelation 20:12–13)

Those standing are those who are unredeemed. They are called dead because death, the cursed consequence of sin, abides within and upon them. These are those who are delivered up from their graves for judgment. They have not passed from death to life. Judgment has not passed over them as was the case of redeemed believers. Their souls or spirits have been released from hades and their bodies have now been resurrected. Jesus, who holds the keys to both death and hades, will at the resurrection use the keys to free these unredeemed prisoners of hades, thus allowing their spirits to return to their bodies to be resurrected.

I am He who lives, and was dead, and behold, I am alive forevermore. Amen. And I have the keys of Hades and of Death. (Revelation 1:18)

Even though those standing before God are called dead because of their spiritual condition, they now have been bodily resurrected and are once again mortally alive, not unlike Lazarus, who was mortally resurrected by Jesus. They now appear before their Creator to be judged. Each individual will be judged according to the works he or she done. *Death* and *hades* have delivered up the spiritually dead that were in them. Death would no doubt indicate the absence of life in the body— that, the grave. Hades is the disembodied state of the spirit after physical death occurs. Here these disembodied spirits have again reunited with their bodies in order to facilitate God's judgment on them. Again, those standing before God are the unredeemed souls, whose disembodied spirits were detained in the hadean prison awaiting final judgment. Now their spirits are again reunited with their resurrected bodies.

Some religious commentators believe the giving up of those in the grave, as well as the spirits released from hades, spoken of in Revelation 20:13 will include both the redeemed and the unredeemed being delivered up together for a final judgment. I disagree with this conclusion. There will be no need for a judgment to determine guilt or innocence for the saved. Can you imagine the righteous being resurrected with immortal bodies and then being sent someplace to determine whether they are saved or lost? Remember, before the Great White Throne judgment will have taken place, Jesus will have already returned to earth and the general bodily resurrection will have already occurred. True, there will be a general resurrection of all of the dead at His coming, both saved and lost; however, the bodily resurrection will be the last similarity between the saved and lost in connection to eternal judgment.

Even though there is no direct mention of the Lord's visible return to earth in Revelation 20, still it is clear He has returned before the Great White Throne judgment in the scriptures referring to the fire He brings with Him. I believe it is the fire Jesus brings, the fire that comes down out of heaven, that will devour the unredeemed people left on the planet.

And to give you who are troubled rest with us when the Lord Jesus is revealed from heaven with His mighty angels, in flaming fire taking vengeance on those who do not know God, and on those who do not obey the gospel of our Lord Jesus Christ. (2 Thessalonians 1:7–8)

The righteous, the camp of the saints, who are alive and remaining on the earth at the Lord's coming will then be changed from mortal to immortal in the twinkling of an eye.

Behold, I tell you a mystery: We shall not all sleep, but we shall all be changed in a moment, in the twinkling of an eye, at the last trumpet. For the trumpet will sound, and the dead will be raised incorruptible, and we shall be changed. (1 Corinthians 15:51–52)

The righteous in the graves will be resurrected to immortality at the same time the unrighteous are resurrected mortally. There is no promise of immortality to lost souls, either to their bodies or their spirits. Immortality has only been promised and will only be given to those redeemed by the blood of Christ. Only those in Christ can have immortality!

For as in Adam all die, even so in Christ all shall be made alive. But each one in his own order: Christ the first-fruits, afterward those who are Christ's at His coming. (1 Corinthians 15:22–23)

The saved, both those changed (those living at Christ's return) and those resurrected to immortality (the righteous dead), will then be caught up together with those changed to meet the Lord in the air, and forever they will be with the Lord. The spirits of those who are changed, who have never died physically, will only have to experience the change from mortal to immortal in respect to their bodies. But *those who sleep in Jesus* (those righteous whose bodies are in the graves and their spirits are in paradise) the Lord will bring with Him when He comes back to earth. They will have been released from the intermediate state to reunite with their bodies. The Holy Spirit, which has already quickened or made alive their human spirit or soul will now make eternally alive (immortalize) their bodies.

For if we believe that Jesus died and rose again, even so God will bring with Him those who sleep in Jesus. For this we say to you by the word of the Lord, that we who are alive and remain until the coming of the Lord will by no means precede those who are asleep. For the Lord Himself will descend from heaven with a shout, with the voice of an archangel, and with the trumpet of God. And the dead in Christ will rise first. Then we who are alive and remain shall be caught up together with them in the clouds to meet the Lord in the air. And thus we shall always be with the Lord. (2 Thessalonians 4:14–17)

The facts surrounding these individual resurrection and judgment events fit with the prophetic words of Paul as he tells the Thessalonian church Jesus is coming back to earth to be *revealed in flaming fire.* I see no purpose of the fire accompanying the Lord's return except to devour or temporarily destroy those who are on earth in an unredeemed state. The writer of Hebrews makes plain those who rebel in willful disobedience to God will eventually suffer God's wrath.

But a certain fearful expectation of judgment, and fiery indignation … will devour the adversaries. (Hebrews 10:27)

Although both redeemed and unredeemed will continue to reside in the hadean realm after physical death until the bodily resurrection, there is obviously a separation in the intermediate realm between the saved and the unsaved. Jesus told the thief on the cross he would be with Him in Paradise the same day they were killed—in other words, immediately after their spirits had been separated from their bodies.

And Jesus said to him, "Assuredly, I say to you, today you will be with Me in Paradise." (Luke 23:43)

In the story of Lazarus and the rich man, a great gulf separated them. Lazarus was being comforted, but the rich man was detained in a suffering condition. The Great White Throne judgment will be for those who have not known God and who have not obeyed the gospel of the Lord Jesus. They will come to their final time of reckoning. Revelation 20:12 says, "the books were opened, and the dead were judged according to their works, by the things written in the books."

THE BOOKS WERE OPENED

And I saw the dead, small and great, standing before God, and books were opened. And another book was opened, which is the Book of Life. And the dead were judged according to their works, by the things which were written in the books. (Revelation 20:12)

There has been much speculation as to the meaning of "and books were opened." Does this mean the books of the Bible? It seems inevitably to include the law of God. However, many people have lived and died never having access to the books of the Bible, especially the completed work we have today. So it must include the laws written in "books" as well as the unwritten laws imprinted on the heart. Paul said in Romans that Gentiles who did not have a written version of God's will or law would be subjected to the natural moral laws of nature.

For when Gentiles, who do not have the law, by nature do the things in the law, these, although not having the law, are a law to themselves, who show the work of the law written in their hearts, their conscience also bearing witness, and between themselves their thoughts accusing or else excusing them in the day when God will judge the secrets of men by Jesus Christ, according to my gospel. (Romans 2:14–16)

Each individual will be accountable to the law God gives to him or her. And unless they are pardoned for their sinful disposition toward God's law, they will be judged by it. All who have not been freed from the law of sin and death and been enabled to walk by the law of the Spirit of life will take part in the Great White Throne judgment. The law of God will be the authoritative standard used to judge sins. And without the atoning merits of the blood of Christ all will fail this judgment test, for all have sinned and fallen short of God's glory. Those standing before the throne of God at this time are accountable without remedy. They stand unredeemed.

It is also reasonable to assume one of the "books" will contain in detail all of the works of each individual life. Jesus made clear all sin—yes, even every idle word spoken—would be accounted for at the judgment.

But I say to you that for every idle word men may speak, they will give account of it in the Day of Judgment. (Matthew 12:36)

All actions and reactions of all unredeemed souls will be compared with God's perfect standard for the life of each individual. These souls, unredeemed by the blood of Christ, will not qualify for God's standard of justice through Christ, being only able to live their lives according to the motions and motives of their fleshly nature. The problem is not that God is partial, unmerciful or unjust. The bottom line is that they never sought to please and worship their Creator.

As a child I felt comfortable with the teachings of my parents and my church. And as previously noted, in all probability, the same was true with my ancestors before me. We usually feel safe when we accept the teachings of the previous generation without question. I think I was mostly honest in my acceptance of these teachings. But the same had been true with those who came before me. It took time, but eventually I realized the answer to my problem was not all that complicated. My problem was this. I was more involved with what people thought than with what God thought. I simply wasn't involved enough with God to look to Him. I was more involved in the service of men. One of the reasons for the New Testament or Covenant was to enable us to have a direct relationship with the Lord.

I will put My law in their minds, and write it on their hearts; and I will be their God, and they shall be My people. No more shall every man teach his neighbor, and every man his brother, saying, "Know the Lord," for they all shall know Me, from the least of them to the greatest of them, says the Lord. (Jeremiah 31:33–34)

We will only have a desire to seek the counsel of God when we are mentally disposed to truly trust in the counsel of God.

"Woe to the rebellious children," says the Lord, "who take counsel, but not of Me, and who devise plans, but not of My Spirit, That they may add sin to sin. (Isaiah 30:1)

Neither my parents nor my church had devised a plan to purposely deceive me. But for a long time I was not receiving most of my information directly from the Bible. I was not looking for spiritual answers directly from God. And I knew this was the problem. I also knew I had not taken up the task to sincerely search for truth. But I had good intentions to look more deeply into the Bible for myself—someday!

Regarding the subject of eternal punishment, I now readily admit my view of was just a secondhand, traditional view. What I firmly believed in childhood now seems very radical and shallow, as well as without scriptural authority or reason. But at that time I sincerely believed an unending living torment was in store for those who missed heaven. I believed this was what the Bible plainly taught. I can't say that I necessarily liked it or that I wanted to focus on it a lot, but I accepted it. And everyone else I knew at the time accepted it as well!

Back then I didn't allow my mind to dwell on the subject of hell or eternal torment. About the only time I would focus on it was when it was unavoidable. I would hear it preached from the pulpit or hear it brought up from time to time in a conversation. But those times were relatively rare. To be honest it actually was rarely discussed, and never with any serious depth of scripture. And I now can see why. It clearly is not a comfortable thought and there isn't a lot of scripture for defending the traditional view. One major reason for an inadequate defense of an unending torment for the wicked is that it just does not seem to be in harmony with the nature of the Creator. Back then it seemed I had to keep God in one part of my brain, but keep those thoughts segregated from the infinite pain and torment the Creator would inflict on lost souls. I think almost everyone felt that way about it. And again, most of the traditional arguments were unbelievably weak and seriously lacking scriptural support.

But I knew no one who believed anything else but endless torture for the lost. At the time, I was simply a product of what had been handed down to me through tradition. No one with whom I was acquainted even entertained the idea that the souls and/or bodies of lost sinners might die completely (the second death), to live no more in the hereafter. On the other hand, virtually everyone believed they would be preserved alive throughout eternity. In fact, to deny the immortality of the wicked seemed almost anathema to a traditional religious mind. Here is my former position stated in just a few words: I was brought up to believe all people who missed heaven would without exception suffer endless misery and torture in hellfire! It wasn't until after my conversion that it occurred to me there might be another answer as to the fate of the wicked.

My journey toward another answer began shortly after my baptism. It happened while in a Bible study with a Christian brother from my congregation. It was at that time an earthshaking question was posed to me. He asked me if I thought there was any possibility the wicked might be eternally destroyed (meaning annihilated) rather than living endlessly in a state of torment. Although my fear of this question seems strange now, at the time I was shaken by it! I remember becoming very uncomfortable and taken aback by the implications of the question. I was shocked at the very thought that anyone could believe God would annihilate lost souls rather than torment them forever. This thinking flew in the face of everything I had ever been taught regarding the punishment of the lost. For me, endless torture of the wicked was one of the unquestioned foundational doctrines of Christianity.

Questioning it was like questioning the authenticity of the Bible. I felt my brother in Christ was carelessly flirting with a dangerous false doctrine! But on the other hand, I was convinced he asked the question in complete sincerity. And I had grown to greatly trust his sincerity and honesty. Nonetheless, I was stunned by his question. Now I realize it was this one question sincerely posed by my loving Christian brother that caused me to rethink my position on this previously unquestioned topic.

THE BOOK OF LIFE

At the end of time only two classes of people will be left: those whose names are written in the Book of Life, and those whose names are not. The scriptures speak of the Book of Life in several places, all in the New Testament. This book is spoken of once in Paul's letter to the Philippians and seven times in the book of Revelation. In Philippians he mentions the necessity of helping the Philippian women of the church, along with Clement and others, who had been his fellow laborers. In doing so, he describes them as those whose names are in the Book of Life.

And I urge you also, true companion, help these women who labored with me in the gospel, with Clement also, and the rest of my fellow workers, whose names are in the Book of Life. (Philippians 4:3)

Notice again what the scriptures say in Revelation 20 about the Great White Throne judgment regarding "the books" and the Book of Life.

And I saw the dead, small and great, standing before God, and books were opened. And another book was opened, which is the <u>Book of Life</u>. And the dead were judged according to their works, by the things which were written in the books. (Revelation 20:12)

Only "the dead" were judged. Nothing is mentioned of the living. This could not have included the righteous who had been changed from mortal to immortal in the twinkling of an eye. These would not have been called dead in any sense of the word for they never came in contact with death. The dead standing before the throne were those whom death and hades had delivered up. And although the passage mentions the Book of Life, these dead were judged according to their works by the things that were written in the books. There is no reference to any of these who are being judged having their names written in the Book of Life.

The sea gave up the dead who were in it, and Death and Hades delivered up the dead who were in them. And they were judged, each one according to his works. Then Death and Hades were cast into the lake of fire. This is the second death. And anyone not found written in the Book of Life was cast into the lake of fire. (Revelation 20:13–15)

After being judged death and hades are cast into the lake of fire. At this point in time death and hades would have nothing to do with the saved because the righteous would have already been resurrected to immortality. But here death and hades are cast into the lake of fire, which is the same place as Satan was cast into in verse 10. He is to be tormented day and night forever and ever. Many take what is said of Satan as applicable to humanity, but the scriptures do not. When lost humanity is cast into the lake of fire the consequence is the second death.

Then Death and Hades were cast into the lake of fire. This is the second death. And anyone not found written in the Book of Life was cast into the lake of fire. (Revelation 20:14–15)

ESCAPING TRADITIONALISM

Once again to reiterate, in my early life I had never even entertained the thought of the annihilation of the wicked. And as I also have said, just hearing the question was unnerving to me. The traditional doctrine was way too rooted in the minds of my spiritual leaders for me to argue with or reject.

These were the leaders I deemed of the *true* Christian community. It was just too much for me to question easily.

But after some time had passed I began to search the scriptures in my private studies. Slowly I was beginning to feel less inhibited and a little more at ease in thinking and studying for myself. My friend's bombshell question was causing me to reconsider my position not only on eternal torment but also other off-limits traditional ideas. It was also at this time when I began to feel the shackles of sectarian traditionalism being very gradually loosened in their grip on me. I still had some fear, but not as much. The abatement of the fear was causing me to be able to begin, and with a greater zeal, to search the scriptures even more for myself. Now the mental burden of preconception was truly beginning to lighten!

While trying to show some semblance of an open mind, I finally answered my friend and brother in Christ. I told him I hadn't given it much thought. But inside of me I was still reeling from his audacity to even ask me such a question. He was actually seeming to suggest the wicked might completely die and be dead forever! If this were true, the worst penalty the wicked would suffer for their sins would be eternal death. They would not be immortal if this were the case. I now realize sin does just that. It indeed brings eternal death to the sinner.

For the wages of sin is death, but the gift of God is eternal life in Christ Jesus our LORD. (Romans 6:23) (NIV)

The ultimate wages of sin is either temporal or eternal death for the individual, because it clearly is death according to Paul. It cannot simply be physical death. If it is physical death, it is merely the death of the body until the resurrection. And in this respect it would be no different for saint or sinner. But if it is eternal death, it is death forever for the individual after the resurrection of the body!

I then asked Brother John if he himself believed in the annihilation of the wicked. He told me he did not but the thought had entered his mind from time to time. From that day forward, although John and I studied together many times, the subject of the wicked being annihilated was never brought up anymore until many years later. But from the time I was asked this question about the eternal consequences of sinners, a small seed of doubt was always present in my mind regarding the doctrine of eternal torture. And as I continued to read and study and ponder this question, I gradually began to realize there was a lot more evidence to consider about it than I previously had thought. Eventually I began to realize although the majority of the Christian world believed in eternal life for the sinner, the Bible wasn't nearly as clear on it as the traditional view might teach.

GOD IS A JUST GOD

I have always truly believed Almighty God is a just God. Nothing else makes sense in light of the Word of God. Nothing else is reasonable. But there were some things I could never quite square with traditional teaching in regard to the fate of the lost. I knew the scriptures explicitly teach God is just. And in regard to this thought my faith has never wavered. However, for a long time, my faith in the justice of God existed without any serious effort to reconcile it with my belief in an unending, torturous existence. I eventually realized I was being faced with that very task.

What is justice? This was the question I ultimately had to answer. And from this question other questions also came to my mind. For example, is God's justice on sin a never-ending process? If so, how could there ever be a time when it could be said God had exacted the penalty of justice on the sinner if in fact the sinner lived forever? After all, the Bible is clear that the penalty is death.

I always believed God would show mercy to saints and execute justice on sinners. And I still believe this. However, few things stand in stark contrast more than mercy and justice. But in my mind, neither equals endless torture. Justice is earned and deserved. This is why death is the "wages" of sin. On the other hand, mercy is unearned and undeserved.

Please pardon a humorous personal reflection that I almost always think about when mercy and justice are mentioned in the same sentence. I was once told about a very rich and vain young woman who paid quite a lot to have a portrait painted of her. The artist chosen was a famous master of his trade. After days of the subject posing for the portrait, it was finally completed and was to be unveiled in a private ceremony. When the cloth was pulled from the canvas, a lengthy hush fell from the crowd of invitees. Finally an elderly lady close to the painting spoke. "Dear, it really does you justice." Toward the back of the room a muffled voice quietly added, "She needs mercy, not justice."

We all stand in need of God's eternal mercy in order to avoid God's righteous justice. To the just God will show mercy, but to the merciless He will render justice.

For the LORD loves the just and will not forsake his faithful ones. Wrongdoers will be completely destroyed; the offspring of the wicked will perish. (Psalms 37:28) (NIV)

I ask again: if the conscious torment of the wicked never ends, when will it be said justice was accomplished? If the process of executing conscious punishment never ends, how could there be a finality of justice? And yet the finality of judgment and justice is surely taught over and over in the scriptures.

For yet a little while and the wicked shall be no more; indeed, you will look carefully for his place, but it shall be no more. (Psalms 37:10)

But the wicked shall perish; and the enemies of the Lord, like the splendor of the meadows, shall vanish. Into smoke they shall vanish away. (Psalms 37:20)

But the transgressors shall be destroyed together; the future of the wicked shall be cut off. (Psalms 37:38)

When the wicked spring up like grass, and when all the workers of iniquity flourish, it is that they may <u>be destroyed forever</u>. (Psalms 92:7)

<u>May sinners be consumed from the earth, and the wicked be no more</u>. Bless the Lord, O my soul! Praise the Lord! (Psalms 104:35)

The Lord preserves all who love Him, But all <u>the wicked He will destroy</u>. (Psalms 145:20)

When the whirlwind passes by, <u>the wicked is no more</u>, but the righteous has an everlasting foundation. (Proverbs 10:25)

<u>The wicked are overthrown and are no more</u>, but the house of the righteous will stand. (Proverbs 12:7)

<u>The soul who sins shall die</u>. The son shall not bear the guilt of the father, nor the father bear the guilt of the son. The righteousness of the righteous shall be upon himself, and the wickedness of the wicked shall be upon himself. (Ezekiel 18:20)

"Do I have any pleasure at all that the wicked should die?" says the Lord God, "and not that he should turn from his ways and live?" (Ezekiel 18:23)

Again, when a wicked man turns away from the wickedness which he committed, and does what is lawful and right, he preserves himself alive. (Ezekiel 18:27)

Say to them: "As I live," says the Lord God, "I have no pleasure in the death of the wicked, but that the wicked turn from his way and live. Turn, turn from your evil ways! For why should you die O house of Israel?" (Ezekiel 33:11)

"For behold, the day is coming, burning like an oven, and all the proud, yes, all who do wickedly will be stubble. And <u>the day which is coming shall burn them up</u>," says the Lord of hosts, "<u>That will leave them neither root nor branch</u>." (Malachi 4:1)

Let him know that he who turns a sinner from the error of his way will save a soul from <u>death</u> and cover a multitude of sins. (James 5:20)

In all of these verses, not once is the idea of unending torment alluded to. God's justice must mean justice for both sin and sinner. What became very important to me was this question. *What is justice* as it concerns the punishment of the lost? Justice is always understood in light of the crime or offense. Is justice to be understood as unending pain and misery for all those who "know not God, and obey not the gospel?" This is what I originally actually thought the Bible taught! This was what traditional teaching had led me to believe. I believed God is God and He alone determines what is just and unjust. Of course, God does determine what is just and what is not just. But are there two standards of justice, one for man and another for God? I don't think so.

Then I wondered. Do I have any business reasoning as to whether God is just? At one time I felt the proper thing was to accept it as a fact rather than to reason or wonder about it. But on the other hand, it felt the Lord was somehow urging me to look deeper into His mercy and justice in the same way as He did with Job of long ago.

But no matter how deeply I studied God's Word, or how intensely I meditated on what I read, being tormented forever continued to seem unjust to my mind. I simply could not square this with the definition of justice. The word *justice* is generally broadly defined. It means fair dealing, being fair, just treatment; it means a deserved reward or punishment. I could not accept anything else as the standard of justice Jesus had taught and had given to his followers. I felt sure Jesus would have me know and understand what is just and right. The orthodox view was beginning to make less and less sense to me.

Was the justice I was expected to perform as a Christian a different standard of justice than the justice a just and merciful God Almighty would exercise on His disobedient creation? Were there two standards of justice, one for man and another for God? This was a concept I could never have imagined! Would the justice for unredeemed sinners, which their Creator would execute in the hereafter, be an unfair and unjust and undeserved punishment? Or would it be death? These were the questions which I needed to answer. Paul told the church this was not the case.

Which is manifest evidence of the righteous judgment of God, that you may be counted worthy of the kingdom of God, for which you also suffer; since it is a righteous thing with God to repay with tribulation those who trouble you, and to give you who are troubled rest with us when the Lord Jesus is revealed from heaven with His mighty angels, in flaming fire taking vengeance on those who do not know God, and on those who do not obey the gospel of our Lord Jesus Christ. These shall be punished with everlasting destruction from the presence of the Lord and from the glory of His power. (2 Thessalonians 1:5–9)

God used Abraham as an example of one who was righteous and just in Genesis 18:19. Listen to how the Lord viewed Abraham.

For I have known him, in order that he may command his children and his household after him, that they keep the way of the Lord, to do righteousness and <u>justice</u>, that the Lord may bring to Abraham what He has spoken to him.

The exercise of justice in the life of Abraham was necessary for the Lord to bless him according to the promises God had given him. This would surely be no less true for the disciples of Jesus living today. Jesus came down very hard on the Jewish religious leaders for substituting legal or traditional gestures of worship in place of justice toward others. Notice how in this verse Jesus couples *justice* with the *love of God.*

But woe to you Pharisees! For you tithe mint and rue and all manner of herbs, and pass by <u>justice</u> and the love of God. These you ought to have done, without leaving the others undone. (Luke 11:42)

It would be mockery before God to profess love without justice. God demands justice of and from his people. But still when I would think these kinds of thoughts an uneasiness that bordered on fear would once again rise up within me. It was not that I now was afraid to reason out these things before God and accept His will. I knew He was the One who had told Israel to reason together with Him and I felt comfortable in doing it.

"Come now, and let us reason together," Says the Lord, "Though your sins are like scarlet, they shall be as white as snow; though they are red like crimson, they shall be as wool." (Isaiah 1:18)

My dread and fear came as a result of what my brethren would think. The question my Christian brother asked me long ago actually led me to begin to break with the orthodoxy of traditional thinking. My mental bondage to tradition was no less than the sectarian mindset the Bible condemns. This way of thinking is not of the Spirit, but of the flesh. The spirit of traditional sectarianism is not only of the flesh, but by the flesh and for the flesh. The flesh desires to be lulled into the comfort of a spiritual slumber. This was the gist of Paul's admonishment to God's people in the early church.

Therefore He says: "Awake, you who sleep, arise from the dead, and Christ will give you light." (Ephesians 5:14)

Although it took years, little by little, by examining the scriptures only and looking only for God's approval, I was beginning a journey with only the Lord. Jesus came into the world to bring the gospel of peace to the poor in spirit, but first the prison bonds must be released. This He was doing with me as well.

"The Spirit of the Lord is upon Me, because He has anointed Me To preach the gospel to the poor; He has sent Me to heal the brokenhearted, to proclaim liberty to the captives and recovery of sight to the blind, to set at liberty those who are oppressed." [Jesus] (Luke 4:18)

To break with tradition by seeking truth does not necessarily always mean the severing of human relationships. But many times it is the price that must be paid. Discipleship comes at a huge cost. And discipleship always means a mind disposed to forsake all in order to serve Jesus the Lord.

THE SATISFACTION OF DIVINE JUSTICE

Innocent human blood is the only thing that will ever satisfy God's divine justice. He has never been satisfied with anything else to eternally atone for sin. From the beginning of creation the Lord made evident the sacredness of blood. After the flood God told Noah and his family life was in the blood and they now were allowed to eat of every living thing, vegetative as well as the flesh of animals.

Every moving thing that lives shall be food for you. I have given you all things, even as the green herbs. But you shall not eat flesh with its life, that is, its blood. Surely for your lifeblood I will demand a reckoning; from the hand of every beast I will require it, and from the hand of man. From the hand of every man's brother I will require the life of man. "Whoever sheds man's blood, by man his blood shall be shed; for in the image of God He made man. (Genesis 9:3–6)

The eating of animals was God's decree only after sin entered into the world and after man's blood was shed by man. The scriptures record the decree only after Noah and his family emerged from the ark after the flood. The worldwide flood may have temporarily destroyed most of the vegetation, making it necessary for Noah to consume animal flesh. This may have been the reason God commanded seven each of the clean animals, whereas only two each of the unclean animals were taken aboard the ark.

You shall take with you seven each of every clean animal, a male and his female; two each of animals that are unclean, a male and his female. (Genesis 7:2)

Whatever the situation was, we can be sure that by the time man's blood was shed by man, sin had come full circle to the shame of humanity. Man had now sinned against both the Creator and the created. Only after Adam's son Cain had killed his brother Abel did God adjust the human diet to include every moving thing. In the beginning, after creation, God only allowed a vegetarian diet for both humans and animals. Scriptural evidence shows God never desired man or animals to be carnivorous.

And God said, "Behold, I have given you every plant yielding seed that is on the face of all the earth, and every tree with seed in its fruit. You shall have them for food. And to every beast of the earth and to every bird of the heavens and to everything that creeps on the earth, everything that has the breath of life, I have given every green plant for food." And it was so. (Genesis 1:29–30)

It may have been that the first blood was shed when the Lord made coats of skin to hide the shame of our Eden parents' nakedness before God. But even after animals were allowed for food, the blood was required to be removed from the animal before the meat could be eaten. God impressed the sacredness of blood continually to His people throughout history. Notice the reaction of God to Cain's murder of Abel.

And He [God] said, "What have you done? The voice of your brother's blood cries out to Me from the ground. (Genesis 4:10)

By shedding his brother's blood, Cain had taken Abel's life. As long as human blood can flow through a human body without being poured out, obstructed or hindered in some way, life continues. God later decreed that when someone's blood was shed by another's hand, the guilty party was to have his blood shed as well. This decree was intended to establish the principle of justice. Making the penalty fit the crime would come to define justice. Any punishment less than the crime would be mercy. But if a punishment is beyond that which is right, it is unjust.

Whoever sheds man's blood, by man his blood shall be shed; for in the image of God He made man. (Genesis 9:6)

Within the general law of justice God has also established a precept of justice that declares that only blood can atone (make amends or reparation) for sin. This law dictates the necessity of only the innocent to be accepted as a sacrifice for the sins of the guilty. It was this concept of justice that was engrafted into the plan of divine atonement. The basic definition of *atonement* is reparation for a wrong or injury. Sin should be thought of as an injury against the sovereign holiness of Almighty God.

So the penalty for sin would be death. The reparation for the wrong or injury against God could only be made through redemption (to redeem means to buy back) with innocent human blood. Under the law of Moses animal blood was used. But atonement by the blood of animals was only a temporary postponement or reprieve from the penalty of sin. Therefore only through the shedding of the blood of the only innocent human—that is, by the blood of Jesus—would there be complete atonement for death that would alleviate the eternal consequence for sin.

When Jesus died on the cross, He died for the sins of the entire world. He died for all sins past, present and future. His death became the only vehicle to allow the divine justice of God to be satisfied. For each individual and for all of humanity, the innocent blood shed on the cross allowed the death of Jesus to have the power of forgiveness for all. And too it would thereby abolish the ensuing eternal death caused by sin, as well as its curse or consequences for all creation.

There was no other way because there was no other, nor would there ever be any other, perfectly innocent human sacrifice. Only by the sacrificed body of the incarnate Word of God could appeasement be made to satisfy divine justice!

Therefore, when He came into the world, He said: "Sacrifice and offering You did not desire, but a body You have prepared for Me. (Hebrews 10:5)

Through the death of Jesus, the only possible way was accomplished for God to forgive and remove forever all sin from the soul of any individual who had ever existed on the planet. The writer of Hebrews compares the temporary rolling forward of sins through the animal sacrifices offered up by the temporary priests of the law of Moses to the eternal redemptive effect of the blood of Christ under His eternal priesthood.

And every priest stands ministering daily and offering repeatedly the same sacrifices, which can never take away sins. But this Man, after He had offered one sacrifice for sins forever, sat down at the right hand of God, from that time waiting till His enemies are made His footstool. (Hebrews 10:11–13)

The death of Christ allowed God's divine justice to be forever satisfied.

But this Man, after He had offered one sacrifice for sins forever, sat down at the right hand of God. (Hebrews 10:12)

It took the resurrection of His sacrificed mortal body to complete the spiritual process for eternal life. The power of sin brought death upon the body of Jesus, but the power of God's Spirit caused it to be resurrected. The power of the same Spirit that raised Jesus will also cause the faithful in Christ to become immortal as well.

But if the Spirit of Him who raised Jesus from the dead dwells in you, He who raised Christ from the dead will also give life to your mortal bodies through His Spirit who dwells in you. (Romans 8:11)

For if when we were enemies we were reconciled to God through the death of His Son, much more, having been reconciled, we shall be saved by His life. (Romans 5:10)

So the death and resurrection of God's Son is the power by which humanity and the whole creation of God can be redeemed or restored. But it was not just the suffering before the death of the Lord that brought salvation. The cost was paid in His death. The Lord Jesus abolished death through His death and resurrection.

But has now been revealed by the appearing of our Savior Jesus Christ, who has abolished death and brought life and immortality to light through the gospel. (2 Timothy 1:10)

Jesus' suffering even up until He died on the cross became a part of the sacrifice of His life, according to the word of Isaiah the prophet. And although the Jews thought they were responsible for the death of the Lord, they only worked to facilitate the work of God the Father who sacrificed His own Son for us. He was "smitten by God, and afflicted."

Surely He has borne our griefs and carried our sorrows; yet we esteemed Him stricken, smitten by God, and afflicted. But He was wounded for our transgres-

sions, He was bruised for our iniquities; the chastisement for our peace was upon Him, and by His stripes we are healed. (Isaiah 53:4–5)

The work of redemption was consummated by His death. True, it was His suffering on the cross that caused His death. But it was His death that paid the price for sin. In His suffering which preceded His death, He was "bearing our griefs and carrying our sorrows," but had He not died, the suffering would have been for naught. His death was the price paid for the satisfaction of divine justice!

Jesus paid all of the costs required by God for sin. But He did not suffer an infinite affliction for sin. This was not necessary. This was not required to satisfy the divine justice of the Father. He temporarily died for the sins of all humanity. But He was made alive again in order to secure everlasting life for those who believe in His name. If the penalty for sin would have been an eternal life in anguish, then that would have been what Jesus suffered. But the scriptures plainly declare that God would not allow Jesus to remain in grip and discomfort of death. He was resurrected to live again.

For You will not leave my soul in Hades, Nor will You allow Your Holy One to see corruption.

The wages (price paid) for sin would be death, determined as justice by the Father. This was fully paid by the Lord's death. This was sufficient. And the same is true with those who will not come to Him for salvation. The penalty will be eternal death. This will be the sufficient penalty required by God.

CONCLUDING THOUGHT

My dear brother in Christ who studied tirelessly with me when I was only a newborn babe spiritually, and who was not afraid to sometimes question and reason outside of prepackaged traditional thought, helped give me courage to do the same. For this I will always be grateful. Not only am I thankful for the example he set for me, an example that gave me the courage to exercise my spiritual senses, but also the example of not being overly weary in my search for the truth of God's will. And though it took many years, we now are in agreement that eternal death means eternal death!

CHAPTER 10
CONDITIONAL OR UNCONDITIONAL IMMORTALITY

THE MORTAL SOUL

Among the world's major religions there are differences as well as similarities in fundamental doctrines. By viewing the various writings connected with the afterlife of lost souls, the imagination can be stretched almost beyond imagination. The view ancient Egyptians held was of a torturous hell of varying degrees for souls of bad people. The degree of torture usually depended on the degree of lawlessness during the lifetime of the subject. The Egyptians believed in order to avoid the agonies of the disembodied state, it was necessary to preserve the body after death. The concept of mummification was developed in Egypt in order to achieve this very purpose.

In contrast to Egypt, within the Mesopotamian cradle of civilization, the ancient Babylonians believed the afterlife held neither punishment nor reward. And although they believed in life after death, their belief was the dead went to a land in the underworld. The superstitious traditions of the Babylonians were many. The following is one such view.

Nevertheless, the condition of the dead was hardly considered the same as the life previously enjoyed on earth: they were considered merely weak and powerless ghosts. The myth of Ishtar's descent into the underworld relates that "dust is their food and clay their nourishment, they see no light, where they dwell in darkness." Stories such as the Adapa myth resignedly relate that, due to a blunder, all men must die and that true everlasting life is the sole property of the gods. (Ancient Mesopotamian religion, afterlife, Wikipedia)

There are differences in teachings regarding eternal punishment in today's Christian community as well, but for the most part a general consistency remains in doctrine. The vast majority of professing Christians cling to the view that both the righteous and unrighteous will be immortal after their earthly existence. Most feel the eternal state of humanity has nothing to do with whether they remain alive forever. Because most professing Christians believe both saved and unsaved will continue to live on forever without end, their main concern is the quality of eternal life. They believe it will be bliss for the righteous but eternal anguish for the unredeemed. This concept fits with the common evangelical saying that everyone will spend a conscious eternity somewhere, either in heaven or hell. This idea has been the majority view for most of Christian history. This belief is called the doctrine of *unconditional immortality*.

The doctrine of *unconditional immortality* teaches all humanity is created with an immortal soul and that at the resurrection both the saved and unsaved will receive an immortal body. They conclude that because people were created with immortal souls, it follows that life cannot end. This in turn creates the unavoidable conclusion that condemned souls will be doomed to an eternal life of misery and torture.

Immortality is defined as deathlessness (incorruptibility, unending existence [*Strong's Concordance*]). The word *immortality* is found about five times in the Bible and the word *immortal* is found one time, all in the New Testament. Immortality conveys the idea of incorruptible perpetuity, which basically means indestructible forever.

In order to establish whether immortality is conditional or unconditional, a basic question must be answered. Is immortality something to be gained after physical birth or creation, or is each soul created inherently immortal? And can we know the answer to this question by the scriptures? I believe the answer to both questions is yes.

If humanity possesses immortality as a part of its created nature, it is unconditional and therefore inherently existing in humans. And if this is the case, then the individual would have to do nothing in order to obtain everlasting life. The reason is because immortality is deathlessness by definition. The doctrine of unconditional immortality invariably leads to the conclusion that there is nothing a person can do to gain immortality and that salvation from sin does not lead to eternal life, but rather to an eternal state of well-being.

If, on the other hand, a person is created with a mortal soul and later gains immortality through some act or endeavor by someone or something, it would be conditional immortality. It would happen as a result of the act or endeavor. Do the scriptures teach some special act or condition causes human immortality? Absolutely! There is one special condition. The only condition revealed by the Holy Scriptures by which a person receives immortality is receiving the atoning merits of the blood of Jesus Christ. The Bible teaches without question that immortality is gained or given only through Christ. It is something sought for. It is not automatic.

Eternal life to those who by patient continuance in doing good seek for glory, honor, and immortality. (Romans 2:7)

The Roman Catholic Church, as well as the majority of protestant denominations, subscribes to the idea of unconditional immortality. The following is an excerpt from Catholic writing.

> The existence of hell is, of course, denied by all those who deny the existence of God or the immortality of the soul. Thus among the Jew the Sadducees, among the Gnostics, the Seleucians, and in our own time Materialists, Pantheists, etc., deny the existence of hell. But apart from these, if we abstract from the eternity of the pains of hell, the doctrine has never met any opposition worthy of mention. (From an article on hell from *New Advent* Catholic Encyclopedia)

In this article it is stated that hell is denied by those who deny the existence of God and those who deny the immortality of the soul. To be sure, it is reasonable to believe those who do not believe in God would also not believe in the existence of hell. However, it is an invalid assumption that a belief in God is incompatible with a belief in conditional immortality (meaning the soul can die). It is not reasonable that Jesus would speak of the destruction or killing of the soul if it was not possible. Yet this is exactly what He does in the following verse. Why would Jesus speak of God being able to kill the soul if God's intentions were to torture it forever? Why wouldn't Jesus have talked about God tormenting the soul forever rather than killing it?

And do not fear those who kill the body but cannot kill the soul. But rather fear Him who is able to destroy both soul and body in hell. (Matthew 10:28)

Some will contend that *destroy* as used in this verse does not include death, but rather living torment. What follows is the definition given in *Strong's Concordance* of the Greek word *apollumi*, translated as destroy. Nothing in the definition precludes the death of both body and soul.

To destroy fully (reflex. To perish, or lose), lit. or fig.: destroy, die, lose, mar. perish.

The verse just cited indicates without doubt that God can kill or destroy both body and soul in hell. Not only are we furnished with scriptural evidence by Jesus to indicate the complete death and destruction of the sinner's soul and body, but the Bible teaches both implicitly and explicitly that without remission of sins it indeed will happen.

Behold, all souls are Mine; the soul of the father as well as the soul of the son is Mine; the soul who sins shall die. (Ezekiel 18:4)

For the wages of sin is death, but the gift of God is eternal life in Christ Jesus our Lord. (Romans 6:23)

Generally speaking, in looking at biblical references for the soul, only the inner being of the individual is suggested. However, sometimes a reference to the soul indicates the whole being. The fact that the *soul* can pertain to the whole being of an individual gives even greater evidence that death is the ultimate result of sin for the whole being of the sinner. Paul speaks of the whole person being sanctified and preserved blameless when the Lord comes back. Sinners will be condemned as completely as the righteous will be sanctified.

Now may the God of peace Himself sanctify you completely; and may your whole spirit, soul, and body be preserved blameless at the coming of our Lord Jesus Christ. (1 Thess. 5:23)

The Bible never speaks of a person's body by itself in connection with salvation, even though the body is included. The primary scriptural emphasis on "the saving of the soul" means the inner person, the soul and/or spirit or the life power animating the whole being. In other words, "the saving of the soul" usually refers to the whole being, but it would always mean at least the soul or inner being. It would be unnecessary to consider the saving of the body alone, since the body without the spirit is dead.

For as the body without the spirit is dead, so faith without works is dead also. (James 2:26)

The Bible also tells us the soul can be saved from things other than death. It can be saved from tribulation and anguish, indicating the minimizing of extreme discomfort as long as it is alive.

Tribulation and anguish, on every soul of man who does evil, of the Jew first and also of the Greek. (Romans 2:9)

Although the soul needs salvation from tribulation and anguish, the ultimate saving of the soul is its salvation from death. Death is not tribulation and anguish. Death is the absence of life. Eternal death will be the result of sin not covered by the blood of Christ. The soul can be saved from death.

Let him know that he who turns a sinner from the error of his way will save a soul from death and cover a multitude of sins. (James 5:20)

Notice the evidence given in the previously referenced *Catholic Encyclopedia* article for belief in *unconditional immortality*. It states, "the doctrine has never met any opposition worthy of mention." While this may be true, it is a very shallow argument. It is also true that throughout history the consensus of the religious masses has never been a good bellwether for doctrinal infallibility. And it is also a fact that a reasonable person could believe in the wicked being cast into the fires of hell and die. After all, the Bible is clear in teaching death as the penalty for sin. One could believe this without believing eternal death is in reality a conscious eternal life. This phrase is a glaring contradiction. The suffering of the wicked in the fires of hell may indeed be taught in the Bible. But the suffering of the wicked, whether it be for a moment or for a thousand years, in no way negates the possibility of eventual loss of life.

Without doubt, the possibility of immortality for the soul of a lost sinner raises many more questions than it answers. One question that comes to mind is whether immortality is predicated on faith in Christ and His blood. Could anyone deny immortality is given as a result of the blood of Christ? Yet this is exactly where belief in unconditional immortality will lead. If the human creation was created immortal, all "lost" souls will have eternal life without the blood of Christ. Those who abide in sin cannot have eternal life abiding in them.

Whoever hates his brother is a murderer, and you know that no murderer has eternal life abiding in him. (1 John 3:15)

THE ORIGIN OF UNCONDITIONAL IMMORTALITY

Who alone has immortality, dwelling in unapproachable light, whom no man has seen or can see, to whom be honor and everlasting power. Amen. (1 Timothy 6:16)

This doctrine of unconditional immortality was deeply etched in Greek philosophic thought at the beginning of the church age. Some early church writing by the fourth century, in regard to the afterlife, should be attributed to the imaginations of Greek philosophers rather than the scriptures. And because of these eschatological writings and teachings many early Christians were influenced by these views as well (*eschatological* refers to a branch of theology concerned with 1: the final events in the history of the world or of humankind. 2: a belief concerning death, the end of the world or the ultimate destiny of humankind [see *Merriam-Webster Dictionary*]).

> The ancient Greek conception of the afterlife and the ceremonies associated with burial were already well established by the sixth century B.C. In the Odyssey, Homer describes the Underworld, deep beneath the earth, where Hades, the brother of Zeus and Poseidon, and his wife, Persephone, reigned over countless drifting crowds of shadowy figures—the "shades" of all those who had died. It was not a happy place. Indeed, the ghost of the great hero Achilles told Odysseus that he would rather be a poor serf on earth than lord of all the dead in the Underworld (*Odyssey*, 11.489–91).

However, it is neither practical nor possible to look into the details of all of these teachings, beliefs and practices of old. Much more can be gained by examining some of the fundamental, traditional thinking throughout the history of the Christian community. We will always be better served to compare our thinking against the clear and explicit language of the Spirit. This should be the goal of every sincere person who seeks to please God.

So where do we start in a quest for truth regarding the questions arising from the doctrine of unconditional immortality? It would seem to me, as we have already indicated, the most important and foundational question is the following. Did God create Adam and all of human creation immortal? This question needs to be answered in order to lay a scriptural foundation for an investigation of the matter of eternal death or eternal destruction. If a person is created immortal, then eternal death and eternal destruction must take on a very different meaning, to say the least. Immortality indicates, by every definition, *deathlessness.*

Many answer these question in the affirmative, truly believing in the inherent and unconditional immortality of a person. They readily affirm all people are created with an immortal soul that cannot die. There are others, albeit a minority in the Christian community, who deny we humans are created immortal. I include myself in the latter group.

Therefore, for a truly honest discussion on the subject of the fate of sinners we must answer this question. Is humanity created mortal or immortal? If this question is not examined in light of the whole counsel of God, it will simply allow conclusions to be formed out of a misty veil of preconception fabricated in our mind by traditions and imaginations of men. So let's look at the scriptures regarding the subject of mortality and immortality.

CREATION AND RE-CREATION

The first words used in the Bible about the creation of Adam are the following.

Then the LORD God formed a man from the dust of the ground and breathed into his nostrils the breath of life, and the man became a living being. (Genesis 2:7)

Adam was formed from the "dust of the ground." He therefore was of the earth. The following words of Paul tend to expand and clarify Genesis 2:7.

So it is written: "The first man Adam became a living being"; the last Adam, a life-giving spirit. The spiritual did not come first, but the natural, and after that the spiritual. The first man was of the dust of the earth; the second man is of heaven. As was the earthly man, so are those who are of the earth; and as is the heavenly man, so also are those who are of heaven. And just as we have borne the image of the earthly man, so shall we bear the image of the heavenly man. I declare to you, brothers and sisters, that flesh and blood cannot inherit the kingdom of God, nor does the perishable inherit the imperishable. (1 Cor. 15:45–50)

Once again notice the first Adam became a living being, the last Adam (Christ), a life-giving spirit. *The spiritual did not come first, but the natural, and after that the spiritual.* I see nothing in the scriptures to indicate the original life God created for Adam and humanity was a spiritual, eternal existence. If Adam had been given immortality at his creation he could never have died. If he had been created immortal and therefore deathless, God would have never pronounced the curse of death upon him when he sinned. Remember the reason God drove the man and woman out of the garden after they had sinned. It was to keep them away from the tree of life. In other words, it was to keep them from becoming immortal.

Then the Lord God said, "Behold, the man has become like one of us, to know good and evil. And now, lest he put out his hand and take also of the tree of life, and eat, and live forever"— therefore the Lord God sent him out of the garden of Eden to till the ground from which he was taken. So He drove out the man; and He placed cherubim at the east of the Garden of Eden, and a flaming sword which turned every way, to guard the way to the tree of life. (Genesis 3:22–24)

So Adam was not created immortal. Immortality means deathlessness, yet Adam, after his fall, was subjected to death by the decree of his Creator. He possessed only a natural, temporal existence. His was a mortal existence.

This mortal existence would endure as long as he remained sinless. But when he sinned the consequences of the sin began its work to cause the deterioration and eventual death of his being. After this, Adam's only hope was in the grace of God by way of redemption.

Mortal is defined as "liable to die" (*Strong's Exhaustive Concordance of the Bible*). And because man's body is liable to die, it will die because of sin. This will invariably happen (he will sin) because of the weakness of the fleshly nature of physically created man. He, through fleshly temptations, sin and rebellion cannot coexist with a perfectly righteous God. The fleshly nature brings enmity with God through sin.

Immortality of the body is conditional and obtained only by the sacrifice of Christ, who is the life-giving Spirit. The weakness of the flesh will fail the test of rising above its fleshly nature. It is corrupted through the sin of a rebellious spirit and therefore dies, and it is separated from its original communion with God. Ultimately this separation will result in eternal death unless there is a way of redemption.

Not only that, but we also who have the first-fruits of the Spirit, even we ourselves groan within ourselves, eagerly waiting for the adoption, the redemption of our body. (Romans 8:23)

This mortal must put on immortality. (1 Cor. 15:53)

So the mortal body will suffer physical death and eventually the second death if not redeemed. The only exception to physical death would be those redeemed persons who are alive at the coming of Jesus for the resurrection. They will be changed to immortality in a moment, in the twinkling of an eye.

Behold, I tell you a mystery: We shall not all sleep, but we shall all be changed … in a moment, in the twinkling of an eye, at the last trumpet. For the trumpet will sound, and the dead will be raised incorruptible, and we shall be changed. (1 Cor. 15:51–52)

It is a natural, mortal body first, and only through the life-giving Christ does it have the ability to become a spiritual immortal body at the resurrection. Some hold that Adam and Eve were immortal until they sinned. But by its very definition immortality (deathlessness) cannot be reversed. If immortality can be reversed, then immortality is meaningless. When Adam and Eve did sin and their sin brought death, this very fact proved they were not immortal.

Once again, and as I have previously stated, the definition of immortality is simply *deathlessness*. The Greek word for immortality is *athanasia*. In 1 Corinthians 15:53–54 the word *athanasia* is rendered "immortality" of the glorified body of the believer (*Vine's Expository Dictionary of New Testament Words*).

Immortality is something given rather than inherently created within the individual. Immortality is given as a result of submission to the will of God. If immortality was unconditional and ever present, it would not be a thing we could put on or strive to obtain. Yet the scriptures teach immortality is to be diligently sought after. God's Word teaches before there can be immortality for God's people, death must be conquered or swallowed up in victory. By man came sin and death, but by Christ came righteousness and eternal life. This was accomplished by Jesus in His death. And the condition for obtaining immortality or eternal life would be trusting in the blood of Jesus and a total surrender of our will in faithful obedience to the will of God. This makes us able to patiently continue in well-doing as we seek glory, honor and immortality.

Eternal life to those who by patient continuance in doing good seek for glory, honor, and immortality." (Romans 2:7)

Paul tells the Corinthian Christians that only by putting off the corruptibility of mortality and putting on the incorruptibility of immortality is death conquered.

For this corruptible must put on incorruption, and this mortal must put on immortality. So when this corruptible has put on incorruption, and this mortal has put on immortality, then shall be brought to pass the saying that is written: "Death is swallowed up in victory." "O Death, where is your sting? O Hades, where is your victory?" The sting of death is sin, and the strength of sin is the law. But thanks be to God, who gives us the victory through our Lord Jesus Christ. (1 Cor. 15:53–57)

The prophet Isaiah foretells a future time when death would be swallowed up by the victory of immortality.

He will swallow up death forever, and the Lord God will wipe away tears from all faces; the rebuke of His people He will take away from all the earth; For the Lord has spoken. (Isa. 25:8)

Therefore immortality is to be attained by those who seek after it. This promise of gaining immortality is only to God's faithful.

Eternal life to those who by patient continuance in doing good seek for glory, honor, and immortality. (Romans 2:7)

Once again, immortality is not inherent in the fleshly nature of humanity; rather it is given to those who strive to do well and seek after it. And the same was true with Adam and Eve before they sinned. If they had been immortal, even sin could not have brought on death. Immortality precludes the possibility of death. Sin brought death upon Adam and Eve because they were mortal. Paul tells the Corinthian Christians, "the spiritual did not come first, but the natural came first, and after that the spiritual" (1 Cor. 15:46). This is another way of saying immortality does not come first. Mortality comes first, and then immortality can come afterward through Christ.

As I continued on in my Christian life I began to realize some religious denominations do teach immortality is conditional. I was somewhat surprised by this. I eventually read some of their literature. But at the time I could not believe my traditional teaching could be wrong, especially on such a seemingly sacred subject as heaven and hell. Although the evidence for conditional immortality began to weigh heavy on the scales of truth within my mind, I still felt somewhat guilty for entertaining the thought that sin might be punished with eternal death rather than eternal torture and anguish. My traditional teaching on this subject was etched in my mind like a brand on cattle. For several years I never revealed my agnosticism toward the eternal torture of the wicked to anyone, not even my wife.

CONCLUDING THOUGHT

By the time I was about thirty years old I began in earnest to throw off the shackles of traditional sectarian dependency in a more complete way. But it didn't happen all at once or in a consistent manner. My mind went back and forth for several years. Every time the bonds of my dependency on tradition would begin to loosen a fear would once again come over me. It came as a feeling of betrayal of my parents, my church and my people. The thought of what my Christian brothers and sisters might think of my breaking ranks in any traditional area gave me considerable pause. And to deny the idea of an endless suffering of the wicked in hell somehow seemed especially egregious. I think many people feel the same way when facing a similar situation. It is impossible to completely free oneself from slavery to men until we first completely enslave ourselves to the Lordship of Jesus Christ! It was this thought that gave me the courage to eventually loose forever my traditional sectarian bonds.

CHAPTER 11
ETERNAL TORMENT
OR ANNIHILATION

I, like the majority of the Christian world, was taught hell is the eternal abode for those who did not go to heaven. Hell was to be forever, and it came with endless misery. This was about all I had heard about hell from traditional church and family teaching. Hell meant two things to me—fire and forever. The vast majority of religious teachings have this same general understanding about the fate of unbelievers. But is this really the way God would have us understand the subject through the teaching of the Bible?

THE ORIGIN OF THE DOCTRINE OF ETERNAL TORMENT

Modern Christianity's general view of everlasting punishment has its roots in pagan religious rites, Greek philosophy, superstitious imaginings and many other non-scriptural schools of thought. But there is little doubt our present day thinking on this subject was solidified through the Roman church–state relationship by the end of the fourth century. The goal of the Roman Empire during the time of the early church period was to conquer the world with carnal weapons of warfare. Later on, much of this would be done through the guise of religion—thus the Holy Roman Empire. It was during this period of Roman conquest that the doctrine of unconditional immortality took deep root in Christian thinking. And out of this doctrine came the idea of eternal torture for the unforgiven sins of the human race.

EARLY CHURCH FATHERS' VIEWS OF ETERNAL PUNISHMENT

The apostolic fathers were the church leaders who lived within about two generations of the apostles. Church tradition accredits them as having been taught by the apostles. Clement of Rome, Ignatius of Antioch and Polycarp of Smyrna were some of the most notable apostolic father of this period. All of those described as *early church fathers* were the influential teachers and writers who lived from the time of the apostolic fathers until about AD 700. (The Church Fathers, Early Church Fathers, Christian Fathers, or Fathers of the Church were ancient and influential Christian theologians and writers. There is no definitive list. The era of these scholars who set the theological and scholarly foundations of Christianity largely ended by AD 700. [Wikipedia]).

The teachings and writings of these early church fathers are deemed authoritative by a lot of religious scholars in consideration of the subject of eternal punishment. Those believing the traditional view (endless sufferings) of eternal punishment as well as those believing the annihilationist view use writings of the church fathers to strengthen their arguments. No doubt there were some in both camps of thought among the Christians in the first few centuries.

Because of the biblical terms used in describing the fate of the wicked, such as *everlasting punishment, unquenchable fire* etc., the writings of the church fathers at first would seem to agree more with the traditional views. These are all scriptural terms. For example, in Matthew 3:12 John the Baptist said of Jesus, "His winnowing fan is in His hand, and He will thoroughly clean out His threshing floor, and gather His wheat into the barn; but He will burn up the chaff with unquenchable fire."

In seeing the words "unquenchable fire" the traditionalist (one who believes in eternal torment) will immediately think of fire that burns forever and burns whatever is in it forever as well. In other words, it is taken as affirming evidence by those who would believe in eternal torture. Annihilationists, on the other hand, look at the context of Matthew 3 and see the "unquenchable fire" will "burn up" chaff. So, in their view, if the verse refers to eternal punishment of the wicked, it would sound a lot more like annihilation than perpetual torment. And the same is true with many of the other scriptures previously dealt with in connection to the punishment of the lost.

Ignatius of Antioch, an early church father, stated that "those who corrupt families will depart into unquenchable fire." Clement of Rome said that "if we neglect his commandments, nothing will rescue us from eternal punishment." Although these phrases may infer an infinite situation, they do not say anything about torture of the wicked. They are not necessarily evidence that these writers are referring to everlasting torture of the wicked. They were simply using Bible phrases without giving their own interpretation.

However, some of the early church fathers did teach eternal torment. They did this by their interpretation of the inspired Word. When this happened, it was usually by invoking the doctrine of unconditional immortality as a biblical truth. The idea of inherent immortality was fairly prevalent in secular and philosophical thinking at the time.

Tertullian (AD 160–230) wrote the tortures of hell would be for the enjoyment of Christians in the hereafter. He believed the Christians who had suffered torture for their faith in this life would be able to watch their tormentors be tormented in fire endlessly. Although Tertullian was probably the first church father to promote this sadistic view of hell, it was also taught by other writers throughout church history. He writes: "How shall I admire, how laugh, how rejoice, how exult when I behold so many proud monarchs, and fancied gods, groaning in the lowest abyss of darkness; so many magistrates, who persecuted the name of the Lord, liquefying in fiercer fires than they ever kindled against the Christians."

The trend toward accepting the idea of eternal torment seems to have begun as early as the late second century. Tatian (ca. AD 120–ca. AD 180) was a Syrian Christian writer who in the second century wrote, "We who are now easily susceptible to death, will afterwards receive immortality with either enjoyment or with pain." This seems to be the first writing to attribute immortality to the unsaved. Therefore the punishment for sin would be pain as endless as immortality. According to this doctrine, eternal life would not just be a gift for the saved, but also the recompense of eternal misery for the unsaved. But the Bible nowhere speaks of immortality or eternal life in this way. It teaches that for the unsaved the wages of sin will be death and that eternal life is a gift from God. The Greek philosophic idea of Plato and others, that the soul was immortal, had infiltrated the mind of the Jews and then the Christians, creating the foundation for the doctrine of eternal torment in the Christian church.

By the beginning of the third century Clement of Alexandria wrote, "All souls are immortal, even those of the wicked, for whom it were better that they were not deathless. For, punished with the endless vengeance of quenchless fire, and not dying, it is impossible for them to have a period put to their misery."

Augustine of Hippo, born AD 354, was an early Christian philosopher from Numidia. His writings made a great impact in the Christian world. As bishop of Hippo Regius in North Africa, he is listed as one of the most important of the church fathers for his writings. Augustine believed, as did many at the time, that some salamanders could live in fire. Therefore he concluded God could make physical human bodies that would be susceptible to pain and yet not be consumed by it. Of course the salamander story was untrue, but the idea gained a following. History shows other church fathers taught the idea about the marvelous fire that burns but does not damage. Augustine became the first Christian theologian to write (in *The City of God*, chapter 21, ca. AD 410) a biblical defense of the view that the lost will suffer forever in hell.

The apostolic fathers (those living most contemporaneously with the apostles of Christ) said very little other than the language of the Spirit in describing eternal punishment. And in the things they have written on the subject there seems to be almost universal silence about eternal torture. Listen to the words of Ignatius of Antioch, said to be one of the students of the apostle John, writing to warn of false doctrines. Notice his reference to the Lord breathing immortality into His church. He says nothing about immortality for the wicked. Here he warns God's people not to "perish" by not recognizing the gift of life or immortality.

For this end did the Lord allow the ointment to be poured upon His head, that He might breathe immortality into his church. Be not anointed with the bad odour of the doctrine of the prince of this world; let him not lead you away captive from the life which is set before you. And why are we not all prudent, since we have received the knowledge of God, which is Jesus Christ? Why do we foolishly perish, not recognising the gift which the Lord has of a truth sent to us?

Ignatius also writes to the Magnesians the following words. In them he gives his opinion that the eternal state of those who reject the mercy of God will cease to be. "Let us not, therefore, be insensible to His kindness; for were He to reward us according to our works, we should cease to be."

Even though some of the early church fathers did appear to teach unending torment, I believe they did it by going beyond what the scriptures show and by adding to the scriptures the idea of unconditional immortality for both saint and sinner.

THE TRADITIONAL VIEW TODAY

Some years back, in reading some of the writings of traditionalists in connection with unconditional immortality, I came upon an article in *Easton's Bible Dictionary* entitled "Eternal Death." After reading this short article I realized this was almost exactly what the vast majority of Christians believe. This was what I was taught in my traditional upbringing. I then decided to study these arguments point by point, offering a rebuttal based on nothing but the authority of the scriptures. Following is the article, and after the article is my rebuttal.

Easton's Bible Dictionary: "Eternal Death"

The miserable fate of the wicked in hell (Matthew 25:46; Mark 3:29; Hebrews 6:2; 2 Thess. 1:9; Matthew 18:8, 25:41; Jude 1:7). The Scripture as clearly teaches the unending duration of the penal sufferings of the lost as the "everlasting life," the "eternal life" of the righteous. The same Greek words in the New Testament (*aion, aionios, aidios*) are used to express (1) the eternal existence of God (1 Timothy 1:17; Romans 1:20, 16:26); (2) of Christ (Revelation 1:18); (3) of the Holy Ghost (Hebrews 9:14); and (4) the eternal duration of the sufferings of the lost (Matthew 25:46; Jude 1:6).

Their condition after casting off the mortal body is spoken of in these expressive words: "Fire that shall not be quenched" (Mark 9:45–46), "fire unquenchable" (Luke 3:17), "the worm that never dies," the "bottomless pit" (Revelation 9:1), "the smoke of their torment ascending up for ever and ever" (Revelation 14:10–11).

The idea that the "second death" (Revelation 20:14) is in the case of the wicked their absolute destruction, their annihilation, has not the slightest support from Scripture, which always represents their future as one of conscious suffering enduring forever.

No matter which side of the argument one might take, almost all would agree on certain biblical words and phrases in connection with the fate of the wicked. Bible believers would agree that the lost will experience "eternal punishment," "unquenchable fire" and "eternal fire." On these terms there could be no rational disagreement. The disagreement is on exactly what these terms mean. This problem can be easily answered by definition, context and the harmony of the scriptures.

Traditionalists maintain that the final punishment for unforgiven sin is some form of eternal conscious torment or misery. It's true that the sinner, while dying, will incur consequences of sin with affliction on body, soul and spirit. However, dying and the pain of dying is not what the Bible says is the penalty for sin. The agony of dying, whether it is by fire, outer darkness or other forms of affliction, may result in the death of the unsaved individual, but the Bible nowhere says torture is the penalty for sin. The Bible clearly teaches *eternal death* is the final state and the ultimate punishment of the unforgiven sinner. And the only reprieve for sin is the redemption that is in Christ. "The wages of sin is death" (Romans 6:23).

But in the mindset of the traditionalist, the phrase "eternal punishment" translates easily into eternal torment. This is because of how the mind has been traditionally programmed to think of a conscious living state of being for the sinner in the hereafter. Therefore the affliction meant to cause eternal death and destruction becomes that which causes an eternal life of misery.

Eternal punishment could mean eternal torture, but this can only be determined by context and scriptural harmony. It is necessary to understand eternal punishment does not necessarily mean endless bodily pain or discomfort. If a person was sentenced to life in prison, he or she would suffer punishment no matter how comfortable (meaning without pain or bodily torture) he or she might be for the rest of his life, as far as bodily pain is concerned. The punishment would be life in prison, not a life of physical torture. In the same way eternal death means absence of life, or being dead forever without any more hope of life.

Arguments in opposition to the traditional view, usually referred to as annihilationism, believe punishment for sin is an unending death or absence of life, thus final destruction or annihilation. Therefore they believe Paul, in speaking to the Thessalonians, is talking about death being the complete and final destruction of those who do not know God and those who do not obey the gospel of Christ.

These shall be punished with everlasting destruction from the presence of the Lord and from the glory of His power. (2 Thessalonians 1:9)

Some very important facts can be gleaned from this verse.

1.   The unsaved will be *punished*.

2.   The punishment *will be everlasting*.

3.   Those punished will be *everlastingly destroyed*. In other words, their destruction will be forever.

4.   Their punishment of everlasting destruction (the second death) will *separate them from the Lord*. The NIV says they will be "shut out" from the presence of God.

An honest look at the sentence construction of this particular verse gives a clear picture of the fate of lost souls in the hereafter, and completely harmonizes with the rest of the scriptures. It teaches the lost will suffer the punishment of being destroyed forever. This is in harmony with the scriptural teaching of death being the final punishment for sin. By virtue of being destroyed forever, the lost will be separated from the power and presence of Almighty God. God's power and presence can only be experienced by the living. God is not the God of the dead. However, if those who are condemned remain alive, as many believe, they surely will only live by the power and presence of Him who gives and sustains life. Is there any life source other than God? If the unrighteous remain alive, the power of their life will certainly be from God. So we must ask this question: will the life of the wicked in the hereafter be sustained when they are separated from God and His power and presence? The very thought of this is unreasonable and foolish from all the scriptures teach.

Jesus, in a conversation with the Sadducees, who believed there was no resurrection of the dead, said the following.

But concerning the dead, that they rise, have you not read in the book of Moses, in the burning bush passage, how God spoke to him, saying, "I am the God of Abraham, the God of Isaac, and the God of Jacob"? He is not the God of the dead, but the God of the living. You are therefore greatly mistaken. (Mark 12:26–27)

In other words, those taking part in the second death, which is eternal death, no longer have a connection with God physically or spiritually, temporarily or eternally. They are no longer among the living. They no longer exist. They are forever separated from the presence of the Lord, and from the glory of His power. It is absurd to believe there could be life absent from the Lord. But this is exactly how it would be if there is a conscious existence of the lost sinner in the hereafter. Paul says they will suffer "everlasting punishment from the presence of the Lord and from the glory of His power." This means they are dead in the most complete sense and without hope of a resurrection or restoration. Not only is their body dead but their body, soul and spirit are destroyed. This is the second death spoken of in Revelation 20. Jesus also spoke of the possibility of this complete destruction in Matthew 10:28.

And do not fear those who kill the body but cannot kill the soul. But rather fear Him who is able to destroy both soul and body in hell.

The *Easton* article begins with: "The Miserable Fate of the Wicked in Hell. (Matthew 25:46; Mark 3:29; Hebrews 6:2; 2 Thess. 1:9; Matthew 18:8, 25:41; Jude 1:7). The Scripture as clearly teaches the unending duration of the penal sufferings of the lost as the 'everlasting life,' the 'eternal life' of the righteous."

This paragraph gives a variety of scripture verses in order to prove the continual torture of the unsaved masses of humanity in the hereafter. However, the view doesn't entertain the idea of death as a penalty for sin, only a torturous, unending life.

The article continues, "The Scripture as clearly teaches the unending duration of the penal sufferings of the lost as the 'everlasting life,' the 'eternal life' of the righteous." Using the same verses, I will endeavor to show by definition, context and harmony of scripture that this is a very misleading and false idea.

One of the dangers of a universal acceptance of doctrine based only on traditional religious views, especially one so profoundly deep and difficult to imagine as eternity and immortality, is the evolution of false doctrine. When universal acceptance occurs it becomes the substitute for a personal search of the scriptures. Paul makes a profound statement bringing the search for truth down to a single verse.

Let God be true, but every man a liar. (Romans 3–4)

He does not say this because everyone is to be classified as liars, but rather with the realization that fallibility exists among all in the fleshly realm. Everything except God's Word is to be taken with guarded suspicion. In this way we can be sure error by acceptance does not replace the search for truth because of pride, complacency, convenience or anything else. And for this reason all testimony of men must be tested by the illumination of the Holy Scriptures.

Now let's proceed to critique the *Easton Bible Dictionary's* (EBD) view of eternal punishment and death.

EBD: (Matthew 25:46) "Then they will go away to eternal punishment, but the righteous to eternal life."

Let's suppose we had never heard or thought of the hereafter with respect to the fate of the wicked. Then let us further suppose we had no other scripture reference on the subject of eternal punishment, death or destruction except this one verse in Matthew 25:46. What could we conclude from this verse as it concerns the unsaved or the wicked? We could reasonably conclude the following two things. (1) There will be punishment for the wicked. (2) The punishment will be unending.

Then they will go away to <u>eternal punishment</u>, but the righteous to eternal life.

I can see no other conclusions that can be drawn from the statement in this verse. On these two facts we should expect unanimous agreement. However, we are given more scriptural information on this subject in this same verse. Not only is the fate of the wicked referenced, but the future of the righteous as well. "But the righteous into <u>life eternal</u>."

Therefore we are enlightened in regard to the future of both groups. However, the contrast is not made in the *quantity* of the judgment between the wicked and the righteous. That is to say, it is not in regard to the duration of future punishment or reward. The future state of the wicked as well as the righteous is eternal or everlasting. The contrast is made in the *quality* (good or bad) of judgment. In this respect the contrast is infinitely distinct.

The *quality* of judgment of the wicked is everlasting punishment. This is in stark contrast to life eternal for the righteous. We can reasonably conclude from this verse that the righteous will not be punished, although this verse does not say that. Why? The primary reason is because they are the righteous. But even if they were not referred to as "the righteous" in the verse, we still could reasonably assume they would not be eternally punished. Why? Because of the contrast in the pronouncement of their future state. They will go into "life eternal."

Throughout the New Testament scriptures the righteous are promised eternal life while the wicked are promised death. Once again notice: "For the wages of sin is death, but the gift of God is eternal life" (Romans 6:23). The two classes will not receive the same judgment. Everlasting punishment is not life eternal and life eternal is not everlasting punishment, and neither group will receive both verdicts.

Although it does not say the righteous will not be punished, it is inferred in the teaching that the wicked will be punished. Neither does it say the wicked will not continue to live forever, but this is the inference since we are told the righteous will go into life eternal. "But he that shall blaspheme against the Holy Ghost hath never forgiveness, but is in danger of <u>eternal damnation</u>" (Mark 3:29). This verse by itself teaches nothing about what the punishment will be for those lost, except that it will last forever. *Damnation* here could be defined simply as judgment. The primary import of this verse is that to "blaspheme against the Holy Ghost" will result in an unforgiven state and will put the subject in danger of eternal damnation judgment.

I will not take up the task of looking at the question of what is meant by blaspheming against the Holy Ghost. However, we might say that as Christians, we must always understand the saving work of God through His Holy Spirit demands our awe and reverence. Without the help of God through His Holy Spirit our finite existence as fleshly creatures would only bring eventual death.

It is the spirit that quickeneth [makes alive]; the flesh profiteth nothing: the words that I speak unto you, they are spirit, and they are life. (John 6:63) (KJV)

Therefore, we must accept the fact that without the Holy Spirit abiding in us we cannot have hope of eternal life. But the point of the EBD article is to prove the verse provides evidence that the wicked will endure conscious punishment throughout eternity. The EBD uses this verse along with others to describe what it refers to as "the miserable fate of the wicked in hell." We can be sure all counted or reckoned sins remaining unforgiven will not go unpunished. This verse points out the unique fact that the sin of blaspheming (speaking against) the Holy Ghost will never be forgiven. Since the wages of sin is death according to Romans 6:23, the unforgiven sin against the Holy

Ghost will bring death. This, however, is true with any sin. The difference with the sin against the Holy Spirit would seem to be the impossibility of receiving forgiveness for it.

Unforgiven sin brings not just physical or temporary death, but eternal damnation or eternal death. So I am in full agreement with the EBD that to blaspheme the Holy Spirit could result in eternal damnation. But the EBD would like for the reader to assume eternal damnation or condemnation is synonymous with eternal torture, which this verse nowhere indicates. Eternal damnation only tells us the recipient will be condemned eternally. With this I concur, and the scriptures clearly bear this out. However, in this verse, the *quality* (how good or bad) of the condemnation is not mentioned, only the *quantity* (eternal).

Of the doctrine of baptisms, and of laying on of hands, and of resurrection of the dead, and of <u>eternal judgment</u>. (Hebrews 6:2)

Once again the EBD uses this verse to point out the already obvious fact of eternal judgment of the wicked in the hereafter. Eternal judgment of the wicked has nothing to do with proving unceasing suffering or torture. The quantity of judgment in respect to duration will be the same for wicked and righteous. The duration will be forever for both classes. This verse does not remotely hint that the wicked will live forever.

In addition, the context of Hebrews 6:2 has nothing to do with proving anything about the fate of the wicked in the hereafter. The writer begins the chapter with an exhortation to the readers of the necessity of moving on from fundamental doctrines to greater perfection in comprehending God's will for their lives.

Therefore, leaving the discussion of the elementary principles of Christ, let us go on to perfection, not laying again the foundation of repentance from dead works and of faith toward God, of the doctrine of baptisms, of laying on of hands, of resurrection of the dead, and of eternal judgment. And this we will do if God permits. (Hebrews 6:1–3)

The writer is speaking to Jewish Christians. Gentile Christians were not a part of the audience for the writing of this epistle. The Jews were familiar, or at least should have been, with the elementary doctrines set forth in Hebrews. Among other teachings, the doctrine of the resurrection of the dead and of eternal judgment was a part of the elementary principles of Christ. This writing was just a simple statement to that effect. Nowhere in this passage is a comment made on the fate of the wicked. However, the passage should be enlightening to the Christian reader in helping to understand the Lord expects continued spiritual progress in His people.

The writer of Hebrews in mentioning eternal judgment has no definition or comment on what the eternal judgment will be. We must learn what is meant here through definition, context and harmony with the full body of scripture. W. E. Vine defines *judgment* in Hebrews 6:2 (Greek *krima*) as "of God's judgment upon men." Still there is no distinction as to whether it concerns the righteous or wicked, or both. It may be true that only the wicked are under consideration in this letter, yet there is no mention as to the type of punishment, only that it is eternal.

Wherefore if thy hand or thy foot offend thee, cut them off, and cast them from thee. It is better for thee to enter into life halt or maimed, rather than having two hands or two feet to be cast into <u>everlasting fire</u>. (Matthew 18:8)

The context surrounding this verse involves offending someone. The Greek word for offend is *skandalizo*. This word is closely associated with our English word *scandalize*. It is defined as meaning to entrap, trip up (make to) stumble, entice to sin.

Earlier in the chapter Jesus says that to offend a little child would be an act that should deserve great punishment. "But whoso shall offend one of these little ones which believe in me, it were better for him that a millstone were hanged about his neck, and that he were drowned in the depth of the sea" (verse 6).

After saying this, Jesus then pronounces woe on anyone who would offend "one of these little ones which believe in me." He says although offenses are something that will happen, "woe to that man by whom the offence cometh!" He then adds, "wherefore if thy hand or thy foot offend thee, cut them off, and cast them from thee; it is better for thee to enter into life halt or maimed, rather than having two hands or two feet to be cast into <u>everlasting fire.</u> And if thine eye offend thee, pluck it out, and cast it from thee; it is better for thee to enter into life with one eye, rather than having two eyes to be cast into <u>hell fire</u>" (Matt. 18:8–9) (KJV)

The main teaching of this passage conveys the severity of offenses (trip up, make to stumble, entice to sin). The snare of deception is not always about one person being deceived by another person. Sometimes self-deception occurs to ensnare the individual. This takes place within the mind of the individual person. This seems to be the case in Matthew 18:8–9. In order to avoid this snare of self-deception that could lead to everlasting fire, the loss of a body member would be a small price to pay.

This brief discourse by the Lord is obviously given to show the small price of living for God when it is compared to serving the desires of the flesh.

For whoever desires to save his life will lose it, but whoever loses his life for My sake will save it. (Luke 9:24)

For what profit is it to a man if he gains the whole world, and loses his own soul? Or what will a man give in exchange for his soul? (Matthew 16:26)

The scriptures explicitly speak of the soul of man as something that can be lost, destroyed, perish or die. The Bible never indicates the soul of an unredeemed man will continue to live. I would not pretend to begin to comprehend the depths of the great truths Jesus taught. But, once again, when this passage is taken in context with the rest of the scriptures, and with its words properly defined, its import becomes much clearer. Matthew 18:8–9 teaches eternal life of the righteous in the hereafter as opposed to eternal punishment for the wicked. But does it teach a conscious, continually living eternity of the wicked? It teaches those impenitent individuals who offend innocent believers can and will be cast into hellfire or everlasting fire. But that is a far cry from endless torture. Jesus calls the fires of hell everlasting fire but nowhere indicates the sinner will be tortured eternally.

Then shall he say also unto them on the left hand, depart from me, ye cursed into everlasting fire, prepared for the devil and his angels. (Matthew 25:41)

The context here shows the separation of the righteous and the wicked in judgment, as I discussed at some length in earlier chapters. In this verse the judgment of the wicked is pronounced by the King (Jesus). This judgment will result in eternal separation also from the King into everlasting fire prepared for the devil and his angels.

But does this verse teach continuous suffering or torture throughout eternity? It does mention everlasting fire and that it is prepared for the devil and his angels. It seems to indicate the everlasting fire was not prepared for humans, but for angels. Could it be that angels and humans will have a different eternal fate? I don't know. However, sometimes when the scriptures speak of the final execution of judgment on wicked humans, Satan and the wicked angels are included. Could it be the fire will last forever to facilitate the judgment of Satan and his host and at the same time annihilate humans? Or could it be language not unlike the writing of Jude, which the EBD uses next?

Even as Sodom and Gomorrah, and the cities about them in like manner, giving themselves over to fornication, and going after strange flesh, are set forth for an example, suffering the vengeance of eternal fire. (Jude 1:7)

I do not know the exact point the EBD is trying to make by using Jude 1:7. This is one of the scriptures the EBD uses to prove the miserable state of the wicked in hell. Surely this must be an oversight by the writer, for this verse is plainly showing a temporal punishment upon these people and upon the wickedness of these cities. Eternal punishment will be executed upon the wicked of these cities only after the resurrection in the hereafter. Everyone was destroyed in the destruction of Sodom and Gomorrah. This included children and mentally challenged individuals along with the rankest of sinners. But the vengeance of eternal fire in the hereafter will not include the innocent children, the disabled etc. The fire at that time was temporary. It has long since gone out and does not continue to burn. The purpose of the fire the Almighty rained down upon these inhabitants was not to cause eternal torment or suffering, but to destroy the wickedness within the cities. Therefore the cities were destroyed along with their inhabitants.

It seems, rather than proving its point, the EBD provides evidence to the contrary. Jude says the destructions of these wicked cities are set forth for an example. What example or examples are set forth? I can think of at least three examples for all to be aware of today. (1) The example of God's intolerance for sin. (2) The example of the severity of God's wrath and vengeance on wickedness. (3) The swiftness and completeness of God's justice.

However, the point that needs to be made to refute the EBD view is that the people in the cities of Sodom and Gomorrah suffered the vengeance of eternal fire in this present life, not in the hereafter. So what is it about the destruction of Sodom and Gomorrah that Jude says is "set forth for an example, suffering the vengeance of eternal fire?" What is it that becomes an example for all other sinners? It simply is this. They perished. They died. They were destroyed. We can see in this verse that the inhabitants of Sodom and Gomorrah and the cities about them suffered the vengeance of eternal fire. We can be sure by the word of this prophetic message that all those like these wicked individuals will suffer a similar fate.

It is amazing the extent to which men will go in order to uphold orthodox views. There are those who believe the fires of Sodom and Gomorrah are still burning on or in the earth. If this were true, there would be folks lined up to see it. Probably an admission fee would be charged. But this is the unbelievable evidence given to show that the fires of Sodom and Gomorrah are eternal and therefore still burning. This, they evidently believe, will in some way give evidence that sinners will suffer a torturous, living existence in the hereafter. But even if these fires had continued to burn on or in the earth for these thousands of years, it gives no substantiation to the doctrine of unconditional immortality.

Obviously the fires of these cities have gone out. But even if they were continually burning even until now, the aforementioned comments from the EBD do not prove the intended point. The people of the cities were destroyed. They were totally and completely burned up. They were no more. This is the point Jude was making, and this was the example for those who would live their lives in sin.

The fires of Sodom were not eternal in the sense of *quantity* or duration. They have long since become ashes and gone out. But rather they were eternal in the sense of *quality*. First, the fires may have been called eternal because of their origin. They came from the everlasting God. They were also eternal in the sense of the *quality* of the destruction of the cities. The cities were destroyed forever! Although the fire did not endure forever, its destruction did. The utter destruction of the cities of Sodom and Gomorrah is an example of the completeness of the destruction forevermore of the wicked in the world to come.

THE UNENDING DURATION OF SUFFERINGS

As we continue our examination of the EBD's definition of the eternal death of the wicked, the next point made by the EBD is the unending duration of sufferings. Much of what I have said up to this point addresses this concern. However, I will examine the following statement made in regard to unending duration of sufferings in other areas I have not yet covered.

The EBD says scripture as clearly teaches the unending duration of the penal sufferings of the lost as the "everlasting life," "eternal life" of the righteous. It further states the same Greek words in the New Testament (*aion, aionios, aidios*) are used to express (1) the eternal existence of God (1 Timothy 1:17; Romans 1:20; 16:26); (2) of Christ (Revelation 1:18); (3) of the Holy Ghost (Hebrews 9:14); and (4) the eternal duration of the sufferings of the lost (Matthew 25:46; Jude 1:6)

The *Strong's Concordance's* definition of *aion* is: an age, a cycle (of time), especially of the present age as contrasted with the future age, and of one of a series of ages stretching to infinity. 165 aiōn (see also the cognate adjective, 166 /aiōnios, "age-long")—properly, an age (era, "time-span"), characterized by a specific quality (type of existence).

Example: Christians today live in the newer age (165 /aiōn) of the covenant—the time-period called the NT. It is characterized by Christ baptizing all believers in the Holy Spirit, i.e. engrafting all believers (OT, NT) into His mystical body (1 Cor. 12:13) with all the marvelous privileges that go with that (Gal 3:23–25; 1 Pet 2:5,9).

The New Testament Greek words (*aion, aionios, aidios*) do express the eternal existence of God, Christ and the Holy Ghost. And although these words may sometimes give evidence of things unending, this in no way proves the unending sufferings of the lost. This is especially true when the subject has to do with nothing connected to the lost or punishment, such as the eternal existence of God. To prove an eternal existence is a far cry from proving unending torture of the wicked.

The words (*aion, aionios, aidios*) do sometimes show unending or eternal punishment, but they in no way define what the unending punishment will be. It might denote torture or suffering without end in the verses cited by the EBD, or in other scriptures that address the matter. But the unending punishment might be unending death. In order to know if it is suffering or torture being addressed in a particular scripture there must be an alluding to suffering or torture in that scripture. The verses cannot simply talk about something eternal and the punishment be understood. Eternal punishment or destruction is not always torture or penal suffering. How do we know this? Because the Bible says the wages of sin is death! Death is the cessation of life. Let's look briefly at the scriptures that have been used.

Now unto the King eternal, immortal, invisible, the only wise God, be honor and glory for ever and ever. Amen. (1 Timothy 1:17)

First of all, the use of this verse to show the eternal existence of God the Father separate from the eternal existence of Christ seems to show a serious lack of research and study. The only wise God in 1 Timothy 1:17 is *The Christ*. This is evident in the verse and in the context.

However, in refuting the idea of God the Father and the Christ being one and the same in this verse, the answer will probably be that the "only wise God" is God the Son (deity), but not God the Father. But this also poses a problem. If "the only wise God" is God the Son (or Christ), does this mean God the Father is not the "only wise God"?

The EBD then uses Revelation 1:18, attempting to show the separate eternal existence of Christ. Either this is an oversight on the part of the EBD, or there are two kings ruling over the kingdom of Heaven, both immortal. Jesus is referred to as the King of Kings in the epistles to the churches and is declared to be the only possessor of immortality. In 1 Timothy 6:14–15, Paul makes this point clear to Timothy the evangelist.

That thou keep this commandment without spot, unrebukeable, until the appearing of our Lord Jesus Christ. Which in his times he shall shew, who is the blessed and only Potentate (ruler), the King of kings, and Lord of lords. Who only hath immortality, dwelling in the light which no man can approach unto; whom no man hath nor seen nor can see; to whom be honor and power everlasting. Amen.

Another thing, perhaps worthy of note, is the fact that among all mortals, only Jesus is said to have attained immortality. The definition of immortality is simply deathlessness. It seems to me that only mortals could put on immortality. We are either mortal or immortal. If we are immortal, immortality cannot be put on because we already possess it. Paul tells the Corinthian Christians incorruption and immortality can be *put on* as a result of Jesus being resurrected to immortality. Thus they could be changed from mortal to immortal.

For this corruptible must put on incorruption, and this mortal must put on immortality. So when this corruptible shall have put on incorruption, and this mortal shall have put on immortality, then shall be brought to pass the saying that is written, Death is swallowed up in victory. O Death, where is thy sting? O grave, where is thy victory? (1 Corinthians 15: 53–55).

The Greek words (*aion, aionios, aidios*), without question, testify to the everlasting duration of the existence of God. However, once again, this gives no evidence of eternal suffering of the wicked. It only speaks to the eternal duration of the sentence. *Easton's Bible Dictionary*, in my opinion, must give greater scriptural evidence than has been brought to light in its statement in order to show the scripture as clearly teaches the unending duration of the penal sufferings of the lost as the "everlasting life" or "eternal life" of the righteous. The evidence of incorruption, immortality and eternal life is explicit throughout the New Testament in regard to the post resurrection of the righteous. But is this promise (or sentence) given to the wicked? I don't think so.

The bottom line is that the scriptures do not promise eternal life or existence for unsaved humanity. Those who advocate eternal suffering for lost souls usually talk about the eternal state of the wicked as an eternal existence rather than eternal life. *Existence* was not a word used by the original English translators. Existence is defined as real or actual being, continued being, living, life. So those seeking to prove eternal torture of the wicked must stress their continued conscious, living existence. But they like to do this without admitting this would be eternal life. What else could it be?

Eternal life is not defined by the *quality* of that life, no more than with physical life. Physical life can be a miserable existence, but it is still life. When is physical life (the life of the body), whether miserable or happy, terminated? Is it not when it is separated from its life source, which is the spirit within it? When this happens, the state of the body is in a state of death whether for a while or forever. Why? It is because death is the absence of life. Jesus said on one occasion that he came to bring life and that it might be more abundant. But think about it! Whether it was more abundant life or less abundant life, would it still not be life? When life is less abundant is it then death? I don't think so. The wages of sin for the wicked is death—eternal death—the second death, not just a tortured life. The gift of God for the righteous is life, eternal life, the second life resulting from being born again. It is a more abundant life. But it is much more than that. It is life without end, eternal life, immortality, deathlessness. On the other hand, the fate of the wicked is death without end, eternal or everlasting death.

Next, the EBD considers the eternal power and the Godhead in trying to prove eternal torment for lost souls.

For the invisible things of him from the creation of the world are clearly seen, being understood by the things that are made, even his eternal power and Godhead; so they are without excuse. (Romans 1:20)

Once again, this speaks clearly to the everlasting nature of the Godhead. But I fail to see a connection with this verse and the eternal suffering of wicked men and women. I will not belabor the other verses given: Romans 16:26, Revelation 1:18, Hebrews 9:14. These verses do show the eternalness of the Godhead. They are proof the Father, Son and Holy Spirit are eternal by the definition of the Greek words (*aion, aionios, aidios*). But I do not think it shows any proof whatsoever that the wicked will suffer endlessly.

I will end by quoting from Dr. Lyman Abbott (1835–1922), a Congregationalist pastor and editor of *Christian Union* and *The Outlook*. He wrote the following:

> Outside of the walls of Jerusalem, in the valley of Gehenna, was kept perpetually burning a fire, on which the offal of the city was thrown to be destroyed. This is the hell fire of the New Testament. Christ warns his auditors that persistence in sin will make them offal to be cast out from the holy city, to be destroyed. The worm that dieth not was the worm devouring the carcasses, and is equally clearly a symbol not of torture but of destruction.

He continues by saying:

> The notion that the final punishment of sin is continuance in sin and suffering is also based in part on, what seems to me, a false philosophy of man. This philosophy is that man is by nature immortal. The conviction has grown on me, that according to the teaching both of science and Scripture, man is by nature an animal, and like all other animals mortal; that immortality belongs only to the spiritual life; and that spiritual life is possible only in communion and contact with God; that, in short, immortality was not conferred upon the race in creation whether it would or not, but is conferred in redemption, upon all those of the race who choose life and immortality through Jesus Christ our Lord.

CONCLUDING THOUGHT

The foundational structure on which the idea of endless torment stands is in the doctrine of unconditional immortality. "You shall not surely die" is the first recorded lie Satan perpetrated on humanity. This was codified in church doctrine hundreds of years ago and has remained alive and well ever since. In order to believe it, we must believe immortality is simply a part of our created nature. If this is true, we then cannot obtain it through Christ. It means we can never die as God told Adam and Eve would happen if they ate of the tree in the garden. And it means Satan was correct in telling them they could not die because of sin. Some folks think it is a stretch to believe in conditional immortality. I think to believe in unconditional immortality is to ignore God's Word of inspiration!

CHAPTER 12

THE RESTORATION OF ALL THINGS

Whom heaven must receive until the times of restoration of all things, which God has spoken by the mouth of all His holy prophets since the world began. (Acts 3:21)

Even the sound of the word *restoration* is beautiful. The word creates an emotion of eager anticipation with thoughts of resurrecting something that is loved, but something that is now deteriorating and dying. It is a thought that can bring feelings of great value, feelings that cannot be expressed in monetary terms. Visions of restoration can resurrect long-held memories deeply etched in our cerebral storehouse; visions can bring our minds back to connect with what once was a cherished treasure. The desire for restoration is a dream for something once cared about very deeply, and now we dream of it being brought back, enabled to live with us once again. Restoration is about bringing something back to the beauty and glory it once knew, a glory always living in our hearts.

One of my father's precious possessions was his father's fiddle. He inherited the fiddle when his father died. It was not valuable in dollars, but it was priceless to my father. I never met Grandpa Richardson. He died about six years before I was born. But as a very small child I often viewed the fiddle in its case hanging on the wall. From time to time Dad would take it out of the case, fondly touching and looking at it. Many times he talked to me and my siblings about Grandpa and his fiddle. I remember him telling us how much he and the family enjoyed Pa playing that fiddle after the evening meal.

But as the years passed, the fiddle began to deteriorate. The wood had become dry and brittle, and eventually it came unglued in several places. This bothered Dad a lot, and he spoke often about desiring to have it restored. But we barely had enough money for necessities. So the unrestored fiddle had to take a back seat to the needs of the family. Once a distant family member told Dad he thought he could restore it. Dad somewhat reluctantly let him take it with him. When he brought it back he told Dad it was beyond his ability to fix. He said there were people who could restore it, but it would be costly. So the fiddle was never restored in my Dad's lifetime. I think Dad continued to think about the restoration of Pa's fiddle as long as he lived.

THE INHERITANCE OF CHRIST

Natural heirs are the truly begotten children of their father. The same is true with God the Father and His Son, Jesus. When we say natural, we mean natural in the sense of being from the parents as opposed to being biologically unrelated. Jesus is the truly begotten and the only natural heir of Almighty God. No one except His only begotten Son can rightly lay any claim to the inheritance of His Father. The inspired Word of God clearly attests to the fact that Jesus was to be the sole inheritor of all things of the Father.

God, who at various times and in various ways spoke in time past to the fathers by the prophets, has in these last days spoken to us by <u>His Son</u>, whom He has appointed <u>heir of all things</u>, through whom also He made the worlds; who being the brightness of His glory and the express image of His person, and upholding all things by the word of His power, when He had by Himself purged our sins, sat down at the right hand of the Majesty on high, having become so much better *than the angels, as He has by inheritance obtained a more excellent name than they. (Hebrews 1:1–4)*

As a man, like all human beings, Jesus was made a little lower than angels.

You have made him [man] a little lower than the angels; You have crowned him with glory and honor, and set him over the works of Your hands. (Hebrews 2:7)

But we see Jesus, who was made a little lower than the angels, for the suffering of death crowned with glory and honor, that He, by the grace of God, might taste death for everyone. (Hebrews 2:9)

So the angels of God were created superior to humans. This doubtlessly is true, especially in respect to intellect. Jesus, because of His humanity, was also made a little lower than the angels when God brought Him into the world. To fulfill God's work of redemption through His Son, it was necessary that His humanity be the same as that of His fellow humans. He was to be like His brethren (fellow humans) in every way.

Therefore, in all things He had to be made like His brethren, that He might be a merciful and faithful High Priest in things pertaining to God, to make propitiation for the sins of the people. (Hebrews 2:17)

It was also necessary for Jesus to be made like ordinary humans in order that He could feel and know the infirmities of humanity.

For we do not have a High Priest who cannot sympathize with our weaknesses, but was in all points tempted as we are, yet without sin. (Heb. 4:15)

The Bible also tells us it was man, rather than angels, who was created in the image of God.

So God created man in His own image; in the image of God He created him; male and female He created them. (Genesis 1:27)

And whatever it means to be *created in the image of God* as humans, this certainly was accomplished in Jesus as well as Adam. Jesus entered the world as a baby with the limitations of humanity. Only after His glorious resurrection and ascension into heaven could it be said He had _become so much better than the angels._ The fact that He had _become_ so much better than the angels shows the completeness of His progression from a fleshly to an immortal existence through perfect obedience to God's will.

The purpose of God in all of creation was fulfilled in and through His Son. In other words, everything that would serve God's purpose in connection to creation would be through, by and for His only begotten Son. It was through the power of the Word of life that Jesus became God's only begotten Son, born of a human woman. It was also by this same power of the Word of life that the worlds were made and all things created.

That which was from the beginning, which we have heard, which we have seen with our eyes, which we have looked upon, and our hands have handled, concerning the Word of life. (1 John 1:1)

And too it was by Him (Jesus) the Word of God's power, that all things are upheld or maintained.

[Jesus,] who being the brightness of His (God's) glory and the express image of His person, and upholding all things by the word of His power, when He had by Himself purged our sins, sat down at the right hand of the Majesty on high. (Hebrews 1:3)

And finally, it was by the sacrifice of the innocent blood of this same Jesus that made possible the forgiveness of sins by God. Jesus became the sole instrument to carry out the will of God in the mystery of the gospel. He then received all the glory of the Father manifested in the power of the Holy Spirit of God, given to Jesus without measure, thus causing Him to become so much better than the angels of God.

Therefore it could truly be said that Jesus has by inheritance obtained a more excellent name than the angels.

Having become so much better than the angels, as He has by inheritance obtained a more excellent name than they. (Hebrews 1:4)

Obtaining a more excellent *name* indicates superiority, excelling in power and glory. This *more excellent name* was achieved because of His inheritance as the Son of God. The angels would not be the rightful heirs of God, but rather it would be and is His Son. He received power above all of creation by virtue of inheritance. He was the heir because He was the only true Son. Jesus was not just a servant in His Master's house, but a Son to receive the inheritance of His Father. For it was by God's power through the Word that was made flesh that the house of God would be built.

Therefore, holy brethren, partakers of the heavenly calling, consider the Apostle and High Priest of our confession, Christ Jesus, who was faithful to Him who appointed Him, as Moses also was faithful in all his house. For this One has been counted worthy of more glory than Moses, inasmuch as He who built the house has more honor than the house. For every house is built by someone, but He who built all things is God. And Moses indeed was faithful in all His house as a servant, for a testimony of those things which would be spoken afterward, but Christ as a Son over His own house, whose house we are if we hold fast the confidence and the rejoicing of the hope firm to the end. (Hebrews 3:1–6)

RESTORATION

The Greek word for restoration or restitution, as found in Acts 3:21, is *apokatastasis*. W. E. Vine defines it as (*apo*), meaning back again, along with (*katastasis*), meaning to set in order. This would seem to indicate something being set back again into its original intended order or design.

Deep down in every soul is a yearning for restoration in some way or other. To the aged, it may be a restoration back to youth. Those who are sick yearn to be restored to their health. To those who are fearful or mentally disturbed, the desire is for restoration back to a peaceful and satisfied mind.

This chapter deals with the idea of the restoration of all things in connection with the whole creation of God and His love for it. Even though angels and the things of heaven are a part of God's overall creative work, for the purposes of this discussion the creation of the things of heaven should be separated from the material universe as we know it. Putting them all in the same creative basket creates the confusion of time with eternity. We know the material universe is bound by the effects of time. It is reasonably safe to assume the things of heaven may not be.

In the book of Mark Jesus is recorded to have left the earth, ascending into heaven.

So then, after the Lord had spoken to them, He was received up into heaven, and sat down at the right hand of God. (Mark 16:19)

Therefore at the present time, He in His glorified immortal state is no longer bound by the limitations of an earthly fleshly existence. He has now been received by heaven. And He is to remain there until the times of restoration of all things.

Whom heaven must receive until the times of restoration of all things, which God has spoken by the mouth of all His holy prophets since the world began. (Acts 3:21)

When the times of restoration of all things are accomplished, Jesus will come back to receive His own inheritance. In pondering this verse in Acts, on various occasions I have wondered aloud to my friends and brethren about its meaning. I wanted to know if it literally means what it says. At the present time, there is clearly not a restoration of all things in any sense of the word. I have read only a few scholarly comments of writers who chose to elaborate on it. However, through the years, in different ways I have received several positions by others as to its meaning. Listed next are a few of them:

1. Universal salvation of all created humankind.

2. The culmination or completion of the work of Christ in the redemption of faithful humanity.

3. The eventual final perfected restoration of all the creation of God, including both humans and angels.

4. The restoration of all the creation of God, with the exception of fallen angels and unredeemed humanity.

In this chapter I plead the case for the last of these position. In doing so, I feel comfortable in my application of scripture. However, my mind is open to other views.

Restoration or "restitution of all things" (KJV) definitely means something! This is one of the passages of scripture many have generally ignored for too long. Spiritual wisdom demands we search God's Word for an understanding of the inspired teachings of the Bible, realizing the acquisition of truth is all important. Its primary importance should be to always bring honor and glory to our Creator. Seeking truth should always result in an honest and humble approach that will please the Lord and bring glory to Him. We need to understand that when we fail to seek the truth we have no promise of ever finding the truth.

Acts 3:21 is but a single verse of scripture. Let's read it once again.

Whom heaven must receive until the times of restoration of all things, which God has spoken by the mouth of all His holy prophets since the world began.

When this one verse is studied and meditated upon, it can open our minds to a spiritual treasure trove. First of all, "all things" are included. So we need to determine what is included in "all things." This will need to be accomplished by examining the scriptural context and viewing the verse in light of other passages of scriptures that deal with the subject.

The backdrop of this verse is quite interesting. The apostle Peter is preaching to those who witnessed the miraculous restoring of a lame man to his natural mobility. As he begins speaking to the audience, Peter gives all glory to the Lord Jesus for this great wonder by saying it was done through faith in His name.

And His name, through faith in His name, has made this man strong, whom you see and know. Yes, the faith which comes through Him has given him this perfect soundness in the presence of you all. (Acts 3:16)

He then charges some who were present, along with their leaders, with their sin of ignorance in taking part in the murder of the Lord.

Yet now, brethren, I know that you did it in ignorance, as did also your rulers. But those things which God foretold by the mouth of all His prophets, that the Christ would suffer, He has thus fulfilled. (Acts 3:17–18)

Through Peter's preaching revealing to them that Jesus was the Messiah, the people begin to see the awfulness of their actions. At this point their consciences are made aware of the truth of their sin, and therefore it became chargeable before God. Next Peter calls on them to repent and be converted in order that "times of refreshing" might come to them when the Lord Jesus comes back at the end of time. Peter tells them Jesus will be sent back from heaven at some future point in order to refresh those whose guilt and sins were blotted out through repentance.

Repent therefore and be converted, that your sins may be blotted out, so that <u>times of refreshing</u> may come from the presence of the Lord, and that He may send Jesus Christ, who was preached to you before, whom heaven must receive until the <u>times of restoration of all things</u>, which God has spoken by the mouth of all His holy prophets since the world began. (Acts 3:19–21)

Even though God's spiritually regenerated people are temporarily refreshed in the kingdom of Christ on earth, the ultimate and eternal refreshing will come from the presence of the Lord after His return to take them home to heaven. The Lord is now in heaven, as Peter tells them, and will remain there until the "times of the restoration of all things."

This is the general context of 1 Peter 3:21. So who or what is included in this restoration of all things? It will obviously not be the salvation of the fallen angels or unrepentant humanity. I say this for the following reasons.

First of all, when Jude wrote his short letter in the first century, the fallen angels were already imprisoned and awaiting the final judgment of an eternally condemning consequence.

And the angels who did not keep their proper domain, but left their own abode, He has reserved in everlasting chains under darkness for the judgment of the great day. (Jude 6)

Neither could it be the eternal fate of those who refuse to retain God in their knowledge and reject the gospel message of grace.

He who rejects Me, and does not receive My words, has that which judges him—the word that I have spoken will judge him in the last day. (John 12:48)

And to give you who are troubled rest with us when the Lord Jesus is revealed from heaven with His mighty angels, in flaming fire taking vengeance on those who do not know God, and on those who do not obey the gospel of our Lord Jesus Christ. These shall be punished with everlasting destruction from the presence of the Lord and from the glory of His power. (1 Thess. 1:7–9)

Jesus is plain in telling us all those in the graves will be resurrected, both the just and the unjust, when the end comes.

For the hour is coming in which all who are in the graves will hear His voice and come forth—those who have done good, to the resurrection of life, and those who have done evil, to the resurrection of condemnation. (John 5:28–29)

Those redeemed by the blood of Christ will be resurrected immortal and will be caught up together in the air to meet the Lord. The unredeemed who have rejected the Lord and have remained unrepentant will suffer the consequence of condemnation. These are destined to be destroyed. I see no scriptural proof of them ever leaving the earth.

Then we who are alive and remain shall be caught up together with them in the clouds to meet the Lord in the air. And thus we shall always be with the Lord. (1 Thess. 4:17)

Paul plainly tells the Gentile Ephesian converts that previous to their spiritual regeneration they were in a state of "having no hope" and without God in the world.

Therefore remember that you, once Gentiles in the flesh—who are called Uncircumcision by what is called the Circumcision made in the flesh by hands— that at that time you were without Christ, being aliens from the commonwealth of Israel and strangers from the covenants of promise, <u>having no hope</u> and without God in the world. But now in Christ Jesus you who once were far off have been brought near by the blood of Christ. (Ephesians 2:11–13)

I do not see the Bible as teaching eternal salvation for unredeemed humanity. But in Acts 3:20–21, Peter gives hope for the "restoration of all things." Therefore, all things must be all things having escaped the eternal consequences of sin. Escaping the consequences of sin can only occur by the forgiveness of that sin or by having not sinned. So all things would mean all creation with the exception of unredeemed humanity and fallen angels.

In using the phrase "restoration of all things" the writer clearly indicates someone or something in addition to redeemed humanity. It doesn't say all men, but all things. It doesn't even indicate just all humanity, or even all living creation. It clearly says the "restoration of <u>all</u> things."

And that He may send Jesus Christ, who was preached to you before, whom heaven must receive until the times of <u>restoration of all things</u>, which God has spoken by the mouth of all His holy prophets since the world began. (Acts 3:20–21)

Therefore I believe there is clear and convincing evidence in the scriptures to uphold the idea of restoration for all nonhuman creation, with the exception of fallen angels.

OPINIONS AND THEORIES

I feel quite sure all of the reasons God created this vast and awesome material universe will never be understood in this life. But I do believe God's

Word allows us to understand the primary reason for it. It is for our Creator to be revered, praised and glorified by his creation. His glory is not just to be extolled by humankind, but by all of His creation. Listen to the beautiful Psalm 148.

Praise the Lord from the heavens; praise Him in the heights; praise Him, all His angels; praise Him, all His hosts! Praise Him, sun and moon; praise Him, all you stars of light! Praise Him, you heavens of heavens, and you waters above the heavens! Let them praise the name of the Lord, for He commanded and they were created. He also established them forever and ever; He made a decree which shall not pass away. Praise the Lord from the earth, you great sea creatures and all the depths; fire and hail, snow and clouds; stormy wind, fulfilling His word; mountains and all hills; fruitful trees and all cedars; beasts and all cattle; creeping things and flying fowl; kings of the earth and all peoples; princes and all judges of the earth; both young men and maidens; old men and children. Let them praise the name of the Lord, for His name alone is exalted; His glory is above the earth and heaven. And He has exalted the horn of His people, the praise of all His saints—of the children of Israel, a people near to Him. Praise the Lord!

Alexander Maclaren (1826–1910) wrote that Psalms 148 continues "a line of thought which runs through Scripture from its first page to its last—namely that as man's sin subjected the creatures to 'vanity,' so his redemption shall be their glorifying."

Noted commentator Adam Clarke sees Psalm 148 as a prophecy to be fulfilled, the fulfillment of which will cause all of creation to praise its Creator. "This call to all creation to praise Yahweh was not an empty wish. Revelation 5:11–13 tells us specifically that it will be fulfilled. 'O what a hymn of praise is here! It is a universal chorus! All created nature have a share, and all perform their respective parts.'"

The inspired exhortation from Psalm 148 allows us to know the Creator's desire is for the whole creation to praise and worship Him. Only among humans and angels do we have scriptural proof of the possibility of eternal destruction. Nowhere else of which I am aware do the scriptures teach the eternal cessation of the rest of creation. With these two exceptions, all of creation was subjected to futility by the curse of sin. Only these two categories of creation are in a position to be lost. This is because of the ability to willingly sin and rebel against God's will.

Among the human and angelic creation will be some of each who refuse to worship the Creator. In the case of humans it will be by making the inexcusable mistake of willfully allowing their minds to reject the knowledge of God. The scriptures tell us this is done by rejecting the obvious evidence of His power as Creator. And since the Creator and the creation (creature) are the only two things existing to be worshipped, many will choose to worship the creature (or what is created) over the Creator. Paul gives witness to this fact in his letter to the Romans. He says the invisible things of the Creator are evident and inexcusable to deny. The eternal power of the Creator is clearly seen in what He has created. To deny this power of creation is to deny the Creator.

For the wrath of God is revealed from heaven against all ungodliness and unrighteousness of men, who suppress the truth in unrighteousness, because what may be known of God is manifest [or evident] in [or among] them, for God has shown it to them. For since the creation of the world His invisible attributes are clearly seen, being understood by the things that are made, even His eternal power and Godhead [or divine nature, deity], so that they are without excuse, because, although they knew God, they did not glorify Him as God, nor were thankful, but became futile in their thoughts, and their foolish hearts were darkened. Professing to be wise, they became fools, and changed the glory of the incorruptible God into an image made like corruptible [or perishable] man—and birds and four-footed animals and creeping things. Therefore God also gave them up to uncleanness, in the lusts of their hearts, to dishonor their bodies among themselves, who exchanged the truth of God for the lie, and worshiped and served the creature rather than the Creator, who is blessed forever. Amen. (Romans 1:18–24)

Does the nonhuman creation praise and worship its Creator? Is this possible? I think this is a perfectly reasonable question to ask. Psalm 148 definitely sends forth a message of the possibility of "the whole creation" praising and glorifying the Almighty. Is it unreasonable to think it was created with this ability?

In the book of Job we are told creation possesses not only the awareness of its Creator's presence but also the ability to teach, tell, speak and explain to humans it knows within God's hands all life is held!

But now ask the beasts, and they will teach you; and the birds of the air, and they will tell you; or speak to the earth, and it will teach you; and the fish of the sea will explain to you. Who among all these does not know that the hand of the Lord has done this, in whose hand is the life of every living thing, and the breath of all mankind? (Job 12:7–10)

As with everything pleasing to the Father, praise of the Creator could only become perfected through His Son. And as with all things connected to pleasing God and doing His will, so also was the perfected glorification of God revealed to all creation by His Son's perfect praise and obedience. In the begetting of the only begotten Son, the physical body of Jesus was prepared for sacrifice by the Creator in order to renew universal praise for Him.

Therefore, when He came into the world, He said: "Sacrifice and offering You did not desire, but a body You have prepared for Me. In burnt offerings and sacrifices for sin You had no pleasure. Then I said, 'Behold, I have come—in the volume of the book it is written of Me—to do Your will, O God.'" (Hebrews 10:5–7)

Blessed be God! It is the perpetual strain of the Old Testament, from Melchizedek down to Daniel, of David in his triumph, and Job in his misery. But not hitherto could men say, blessed be "the God and Father of our Lord Jesus Christ!" He was "the Most High God, the

God of heaven,""Jehovah, God of Israel, who only doeth wondrous things,""the Shepherd" and "the Rock" of His people, "the true God, the living God, and an everlasting King"; and these are glorious titles, which have raised men's thoughts to moods of highest reverence and trust. But the name of "Father," and "Father of our Lord Jesus Christ," surpasses and outshines them all. With wondering love and joy unspeakable St. Paul pronounces this "Benedictus." God was not less to him the Almighty, the High and Holy One dwelling in eternity, than in the days of his youthful Jewish faith; but the Eternal and All-holy One was now his Father in Jesus Christ. Blessed be His name: and let the whole earth be filled with His glory! (Expositor's Bible Commentary)

Fleshly men invariably become wise in their own opinions (i.e., conceits). With man's wisdom there is usually gravitation toward a diminishing praise of the love, mercy and power of the Creator. Carnal men walk by sight. But those who are spiritual trust in the Lord to lead them. To trust in God is to trust in His Word. To trust in His Word is to trust in His Christ, who was and is His Word incarnate. We, by faith, do this even when we have no idea how God might cause something to happen or how it might be fulfilled according to His promise.

One example of trusting without visible evidence might be in Paul's message to the Roman church regarding whether the spiritual blindness of the children of Israel would remain forever or the veil of unbelief would eventually be lifted from their eyes. Even though we may not understand this mystery, we should believe the word of prophecy until or when we receive revelation of how it will be accomplished. We should never deny or dismiss what the Lord has spoken by being blinded through religious dogma.

Even though we may never understand how the restoration of Israel could be fulfilled, faith compels us to believe just as Abraham believed God. To discount the scriptures, dismissing any part of God's will as undoable, is to trust in the flesh rather than the power of Almighty God. With God all things are possible!

For I do not desire, brethren, that you should be ignorant of this mystery, lest you should be wise in your own opinion, that <u>blindness in part</u> has happened to Israel until the fullness of the Gentiles has come in. And so all Israel will be saved, as it is written: "The Deliverer will come out of Zion, and He will turn away ungodliness from Jacob; for this is My covenant with them, when I take away their sins." (Romans 11:25–27)

We can be sure that when Paul penned these words, in some way Israel was in a state of blindness in part. This condition would continue until "the fullness of the Gentiles has come in." Just because we haven't received a revelation of how it could happen doesn't detract from its truthfulness. Wisdom from above will always cause us to more fully realize the true and loving nature of the Creator toward His creation. But it will only happen by carefully observing and clinging to the promises of His Word.

Whoever is wise will observe these things, and they will understand the lovingkindness of the Lord. Psalms 107:43

When we seek truth by setting our minds on worshipping and revering the wisdom of the created rather than the Creator, we will be lifted up with pride in the created. This begins a process of sure destruction for our souls. Our association with those of like precious faith in spiritual things, by communicating the things of God with those who have also been humbled by the knowledge of God's power, will help to ensure our faith.

Be of the same mind toward one another. Do not set your mind on high things, but associate with the humble. Do not be wise in your own opinion. (Romans 12:16)

Unregenerate minds of men always desire to bow down to the opinions of men. In the end this means the worship of the creature rather than God.

INSTINCTIVE OR LEARNED BEHAVIOR

Instinctive behavior is probably the most common reason given by the scientific community in trying to show the intellectual disadvantages of the nonhuman creation as opposed to humans. The idea of instinctive behavior advocates the theory that certain actions are performed by members of each creature or species through powerful impulses. The action is theorized to be a fixed action pattern (FAP) occurring as the result of a specific stimulus. Fixed action pattern behavior, the scientific community contends, differs from learned behavior. The difference is that with instinct there would be little or no need to possess abilities to reason and learn. Basically, this behavior would differ little from a preprogrammed robot.

But how do humans know the nonhuman creation is merely instinctively controlled without a need to reason or learn? Humans do not even know what is in the minds of other human beings. So how would it be possible for them to know what is in the minds of nonhuman creatures? The concept of instinctive behavior at first seems plausible. But I believe it is accepted mainly because of the difficulty of disproving it. A lot of things can seem reasonable when we have no real way to know their causes. So maybe the theory about instinct is correct or maybe it is not. But it is a theory, not a proven fact.

One reason instinctive behavior seems reasonable is because we live only in our own minds. We cannot know what is in the mind of another unless it is revealed to us by a power higher than ourselves. Outside our minds we can observe, calculate, deduct and reason with our natural sensory perception. But we can't get into the minds of anything else by way of our natural senses. We can sense things about people and the rest of God's creation. And after sensing, we may then reason and make deductions about why the behavior is this way or that way. In other words, we may see what is done, but we cannot be sure as to why. No one but the Creator knows the mind.

For what man knows the things of a man except the spirit of the man which is in him? Even so no one knows the things of God except the Spirit of God. (1 Cor. 2:11)

But we can know something about human thought, action and reasoning because we have human minds. We can tell a lot about other people by how we are. And by God's Spirit we can also have the counsel of God to teach us about our own human thinking, acting and reasoning.

However with animals and the rest of the creation, we only know what we can observe with our finite senses. We can see what they do and how they act and react. But we cannot know what they think, why they act as they do or to what extent they reason. We assume a lot, but we know very little about the causes of the behavior of other creatures. The wisdom of this world does a lot of guessing, even regarding human behavior. Once again, only our God knows the minds of His creation.

Is it possible that animals behave because of a special divinely preprogrammed system governing their behavior? And could this behavior be governed by a completely different set of laws unimaginable to understand with human ability? Could it be that the nonhuman creation behaves neither by instinctive or learned behavior but according to a completely different system? It is entirely possible the Creator created a different way in which to communicate His purpose to the rest of the creation. If this is the case no human would ever know why animals behave as they do without divine inspiration revealing it to their minds. This kind of spiritual "technology" would be far beyond the created capabilities of humans. But we can be certain that with God all things are possible!

And what do we know about angels? Do angels behave instinctively or is their behavior learned? Or could it be a learned behavior, but a different kind of learned behavior than that of humankind? Is it possible God created angels without either instincts or learned behavior? This might be accomplished by making their minds mature (fully programmed with the knowledge they need) from the beginning of their creation. Humans are born as immature beings. They obviously do possess some instinctive behavior at birth but gradually grow into a knowledge-based behavior that is gradually less dependent on instincts. This enables choice of thought and reaction through the power of reasoning rather than through mere instinct or impulse.

Angels are different than people in many ways. One way, as previously noted, would seem to be by being created fully mature. Angels obviously are without gender, according to what Jesus says in the gospels.

Jesus answered and said to them, "You are mistaken, not knowing the Scriptures nor the power of God. For in the resurrection they neither marry nor are given in marriage, but are like angels of God in heaven."

Angels would seem to have been created with all the knowledge needed to serve the purpose of the Creator. This would be an entirely different situation than with mankind, who knows virtually nothing at the time of creation. There is nothing that I am aware of in the scriptures about immature angels. This would seem to indicate maturity of knowledge from their creation. Maturity of knowledge would erase the need for learning.

There is also nothing in the scriptures telling us the Creator has to divulge His creative mysteries to the created. We can build schools of thought, we can have opinions, we can surmise elaborate theories, we can postulate tantalizing arguments, but in the end it is God and only God Who knows His ways. We can only know what He chooses to reveal through His inspired word.

Oh, the depth of the riches both of the wisdom and knowledge of God! How unsearchable are His judgments and His ways past finding out! "For who has known the mind of the Lord? Or who has become His counselor?" "Or who has first given to Him and it shall be repaid to him?" For of Him and through Him and to Him are all things, to whom be glory forever. Amen. (Rom. 11:33–36)

Those who are truly faithful to their calling as children of God should know the power of the Almighty is without limits and His ways are unsearchable.

Have you not known? Have you not heard? The everlasting God, the Lord, The Creator of the ends of the earth, neither faints nor is weary. His understanding is unsearchable. (Isa. 40:28)

At this point, once again, we need to ask: does true revelation come from the minds of men or from God? We can safely conclude the source of all truth flows from the divine mind of our Creator. So in making my case for the "restoration of the whole creation," I stand firmly on a divine statement from Jesus. *With God all things are possible!*

But Jesus looked at them and said to them, "With men this is impossible, but with God all things are possible." (Matt. 19:26)

The point is simply this: humans have very limited knowledge, even though many times they seem so ignorant of this fact. History books are filled with oceans of evidence that makes it glaringly obvious humanity has foolishly and continually overrated its own wisdom. But when some men are seen by others to have great intellectual powers, usually many tend to follow their lead. This is true even when those with perceived wisdom are only proponents of untested or unprovable theories. And most of man's opinions and theories in connection with the creation and sustaining of our material universe remain unproven or unprovable. The mode of operation within the scientific community is to postulate a theory until something is proven or disproven. But the spiritual mind is different. It will continue to look to the counsel of God, neither embracing nor denying theories of men when the scriptures are silent on a particular matter. The spiritual mind realizes some things will never be revealed. This is especially true with the things that belong to God only.

The secret things belong to the Lord our God, but those things which are revealed belong to us and to our children forever, that we may do all the words of this law. (Deut. 29:29)

Now notice carefully the exposition of Paul to the Romans in regard to the restoration of God's creation as we study Romans 8.

GLORY THROUGH SUFFERING

For I consider that the sufferings of this present time are not worthy to be compared with the glory which shall be revealed in <u>us</u>. (Romans 8:18)

In examining the context of Romans 8 there are two distinct areas of concern. The first is in the suffering that Adam's sin caused for the whole creation of God. The suffering was not just man, even though man was the guilty party, in bringing about the curse of sin. But because of Adam's fall the whole creation suffered as well as man. In verse 18 the apostle gives us the following information. He says the present sufferings cannot be compared with the future glory to be revealed in God's redeemed humanity.

In this verse he may be speaking only of the sufferings of mankind, or it may include the entirety of the whole creation. But whichever it is, it is made clear the sufferings will be light and insignificant when compared with the eternal weight of glory to be finally realized in the deliverance of those in bondage.

For our light affliction, which is but for a moment, is working for us a far more exceeding and eternal weight of glory. (2 Cor. 4:17)

The "us" in Romans 8:18 is obviously to be understood as redeemed humanity, those saved by the blood of Christ. A wondrous glory is to be revealed in the redeemed children of God. It is a glory so magnificent it could never be compared with all the ongoing sufferings of mortal existence. The afflictions of the faithful are as a moment of light affliction in comparison with the eternal weight of glory revealed in the hereafter. Afflictions and sufferings with Christ are prerequisites to glorifying God. In order to share in the glory, God's people must share in the sufferings of Christ.

This is a faithful saying: For if we died with Him, we shall also live with Him. If we endure, we shall also reign with Him. If we deny Him, He also will deny us. (2 Timothy 2:11–12)

Yet if anyone suffers as a Christian, let him not be ashamed, but let him glorify God in this matter. (1 Peter 4:16)

For Christians who take part in the first resurrection and spiritual reign with God's Son, becoming heirs of God and joint heirs with Christ is not a new concept. Shared glory through suffering is a main theme of the Christian experience. At the end of time, and after the bodily resurrection of the redeemed to immortality, the revealing of the glory of the redeemed in Christ will be seen by the whole creation.

For the earnest expectation of the creation eagerly waits for the revealing of the sons of God. (Romans 8:19)

This revealing will have been accomplished as a result of lives that were once enslaved to sin, but were then made free by the blood of Christ to subsequently become enslaved to the discipleship of Jesus. The adopted sonship through Christ will result in a joint inheritance with the Lord Jesus.

And if children, then heirs—heirs of God and joint heirs with Christ, if indeed we suffer with Him, that we may also be glorified together. (Romans 8:17)

Glory through suffering with Christ is the grand story of the human experience. The redeemer and the redeemed will all be the same in future revealed glory. The writer of Hebrews writes beautifully of the ultimate common inheritance of the Sanctifier and those who are being sanctified, showing Jesus was perfected through suffering. In every way Jesus will become a brother to those redeemed by His blood, sharing His inheritance with them. Jesus insisted that in *all things* His desire was to be made like His brethren.

For it was fitting for Him, for whom are all things and by whom are all things, in bringing many sons to glory, to make the captain of their salvation perfect through sufferings. <u>For both He who sanctifies and those who are being sanctified are all of one</u>, for which reason He is not ashamed to call them brethren, saying: "I will declare Your name to My brethren; In the midst of the assembly I will sing praise to You." And again: "I will put My trust in Him." And again: "Here am I and the children whom God has given Me." Inasmuch then as the children have partaken of flesh and blood, He Himself likewise shared in the same, that through death He might destroy him who had the power of death, that is, the devil, and release those who through fear of death were all their lifetime subject to bondage. For indeed He does not give aid to angels, but He does give aid to the seed of Abraham. Therefore, in all things <u>He had to be made like His brethren</u>, that He might be a merciful and faithful High Priest in things pertaining to God, to make propitiation for the sins of the people. For in that He Himself has suffered, being tempted, He is able to aid those who are tempted. (Hebrews 2:10–18)

One of my favorite passages of scripture, which sums up the final glory to be revealed in the children of God, is found in 1 John 3.

Behold what manner of love the Father has bestowed on us, that we should be called children of God! Therefore the world does not know us, because it did not know Him. Beloved, now we are children of God; and it has not yet been revealed what <u>we shall be</u>, but we know that when He is revealed, we shall be like Him, for we shall see Him as He is. And everyone who has this hope in Him purifies himself, just as He is pure. (1 John 3:1–3)

The revelation of the glory of God's redeemed will come only after the bodily resurrection to immortality. But we can know that whatever <u>we shall be</u>, it will be like our Lord. He suffered the pain and death meant for us because of our sin. He died for us in order that we might be worthy to live for Him. He was put to death in the flesh, but made alive by the Spirit. Only by His death are we enabled to die to the flesh and to be made alive by the Spirit.

For Christ also suffered once for sins, the just for the unjust, that He might bring us to God, being put to death in the flesh but made alive by the Spirit (1 Peter 3:18)

Now to Him who is able to do exceedingly abundantly above all that we ask or think, according to the power that works in us, to Him be glory in the church by Christ Jesus to all generations, forever and ever. Amen. (Ephesians 3:20–21)

THE EXPECTATION OF THE CREATION

For the earnest expectation of the creation eagerly waits for the revealing of the sons of God. (Romans 8:19)

Expectation can arouse human emotions to the point of jubilation, or it can create great fear and dread. An example of the difference might be a four-year-old child joyfully opening a birthday present from her parents, as opposed to sobbing vehemently when being separated from her parents by immigration authorities. Expectation may bring either joy or fear, but it will always bring an emotional response.

When we expect something, it will either be something we desire or the opposite. Expectation will create either joy or dread. Hope, the anchor of the soul, is born out of expectation. But in order for expectation to produce hope, it has to be accompanied by desire. We will not be hopeful about a thing that is undesirable to us. The scriptural fact that the "earnest expectation" of the creation "eagerly waits …" attests to the hope of the thing waiting. In this case, because the creation "eagerly" waits, we know there is a desire in its expectation.

And what is the earnest expectation of the creation? It is "the revealing of the sons of God." This means the creation spoken of in verse 19 is obviously God's creation, but it does not include the sons of God (i.e., those who are sanctified and redeemed). This is made even clearer later on in the chapter. The *creation* would almost surely mean *all* God created in the natural or the material universe that was either untouched by sin or redeemed from it. By the wording of the verse 19 we are made to understand the revealing of the sons of God is very important to the rest of creation. There is an earnest expectation on the part of the nonhuman creation. And because of its earnest expectation, the creation is eagerly waiting for something. The thing the creation is earnestly expecting and eagerly waiting for is the revealing of the sons of God.

When someone or something is in earnest expectation, eagerly awaiting a particular event, this necessitates some form of communication for it to consciously expect the event. It would obviously also necessitate a degree of knowledge and reason. And any possibility for any created thing to know, reason and communicate would come from the power of God, which is now completely vested in His Son.

And Jesus came and spoke to them, saying, "All authority [power] has been given to Me in heaven and on earth. (Matthew 28:18)

Man can only communicate to the extent that God will grant the ability to do so. The simple definition of communication is the sharing of information. God gives humans five primary senses or sensors in order to be able to communicate. However, the rest of the creation of God, especially those deemed to be living, possess various kinds of senses with which to communicate.

The following article is about the communication and socialization abilities of whales. This is just one of perhaps millions of ways God has designed His creation to communicate.

Whales are very social creatures that travel in groups called "pods." They use a variety of noises to communicate and socialize with each other. The three main types of sounds made by whales are clicks, whistles, and pulsed calls.

Clicks are believed to be for navigation and identifying physical surroundings. When the sound waves bounce off of an object, they return to the whale, allowing the whale to identify the shape of the object. Clicks can even help to differentiate between friendly creatures and predators. Clicks have also been observed during social interactions, suggesting they may also have a communicative function.

Whistles and pulsed calls are used during social activities. Pulsed calls are more frequent and sound like squeaks, screams, and squawks to the human ear. Differing vocal "dialects" have been found to exist between different pods within the same whale population. This is most likely so that whales can differentiate between whales within their pods and strangers.

Whales also use their tails and fins to make loud slapping noises on the surface of the water to communicate nonverbally. The sound can be heard for hundreds of meters below the surface and may be a warning sign of aggression or a tool to scare schools of fish together, making them an easier meal.

In the Stellwagen Bank National Marine Sanctuary, NOAA scientists attached sensors to whales in order to track their movement patterns. They hope to learn about the whales' behavior and communication as well as to observe how human interaction affects their behavior. ("Why Do Whales Make Sounds?" National Ocean Service [NOAA], US Dept. of Commerce)

Humans know very little about how God deals with His nonhuman creation. Normally when we assume something is impossible, it's just that—an assumption. Do you think people who lived during American colonial times could have ever been convinced a man would walk on the moon? Could they have conceived that we could communicate with a loved one hundreds of miles away and that we could hear their voices from that distance or see a video of them speaking?

Only God is a creator. Man creates nothing. Man only discovers a few of the multiplied billions of things the Almighty Creator has created. Beyond the relatively few scientific discoveries, there are infinite possibilities within the created universe only the Creator knows about. Man will come to know only a few of the things that could be known. But we can know through His Word that the Creator cares about *all* of His creation.

Are not five sparrows sold for two copper coins? And not one of them is forgotten before God. (Luke 12:6)

Who among us, having the slightest knowledge of the loving and merciful nature of our Heavenly Father, would say He is unconcerned about the nonhuman creation? Also, which of us would be willing to say God created the nonhuman creation only for a purpose to be used, abused and eventually to be destroyed forever?

For these reasons I am totally convinced the Lord not only is concerned with the consequential inabilities of man in dealing with his sinful nature, but He communicates and directs the entire natural universe in matters connected to the effects of man's sin. It is reasonable to assume a part of this communication would be that the creation knows of its condition, as well as having an understanding to give them hope of restoration through the blood of Jesus. I believe this is exactly what Romans 8 teaches.

THE CREATION IS SUBJECTED IN HOPE

For the creation was subjected to futility, not willingly, but because of <u>Him</u> who subjected it in hope. (Romans 8:20)

Man has been subjected to the futility of sin's curse by the power of his own will and choice. Humanity is powerless except for the power to choose to submit to the power of God. By sinning against God man chose to defy the authority of God. This was not the case with the rest of God's earthly creation. All of the rest of creation was subjected to the futility or vanity that man's sin brought into the world, but theirs was *not willingly*. Those making up the nonhuman creation were subjected to sin's curse of pain, degradation and death because of it being allowed of God in the service of His divine purpose. It was because of Him (God) that they were subjected to this groaning and travailing in pain until now. The pain began when Adam sinned, and it will continue until the Lord returns.

For we know that the whole creation groans and labors with birth pangs together until now. (Rom. 8:22)

God does not act purposelessly. We may never fully know God's purpose to subject the creation to sin's curse, but it was done with purpose by a Creator with complete foreknowledge. Why, then, would anyone think it a radical idea that the Creator would deliver His creation out of this corruptible situation that man's sin caused? But what else could it mean in that He subjected it in hope? Where is the hope in a miserable present existence and eternal death in the future, especially as we see their bondage was allowed by the Creator? Is it an absolutely reasonable thought to think their Creator would not desire their eternal destruction? Only He Who has subjected these creatures to this bondage can deliver them from it. Will their Creator allow them to be used, abused and finally permanently destroyed? Are these not reasonable questions for the minds of those who are partakers of the divine nature of Christ to entertain?

The majority of the Christian community obviously gives little thought to the mercy of God in connection with delivering the creation out of its misery. I say this because of the minimal amount of written attention given to the fate of the nonhuman creation. And even more surprising is that it happens even in the face of so much scriptural evidence teaching the restoration of the creation in very literal and explicit language. Almost all religious students and teachers concentrate on the ability of the blood of Christ to deliver the human family. And although this might seem to be the thing of primary concern, this should not diminish our attention concerning the mercy of the Creator toward all creation. The idea that the blood of Christ could have the power to deliver the rest of creation is rarely mentioned. I believe the honest students of the Word, those seeking its truths, should readily agree with the following statements.

1. If the Lord chooses to deliver the rest of the creation through the atoning merits of the death of Christ, no harm will be done to anyone or anything else.

2. The restoration of the creation will in no way diminish the power of the blood of Christ, but rather serve to further show its power, if by it all of the nonhuman creation is delivered and restored.

3. Neither will it diminish the power of God's love and mercy for His creation if complete restoration occurs, but only serve as a greater witness to it.

4. From the beginning of creation God's desire was never for any of His creation to suffer and die.

Is there anything in the language of the Holy Spirit to cause one to believe the Creator is willing for any of His innocent creation to suffer eternal death? Paul tells the Roman church the *whole creation* will be delivered.

Because the creation itself also will be delivered from the bondage of corruption into the glorious liberty of the children of God. For we know that the whole creation groans and labors with birth pangs together until now. Not only that, but we also who have the first-fruits of the Spirit, even we ourselves groan within ourselves, eagerly waiting for the adoption, the redemption of our body. (Romans 8:21–23)

The reason for basically discounting the value of the rest of the creation has much to do with religious doctrinal tradition, which is always the case when parts of the Bible are circumvented, watered down and ignored. Open spiritual minds desire to know the truth of God's will at any cost. The sectarian mind wants to defend its doctrines at all costs. The sad truth is that traditional religious thinking spends very little time on glorifying and extolling the love and mercy of the Creator. But no matter how long it might be ignored, God's Word will continue to say *all things* in heaven and on earth will be *gathered together* in Christ!

That in the dispensation of the fullness of the times He might <u>gather together in one all things in Christ</u>, both which are in heaven and which are on earth—in Him. (Ephesians 1:10)

So the Creator has subjected the creation to its present pain brought on by the consequences of human sin. This is the bad news for the present. But there is glorious hope for the future! The hope lies not in the ability of the creation to deliver itself from the corruptive consequence of sin. It has been given no power in this respect. Nor is the hope in waiting for fallen man to regenerate and purify his own heart or to devise a plan for his own deliverance. Rather, the hope is in the love of God through His Son. It will be *in Christ* that the power of "gathering together in one all things" will be made possible for man and the rest of the creation, both in heaven and on earth. All things in heaven and on earth have been subjected to the awful deteriorative effects of man's sin. And all will be blessed through the power of Christ's sinless life and sacrificial death!

For we know that the whole creation groans and labors with birth pangs together until now. Not only that, but we also who have the first-fruits of the Spirit, even we ourselves groan within ourselves, eagerly waiting for the adoption, the redemption of our body. (Romans 8:22–23)

Therefore the creation, by not willingly (not because of its own sin) having been party to the corruptive influence of sin, has been subjected in hope during this bondage caused by sin. And because of having been subjected in hope, the creation will be delivered, according to the true Word of God, from corruption into the glorious liberty of the children of God!

For the creation was subjected to futility, not willingly, but because of Him who subjected it in hope; because the creation itself also will be delivered from the bondage of corruption into the glorious liberty of the children of God. (Romans 8:20–21)

Any deliverance for any of creation, including humanity, will be only by the atoning merits of the blood of Christ. Reconciliation, resurrection and restoration will be accomplished only by the innocent sacrifice of Jesus, the Lamb of God. There is no other power to satisfy divine justice in the performance of cleansing from sin and its consequences. Blood was always the ultimate cleansing agent used by the Lord God to cleanse and nullify the condemnation of sinful rebellion against His will. After Adam and Eve had sinned against God's law in the Garden of Eden, they were given garments to wear. The garments were made of animal skins designed by God Himself and given for the purpose of hiding the shame of their nakedness.

Also for Adam and his wife the Lord God made tunics of skin, and clothed them. (Genesis 3:21)

Their eyes had been opened to the shame of being naked before God. The sacrifice of the innocent life from among God's creation was the first scriptural account of bloodshed within the entire community of the creation of God. It was also the beginning of the awful consequences of the curse God placed on the creation because of man's sin.

Another example of the power of blood, symbolic of the blood of Christ, is when God sent plagues upon Egypt in the deliverance of the children of Israel from Egyptian bondage. The account of this story is found in the book of Exodus.

For I will pass through the land of Egypt on that night, and will strike all the firstborn in the land of Egypt, both man and <u>beast</u>; and against all the gods of Egypt I will execute judgment: I am the Lord. Now the blood shall be a sign for you on the houses where you are. And when I see the blood, I will pass over you; and the plague shall not be on you to destroy you when I strike the land of Egypt. (Exodus 12:12–13)

The blood of a sacrificed lamb was to be placed on all of the houses of God's people. The presence of the blood was to identify them in order for the death angel to pass over the house, preventing the destruction of the firstborn son of the family inside. The Egyptian people were not given this message. And as a result every firstborn Egyptian son died on that fateful night.

But it was not just the human firstborn sons of the Egyptians who suffered death. It included "both man and beast; and against all the gods of Egypt." Therefore the presence of the blood saved the firstborn animals of the Israelites from death.

A key to understanding any Bible verse or passage is being careful not to dismiss as impossible that which is being said, but rather to continue to gather information, accepting any and all scriptural evidence for or against it before making conclusions. Many things in the Bible are very clear. These things must be taken at face value until or unless other proofs are given to modify or clarify.

For example, it is clear what the Bible says in Acts 3:21 about restoration. It says there will be the restoration of all things. We have no choice but to accept all things to mean all things unless there are exceptions given elsewhere in the Bible. We may find cause to argue about what all things means in the context given, or by the evidence of other scriptural information, but we cannot honestly argue it is meaningless or unnecessary. If it was meaningless or unnecessary it would have never been written by the inspiration of God's Spirit. But we actually do count it meaningless and unnecessary when we choose to ignore it for fear of disturbing preconceived sectarian notions. Think about this. How many sermons have you heard about the restoration of all things from Acts 3 or elsewhere in the Bible? If the answer is never, it's certainly not because it is not addressed in the Word. But there must be a reason if you've never heard any teaching on this subject, as important as it is to the heart of God.

How many people talk about God's creation being "delivered from its bondage of corruption into the glorious liberty of the children of God?" This is something God's Word clearly talks about. Some older commentaries make a few comments on this subject. But mostly they ignore the idea of the restoration of creation by indicating the scriptures don't mean what they say. Traditional church doctrine has not included, for the most part, the restoration of all things in its teachings. However, since there is something being taught and something to be revealed in Romans 8, we need to harmonize the scriptures around the passage and find the truth of its teaching.

By taking Acts 3:21, which says "the restoration of all things," and putting it together with the information Paul gives in Romans 8, we can begin to draw some very solid conclusions. Romans 8 talks about the "bondage of corruption" and the groaning and travailing of creation. Verse 22 tells us "the whole creation groans and labors with birth pangs together until now." This curse was brought on all of the earthly creation when man sinned. The curse had continued up until Paul wrote the letter to the Romans, and it remains today. So by the foregoing statements it is beyond reasonable to conclude the whole creation is under consideration. But what does this actually mean? Is it really teaching that all of the whole creation that has no sin is to be restored?

The second part of the context in Romans 8 is the revealing of the glory of the children of God through Christ's suffering death, burial and resurrection to an immortal existence.

THE GLORY REVEALED IN US

For I consider that the sufferings of this present time are not worthy to be compared with <u>the glory which shall be revealed in us</u>. (Romans 8:18)

This is a very important point. The fact that Jesus could suffer death but overcome it through a sinless life meant hope for all those willing to suffer and identify with Him. The scriptures have quite a lot to say about the revealing of God's people by way of identifying with Christ in His death. The glory of the Lord that would be revealed through the redemption in Christ was spoken of by the prophets.

The glory of the Lord shall be revealed, and all flesh shall see it together; for the mouth of the Lord has spoken. (Isaiah 40:5)

It is noteworthy that "all flesh" together would witness the glory of the Lord revealed. In the same way as God had decreed that He would pour out His Spirit upon all flesh in Joel 2, He has also decreed that His glory would be revealed to all flesh and they would see it together. It would not be revealed just to the Jews but to the Gentiles as well. The gift of His Holy Spirit (Acts 2:38) made His glory known.

We do, however, speak a message of wisdom among the mature, but not the wisdom of this age or of the rulers of this age, who are coming to nothing. No, we declare God's wisdom, a mystery that has been hidden and that God destined for our glory before time began. None of the rulers of this age understood it, for if they had, they would not have crucified the Lord of glory. However, as it is written: "What no eye has seen, what no ear has heard, and what no human mind has conceived" the things God has prepared for those who love him—these are the things God has revealed to us by his Spirit. The Spirit searches all things, even the deep things of God. (1 Cor. 2:6–10)

From the beginning of time the revealing of God's mystery of redemption had been hidden from the minds of men, even though God's redemptive work through Christ was destined for our glory before time began. Before Christ, the mind of humanity was in darkness as to how God would ultimately deal with the consequence of eternal death brought on by sin. Those living in the days of Noah only knew physical death as an expiration of life, without any hope of redemption. No doubt some of them longed for a restoration of life, but no explicit promise was given from God that would give clear evidence of immortality, or how that might be accomplished. Only through Jesus were life and immortality brought to light.

But it has now been revealed through the appearing of our Savior, Christ Jesus, who has destroyed death and has brought life and immortality to light through the gospel. (2 Timothy 1:10)

A path leading to deathlessness was spoken of in the book of Proverbs. But the way God would devise redemption through Christ was not clear.

In the way of righteousness there is life; along that path is immortality. (Proverbs 12:28)

Job believed his eyes would see God because of his trust in the mercy of his Creator. This was the situation with all of the heroes of faith mentioned in the Old Testament.

And after my skin has been destroyed, yet in my flesh I will see God. Job 19:26

The eternal glorious hope of the righteous, through faith in Christ, is tied to the willingness to suffer with and for Christ. When the sacrificial sufferings of Jesus truly become our hope, and when we gladly partake of His suffering love, we then can expect to be glorified by it.

But rejoice to the extent that you partake of Christ's sufferings, that when His glory is revealed, you may also be glad with exceeding joy. (1 Peter 4:13)

In Romans 8:18 Paul tells of the glory that shall be revealed in us. This is not glory to be revealed for us, but in us. The righteous saved of Christ will be a product of glory!

CONCLUDING THOUGHT

A lot of people question whether the nonhuman creation will be restored. Ask yourself three questions. Does God love all of His creation? Does God have the power to restore all of His creation? Since the creation was subjected to the curse of man's sin and has groaned in pain and death since, why would God eternally destroy it?

CHAPTER 13

WHEN WILL THESE THINGS BE?

NO ONE KNOWS

I was born and raised in the Ozarks of Missouri. In the 1950s this region of the country experienced several years of severe heat and drought. One day during this time, Dad told Mom about a religious neighbor with whom he'd had a conversation. And because Dad had quite a lot of faith in the biblical knowledge of this man, he was somewhat disturbed the man had told him the ensuing drought was a sign of the end. He told Dad the Bible prophesied seven years of drought shortly before the Lord came back.

The extremely hot and dry weather pattern had gone on for several years. Dad's corn crop, which accounted for much of our livelihood, was at the point where a few more rainless days would have done it in. However, a few days after Dad's speaking with the man, the windows of heaven seemed to open up to give us the much-needed rain for our corn crop.

I remember being in the house with my parents and siblings as the rain poured down for several hours that day. We all were very excited the rain had finally come. After it had rained hard for most of the day and Dad was totally convinced the drought had been broken, he began to speak to Mom about the man who had prophesied the end. In the midst of our family's happy conversation of thankfulness about the rain, Dad's voice suddenly took a very serious tone. He said, calling out the neighbor's name, "He didn't know what he was talking about. I doubt if the Bible even says that."

END TIME VERSUS THE DESTRUCTION OF JERUSALEM

There can never be enough emphasis put on trusting the Word of God over the word of man. No matter how well intentioned, most folks are hindered by the impulses of the flesh in their expressions of knowledge. When we are only counseled by humans, no matter how sincere they may be, we need to consider the limits of their intellectual abilities and traditional backgrounds. But when we allow God's Word to guide us, our spiritual mind can come to know some things regarding the time frames of prophetic events mentioned in the Bible. But these will never be discerned by simply accepting a sectarian doctrine that has evolved by tradition. Neither will they ever be understood by way of an unregenerate or fleshly mind. And they will not be revealed in a personal miraculous revelation from the Lord that circumvents His inspired written word. Learning about God's revealed will takes spiritually minded desire along with study, prayer and meditation. The Lord has chosen to give His revelation through the rightly divided Word of God.

Be diligent to present yourself approved to God, a worker who does not need to be ashamed, rightly dividing the word of truth. (2 Timothy 2:15)

All Scripture is given by inspiration of God, and is profitable for doctrine, for reproof, for correction, for instruction in righteousness, that the man of God may be complete, thoroughly equipped for every good work. (2 Timothy 3:16–17)

An important key in studying God's word is to let the Bible be its own commentary. When we rightly divide the word of truth, we do this very thing. Dependency on man-made ideas and doctrines closes off the desire to look directly at the Bible. It is always good to listen to other opinions and interpretations of the scriptures. But what we read or hear from the minds of men should always be tested and proved by the Word of God.

Test all things; hold fast what is good. (1 Thess. 5:21)

The Bible itself gives clues of interpretation. For example, the seventy weeks of Daniel gives clues to the understanding of some prophesies relating to certain time periods. It is almost universally accepted that a day represents a year in calculating the fulfillment of this prophecy (Dan. 9:24–27). The day–year principle is a method in the interpretation of Bible prophecy in which a day in prophecy is considered symbolic of a year of actual time. We can be certain some of the days of prophecy represent years because the Bible actually tells us this.

But neither the disciples of Jesus nor the early church were allowed to know the exact time when certain events would occur. Jesus makes this clear with the following information about an event He speaks to His disciples about.

But about that day or hour no one knows, not even the angels in heaven, nor the Son, but only the Father. (Matt. 24:36)

Therefore keep watch, because you do not know the day or the hour. (Matt. 25:13)

In these verses Jesus may have been referring to the end of the last age, when He visibly returns to earth for His people, or perhaps this was a reference to the destruction of Jerusalem in AD 70. Most Christians probably believe this event to be the Lord's visible return to earth at the end of the world. Some believe this refers to the destruction of Jerusalem, which happened within the lifetime of some of Jesus' listeners. Both views can seem plausible when casually reading this part of the gospel of Matthew. Those believing it to refer to the end of time might argue Jesus surely would know the exact time of the destruction of Jerusalem. This may or may not be true. But the same argument could be made about the end of time. Why would Jesus know the exact time of the destruction of Jerusalem, but not the time of the end of the world? Both views have a certain amount of plausibility, but both views are not correct. It takes a lot of time, study and meditation to discern the prophecies of these two events. Most people are not willing to put forth the effort needed to arrive at an educated conclusion. I certainly do not profess to know all the answers.

Daniel was not to know when his own vision would be fulfilled (Daniel 12:8–10), but he was told it would be revealed to God's people at a later date. Some things cannot be understood in the present moment. This is true simply because it is not time for God to reveal it. But sometimes this is not the problem. The problem is sometimes simply a mind lacking the spiritual capacity to be enlightened by the Word.

In Matthew 24, as well as the other gospels dealing with the AD 70 destruction of Jerusalem, Jesus speaks rather specifically about events that would lead up to this event. Probably one of the reasons for a greater degree of specificity was because it was necessary for Jewish Christians in Jerusalem to know about the events leading up to this destructive event in order to escape its peril. On the other hand, in connection to the Lord's visible return to earth, it was not necessary to warn the disciples living at the time Jesus spoke, for their lives would have long since passed when the end of the world would occur. So for this reason and for other reasons I will discuss, I believe Jesus primarily referred to the destruction of Jerusalem. But this does not mean the chapter has nothing to do with the end of time.

In regard to the destruction of Jerusalem, the Lord leaves little doubt this event would take place within the lifetime of some of those with whom He was speaking. He therefore gave them specific instructions as to what they would see and should speak, as well as where they should go and what they should do. Because this was a warning of almost immediate consequence, it would warrant immediate and detailed instructions in order to ensure deliverance for the faithful of Israel.

So when you see standing in the holy place "the abomination that causes desolation" spoken of through the prophet Daniel—let the reader understand— then let those who are in Judea flee to the mountains. Let no one on the housetop go down to take anything out of the house. Let no one in the field go back to get their cloak. How dreadful it will be in those days for pregnant women and nursing mothers! Pray that your flight will not take place in winter or on the Sabbath. (Matthew 24:15–20) (NIV) (*Abomination* in the Greek indicates that which is disgusting and is usually associated with that which defiles or is idolatrous. The Hebrew meaning is associated with pagan idols.) Desolation is an uninhabitable and devastated condition. The great prophet Daniel spoke of the abomination of desolation in three different chapters in the book of Daniel. He was speaking of the same event Jesus had talked about to His disciples. We know this because the Lord said, "When you see the abomination of desolation spoken of by Daniel the prophet."

In Daniel 9 the prophet talks about a covenant being confirmed with many for "one seven," or for one week as in the KJV. In the middle of the week an end would come to "sacrifice and offering." He says it would be "at the temple" that the abomination causing desolation would be set up. And he seems to say there would be an end "decreed" (commanded or directed) and "poured out on him" who causes the abominable action.

He will confirm a covenant with many for one "seven." In the middle of the "seven" he will put an end to sacrifice and offering. And at the temple he will set up an abomination that causes desolation, until the end that is decreed is poured out on him. (Daniel 9:27) (NIV)

His armed forces will rise up to desecrate the temple fortress and will abolish the daily sacrifice. Then they will set up the abomination that causes desolation. (Daniel 11:31) (NIV)

From the time that the daily sacrifice is abolished and the abomination that causes desolation is set up, there will be 1,290 days. (Daniel 12:11) (NIV)

However, without careful consideration of other prophetic scriptures, the destruction of Jerusalem and the Lord's visible coming can be easily confused in some passages. A lot of the things the Lord said about the destruction of Jerusalem are easily mistaken for references to the end of the world. Nonetheless, the destruction of Jerusalem is clearly the primary focus of the Lord's directives and warnings in these gospel accounts. Any words that might have been spoken by the Lord in regard to the end of time would probably be applicable to the entirety of the Christian age.

The statements of Jesus in Matthew 24, as well as the other gospel accounts mentioning the impending doom of the Jews and Jerusalem as opposed to the signs of the end of time, have been a mystery to many from the beginning. The Lord's disciples were perplexed when trying to differentiate between these two prophetic events, and Bible scholars have remained puzzled throughout the history of the church when they have tried to separate the two contextually in the gospels. The destruction of Jerusalem in AD 70 was probably a type of the end of the world.

However, one thing is evident: both events deal with God's wrath upon sin and the rejection of His Son. Both also deal with the monumental consequences of failing to heed God's warnings against unbelief. The warnings of the destruction of Jerusalem were intended only for the Jews, whereas the warnings of the end of the world would probably be directed more to the Gentiles or to the whole world. I would not profess to be sure about what specifically pertained to the downfall of the Jewish polity in all instances of prophecy, as opposed to the final destruction of the world at the end of time. But it is clear the Lord warns about both events.

The epistles of Paul and Peter deal extensively with God's wrath on a sinful world that unceasingly caused tribulation for the people of God. The vengeance of the Lord on evil in the final chapter of God's wrath will be inflicted as a result of not knowing God and not obeying the gospel of our Lord Jesus Christ. Unlike the destruction of Jerusalem, the vengeance of the Almighty at the end of time will not just be a temporary physical punishment, but *eternal destruction from the presence of the Lord and from the glory of His power*. It will not just kill the body of the wicked but it will also *destroy both body and soul in hell*. The coming of Jesus at the end of time is made clear in the apostolic letters to the church. Paul's letter to the Thessalonian church is one example.

And to give you who are troubled rest with us when the Lord Jesus is revealed from heaven with His mighty angels, in flaming fire taking vengeance on those who do not know God, and on those who do not obey the gospel of our Lord Jesus Christ. These shall be punished with everlasting destruction from the presence of the Lord and from the glory of His power, when He comes, in that Day, to be glorified in His saints and to be admired among all those who believe, because our testimony among you was believed. (2 Thess. 1:7–10)

THE DAY OF THE LORD

The phrase "the day of the Lord" is used throughout the scriptures. Although this phrase has been used to predict the visitation of God's wrath on the sins of Israel and other nations at various times for temporal punishment, Peter obviously has the climatic final judgment in mind in the following passage.

But the day of the Lord will come as a thief in the night, in which the heavens will pass away with a great noise, and the elements will melt with fervent heat; both the earth and the works that are in it will be burned up. Therefore, since all these things will be dissolved, what manner of persons ought you to be in holy conduct and godliness, looking for and hastening the coming of the day of God, because of which the heavens will be dissolved, being on fire, and the elements will melt with fervent heat? Nevertheless we, according to His promise, look for new heavens and a new earth in which righteousness dwells. (2 Peter 3:10–13)

This clear passage of scripture tells us what will happen on that final day, the day of the Lord. It tells us the day of the Lord will come as a thief in the night. Jesus is coming back to earth and His arrival will be unexpected to the vast majority of humanity. There will be a great noise and the elements will melt with fervent heat. Nothing could be plainer. When the heavens pass away it will cause a great noise and they will melt and be dissolved. They will be on fire. They will be destroyed, but they will be replaced with new heavens and a new earth made not with temporal elements, but with that which is indestructible. Righteousness will replace sin and evil on the new earth.

However, the scriptures do not give us the exact time (day or hour) of the end of the world. Ample prophetic warnings are given in both the Old and New Testaments concerning the coming finality of God's wrath on the world. These warnings are given in much the same way as Jesus warned of the destruction of Jerusalem in the gospels. But, regarding the end of the world, the warnings are not given with the immediate consequences that seem to be shown in Jerusalem's destruction. Instead, there seems to be only the warnings of certain woeful signs and conditions preceding the end of time, most of which are spiritual rather than earthly calamities. Paul speaks of some of the signs occurring in the last days before the Lord comes back to earth. These signs speak to the increasing moral depravity that will exist, not unlike the condition of the world in the days of Noah.

But know this, that in the last days perilous times will come: For men will be lovers of themselves, lovers of money, boasters, proud, blasphemers, disobedient to parents, unthankful, unholy, unloving, unforgiving, slanderers, without self-control, brutal, despisers of good, traitors, headstrong, haughty, lovers of pleasure rather than lovers of God, having a form of godliness but denying its power. And from such people turn away! (2 Timothy 3:1–5)

Rather than speaking about the "end of time," Daniel speaks of the "time of the end" by citing periods of events and conditions rather than an exact time or of the end being of immediate consequence. He is told to shut up the words and seal the book until the time of the end. This seemingly looks forward to a certain point near the end of time.

But you, Daniel, shut up the words, and seal the book until the time of the end; many shall run to and fro, and knowledge shall increase. (Daniel 12:4)

However, as we read in Daniel 12:8–10, it seems to infer that at the time of the end the mystery would be revealed to God's people by Daniel saying the wise shall understand.

Although I heard, I did not understand. Then I said, "My lord, what shall be the end of these things?" And he said, "Go your way, Daniel, for the words are closed up and sealed till the time of the end. Many shall be purified, made white, and refined, but the wicked shall do wickedly; and none of the wicked shall understand, but the wise shall understand." (Daniel 12:8–10)

In chapter 11 we find a narrative of world events that seem to begin with the then present day, but that would eventually lead up to the general bodily resurrection as chapter 12 begins. Almost certainly this foretells the general resurrection of the dead at the second coming of Christ.

At that time Michael shall stand up, the great prince who stands watch over the sons of your people; and there shall be a time of trouble, Such as never was since there was a nation, even to that time. And at that time your people shall be delivered, everyone who is found written in the book. And many of those who sleep in the dust of the earth shall awake, some to everlasting life, some to shame and everlasting contempt. Those who are wise shall shine like the brightness of the firmament, and those who turn many to righteousness like the stars forever and ever. (Daniel 12:1–3)

The writing of Daniel tells us the Babylonian Empire under King Nebuchadnezzar was the foremost world power when Daniel and the Jews were taken into Babylonian captivity. Later, during the reign of Belshazzar, who was probably the grandson of Nebuchadnezzar, the mighty Babylonian power was lost to the Medes and Persians. Eventually the kingdom fell to the rule of the Greeks and then to the Romans.

In chapter 10 Daniel begins the account of the vision he received from God. And here he seems to be given a clear understanding of the things pertaining to certain world events that would continue until the end of time. And as I noted earlier, this vision would span time from the then present day and continue forward until the bodily resurrection of the dead, which is spoken of as chapter 12 begins. This is one of the few times, if not the only time, that the general resurrection of the dead is specifically alluded to in the Old Testament. Notice Daniel was given to understand that "the appointed time was long," meaning far out into the future. But he evidently was not given an exact way to calculate specifically when the end would come. We know this by his question to the messenger concerning what shall be the end of these things. But this seems to be the same end Paul writes about in 1 Corinthians, which was the end of the world at the resurrection.

For since by man came death, by Man also came the resurrection of the dead. For as in Adam all die, even so in Christ all shall be made alive. But each one in his own order: Christ the first fruits, afterward those who are Christ's at His coming. Then comes the end, when He delivers the kingdom to God the Father, when He puts an end to all rule and all authority and power. (1 Corinthians 15:21–24)

So Daniel understood the general message of the vision, but was not given an exact time when the end would be, only that the appointed time was long.

In the third year of Cyrus king of Persia a message was revealed to Daniel, whose name was called Belshazzar. The message was true, but the appointed time

was long; and he understood the message, and had understanding of the vision.
(Daniel 10:1)

Whatever the implications of the prophetic message received by Daniel, it caused him great pain. And because of the revelation Daniel went into a state of mourning and fasting for three weeks. Let's reiterate the scene in chapter 10.

In the third year of Cyrus king of Persia a message was revealed to Daniel, whose name was called Belshazzar. The message was true, but the appointed time was long; and he understood the message, and had understanding of the vision. In those days I, Daniel, was mourning three full weeks. I ate no pleasant food; no meat or wine came into my mouth, nor did I anoint myself at all, till three whole weeks were fulfilled. (Daniel 10:1–3)

Daniel received this visionary revelation through angelic messengers from the Lord.

While he was by the side of the Tigris River he beheld a man clothed in linen. The man was girded with gold, his body was like beryl, and his face had the appearance of lightening, his eyes like torches of fire, with arms and feet like the color of bronze, and his words sounded like the voice of a multitude. (Daniel 11:4–6)

The key to understanding the mystery of how long until the end was obviously understanding the symbolic words of the messengers from God. Listen to the answer of one of the heavenly messengers as someone else asks how long it would be until the complete fulfillment of the vision. In order to understand the fulfillment of the vision, the reader must understand the following prophecy of chapter 12.

Then I, Daniel, looked; and there stood two others, one on this riverbank and the other on that riverbank. And one said to the man clothed in linen, who was above the waters of the river, "How long shall the fulfillment of these wonders be?" Then I heard the man clothed in linen, who was above the waters of the river, when he held up his right hand and his left hand to heaven, and swore by Him who lives forever, that it shall be for a time, times, and half a time; and when the power of the holy people has been completely shattered, all these things shall be finished. Although I heard, I did not understand. Then I said, "My lord, what shall be the end of these things?" And he said, "Go your way, Daniel, for the words are closed up and sealed till the time of the end. Many shall be purified, made white, and refined, but the wicked shall do wickedly; and none of the wicked shall understand, but the wise shall understand. And from the time that the daily sacrifice is taken away, and the abomination of desolation is set up, there shall be one thousand two hundred and ninety days. Blessed is he who waits, and comes to the one thousand three hundred and thirty-five days. But you, go your way till the end; for you shall rest, and will arise to your inheritance at the end of the days." Daniel 12:5–13

This brings us to the words of Jesus, that no one knows when the coming of the Son of Man will be. And although this passage may have an application to the destruction of Jerusalem, it seems to also reference the second coming of the Lord.

But about that day or hour no one knows, not even the angels in heaven, nor the Son, but only the Father. As it was in the days of Noah, so it will be at the coming of the Son of Man. For in the days before the flood, people were eating and drinking, marrying and giving in marriage, up to the day Noah entered the ark; and they knew nothing about what would happen until the flood came and took them all away. That is how it will be at the coming of the Son of Man. (Matthew 24:36:39) (NIV)

But in contrast to not knowing when the coming of the Lord would happen, Jesus speaks of the destruction of Jerusalem in terms of almost immediate fulfillment. In Matthew 23 Jesus concludes his speech to His disciples at the temple with these words of warning to the Jews. He said *all this will come on this generation.* Jesus strongly infers it would have at least some bearing on the destruction of Jerusalem in AD 70. But we could take this statement to also mean the forthcoming desolation of the Jewish people. The Lord's most dire warning of doom for these Jews comes when He says, "For I tell you, you will not see me again until you say, 'Blessed is he who comes in the name of the

Lord.'" In other words, the destruction of Jerusalem was only the beginning of sorrows for God's chosen people. Their chastening from God because of their failure to embrace His Son would continue for hundreds of years in the future. The word *generation* probably implies their race or nationality rather than a generation in their life span.

Truly I tell you, <u>all this will come on this generation</u>. "Jerusalem, Jerusalem, you who kill the prophets and stone those sent to you, how often I have longed to gather your children together, as a hen gathers her chicks under her wings, and you were not willing. Look, your house is left to you desolate. For I tell you, you will not see me again until you say, 'Blessed is he who comes in the name of the Lord.'" (Matthew 23:36–39) (NIV)

Usually the events foretold by God's prophets are foretold for the purpose of warning, especially those who would resist the will of the Lord. But some events foretold are promises to encourage and give hope to the faithful. However, whether it is promises given to the faithful or warnings given to the evildoers, in this last age the warnings are much more of an eternal or spiritual nature than something temporal or earthly. This is not to say there are no biblical warnings about natural disasters and such things, especially in the Old Testament.

Basically I am of this general persuasion: the things connected with the destruction of Jerusalem were given to allow the hearers or readers the opportunity to know when the destruction was coming, at least within a reasonable time frame. The things Jesus spoke of in connection with final judgment are without specific information as to when they will occur (see Matt. 24:36, 25:13).

Another thing that gets in the way of a better understanding of prophecy is taking too literally the figures and symbols from the book of Revelation and the Old Testament books of prophecy. Revelation is almost entirely given in figurative language, as are a lot of the prophecies of the Old Testament.

QUESTIONS ABOUT THE END

Then Jesus went out and departed from the temple, and His disciples came up to show Him the buildings of the temple. And Jesus said to them, "Do you not see all these things? Assuredly, I say to you, not one stone shall be left here upon another, that shall not be thrown down." Now as He sat on the Mount of Olives, the disciples came to Him privately, saying, "Tell us, when will these things be? And what will be the sign of Your coming, and of the end of the age?" (Matthew 24:1–3)

When a discussion takes place regarding the end of the world, Matthew 24 and parallel passages from the other gospels are usually some of the first scriptures considered and presented as evidence of the Lord's return and the end of time. And unless it would be from the book of Revelation, where end-time prophecy is conveyed in figures and symbols, there may be no greater Bible passage dealing with eschatology than Matthew 24.

Some prophecies can be calculated as to the time of their fulfillment by the information given in the scriptures, but this is not the case with the visible return of Jesus at the end of time. No one knows the exact time of the Lord's coming back to earth in order to execute vengeance on the wicked and to raise the dead.

But about that day or hour no one knows, not even the angels in heaven, nor the Son, but only the Father. (Mark 13:32)

And even though the parallel accounts found in Matthew 24, Mark 13 and Luke 21 tell us Jesus is coming back, it is made clear the time will be unexpected by many, if not all. Even with those closest to Him, Jesus simply admonished them to watch and pray that they might be counted worthy to stand before Him on that day. However, true believers will be enlightened to many of these prophetic events as the end draws near. I am convinced that one of the keys to understanding more about the time of the end of the world is a proper understanding of the kingdom of God.

When the prophet Daniel received the end-time vision from heaven he was puzzled as to its meaning. He was informed he would not know the complete meaning of the vision, but it would be known to God's people when the proper time came.

I heard, but I did not understand. So I asked, "My lord, what will the outcome of all this be?" He replied, "Go your way, Daniel, because the words are rolled up and sealed until the time of the end. Many will be purified, made spotless and refined, but the wicked will continue to be wicked. None of the wicked will understand, but those who are wise will understand." (Daniel 12:8–10) (NIV)

Much of the prophecy of Jesus in Matthew, Mark and Luke was fulfilled within the lifetime of the disciples to whom Jesus spoke. I think the idea that much of Matthew 24 would soon come to pass confuses a lot of people, but it is made very clear by the Lord.

Even so, when you see all these things, you know that it is near, right at the door. Truly I tell you, this generation will certainly not pass away until all these things have happened. (Matt. 24:33–34) (NIV)

In the gospel accounts of Matthew, Mark and Luke the Lord's discourse is prefaced by a prophetic message of coming doom on the Jews, who were the children of the first covenant. So in order to understand the context of this message it becomes necessary to back up and review the Lord's previous teachings.

Jesus was entering the last phase of His personal ministry on earth when He spoke of the coming judgment upon the Jews in Matthew 23. He had been very critical of the Jewish religious leaders, especially the scribes and the Pharisees, for the year previous to the dire warning He pronounced on them in Matthew 23. After a scathing condemnation of the house of Israel throughout chapter 23, He ends His remarks with the follow declaration.

See! Your house is left to you desolate, for I say to you, you shall see Me no more till you say, "Blessed is He who comes in the name of the Lord!" (Matthew 23:38–39)

The gospels of Matthew, Mark and Luke give an account of the questions the disciples asked after leaving the temple and removing themselves to the Mount of Olives nearby. In all three of the gospels the disciples asked, "When shall these things be?" As the questioning continues in Matthew, Jesus is asked, "And what shall be the sign of thy coming, and of the end of the world?" Mark says, "And what shall be the sign when all these things shall be fulfilled?" Luke records, "What sign will there be when these things shall come to pass?"

Matthew 24: *And as he sat upon the Mount of Olives, the disciples came unto him privately, saying, tell us, when shall these things be? And what shall be the sign of thy coming, and of the end of the world?*

Mark 13: *And as he sat upon the Mount of Olives over against the temple, Peter and James and John and Andrew asked him privately, tell us, when shall these things be? And what shall be the sign when all these things shall be fulfilled?*

Luke 21: *And they asked him, saying, Master, but when shall these things be? And what sign will there be when these things shall come to pass?*

It is these questions Jesus answers at length in the accounts of the three parallel gospels. I begin by analyzing the questions in order to find out just what the disciples of Jesus wanted to understand. It is obvious that the first question, "When shall these things be?" was asked primarily as a result of what Jesus had told the disciples earlier.

And as some spake of the temple, how it was adorned with goodly stones and gifts, he said, As for these things which ye behold, the days will come, in the which there shall not be left one stone upon another, that shall not be thrown down. (Luke 21:5–6) (KJV)

The disciples concern was "when shall these things be" or when the temple would be destroyed. They no doubt had in mind the destruction of Jerusalem and the restoration of an earthly kingdom in Jerusalem in which the Messiah would reign. But if we pay attention to the words of Jesus, we can clearly see His kingdom is not of this world in any way.

You are from below; I am from above. You are of this world; I am not of this world. (John 8:23) (NIV)

My kingdom is not of this world. If it were, my servants would fight to prevent my arrest by the Jewish leaders. But now my kingdom is from another place. (John 18:36) (NIV)

This is what much of the Christian world is waiting for today, the restoration of an earthly kingdom. Some think it will be in Jerusalem. Others are waiting for the Messiah to come and set up a kingdom elsewhere on earth. I am fully persuaded that many in the Christian world are mistaken.

CONCLUDING THOUGHT

We do not know when Jesus will come back to earth, or when time as we know it will end. Just as it is with the changing of the seasons, we might be able to tell spring is near, but we will never be able to know the exact day or hour. It is amazing that even Jesus did not know the exact time of the end. This was something only our God the Creator would know and determine.

But it is not necessary for us to know some things. We are to believe what is written about them, but not to be overly concerned about those things that are not revealed. Whether it was warnings and signs given by Jesus to the Jews about the physical destruction of Jerusalem, or the destruction of the material heavens and the earth at the end of time written by the apostle Peter, we would do well to listen to the words of Jesus.

Take heed, watch and pray; for you do not know when the time is. (Mark 13:33)

Watch therefore, and pray always that you may be counted worthy to escape all these things that will come to pass, and to stand before the Son of Man. (Luke 21:36)

CHAPTER 14
ETERNAL BLISS

ENDLESSNESS

I vividly remember the warm country summer nights I experienced as a child in south central Missouri. I loved them. I, along with my brothers and sisters, usually played outside until Mom would make us come in and bathe and get ready for bed.

One night my older sister Maxine began to talk to me about the constellations. She had learned about them in her science class. She pointed out the Big Dipper and told me some of the stars are so far away it takes thousands or millions of years for the light from them to reach the earth. I was amazed! This was quite a revelation for me. And although I could not comprehend the magnitude of that time and distance, I realized there was something very amazing about the universe. It must be a lot bigger than I had ever thought. The thought made me excited and a little scared at the same time. Some things are too marvelous for little minds.

The deep mysteries of God's universe will never be known in this life by observing the creation. And even with the things we can come to understand, it still is difficult to imagine that it's real! No matter how far the biggest and most powerful telescopes can penetrate into space, and no matter how far the human imagination can be stretched, God's creative work will still continue far beyond! We simply cannot understand it. And it's not meant for us to understand. But if we are honest with ourselves we must believe the scope of the Creator's creation is somehow infinite. And by this we can know by faith there is a God who is almighty, knowing and seeing all. He is the Great I Am who sees the end from the beginning.

Our sun is the only star in our solar system. It is orbited by nine known planets. Planet Earth has one moon approximately 240,000 miles away. The sun is approximately 93,000,000 miles from the earth. Light travels at approximately 186,000 miles per second, meaning it takes about eight minutes for the light from the sun to reach the earth. All of this is amazing in itself.

But far beyond this, it is estimated there are about 100 billion stars in our galaxy, the Milky Way. Our galaxy is one of billions of observable galaxies. The closest star from our solar system is trillions of miles away!

In 2021, data from NASA's New Horizons space probe was used to revise the previous estimate to roughly 200 billion galaxies (2×1011), which followed a 2016 estimate that there were two trillion (2×1012) or more galaxies in the observable universe. (Wikipedia, "Galaxy" https:// en.wikipedia.org › wiki › Galaxy)

Of course these would be of relevance only if there was an end to space with the assumption that the universe is finite. It is impossible to imagine the size of the universe with the human mind. Even more inconceivable is an ending of space or an ending of the universe. But perhaps the greatest mental task is to imagine it has no end.

But whether we think about the big things or the small things of creation, we are forced into a mental state that embraces the idea of infinity. It is inescapable! The following remarks on the infinite smallness of the smallest part of the elements of creation help bring these thoughts into greater perspective.

The answer to the enduring question of the smallest thing in the universe has evolved along with humanity. People once thought grains of sand were the building blocks of what we see around us. Then the atom was discovered, and it was thought indivisible, until it was split to reveal protons, neutrons and electrons inside. These too seemed like fundamental particles, before scientists discovered that protons and neutrons are made of three quarks each.

"This time we haven't been able to see any evidence at all that there's anything inside quarks," said physicist Andy Parker. "Have we reached the most fundamental layer of matter?"

And even if quarks and electrons are indivisible, Parker said, scientists don't know if they are the smallest bits of matter in existence, or if the universe contains objects that are even more minute. ("What Is the Smallest Thing in the Universe?" www.livescience.com/23232-smallest-ingredients-universe-physics.html)

When the imaginations of our minds have expanded as far as possible in thinking of the sheer awesomeness of God's creation, we still have considered only the temporal things in the Creator's work. The unknown things of spiritual regeneration, redemption and restoration would cause our most expanded imagination to pale in comparison with what can be naturally discerned even with the most sophisticated scientific technology. We only consider the seen and the imaginable (natural things) from a scientific point of view. But through spiritual regeneration, by partaking of the divine nature, we can be empowered to receive beyond the power of the natural senses. This happens simply by believing and trusting in what God says. We are convinced there is a Creator. Believers trust in the Word of the Creator. Of course this trust comes by faith and not by sight because our physical senses are limited to the power of our senses.

While we do not look at the things which are seen, but at the things which are not seen. For the things which are seen are temporary, but the things which are not seen are eternal. (2 Corinthians 4:18)

We have yet to explore and contemplate that which will at some point be revealed to us by our Creator; the things far beyond time and beyond this temporary system of things. This will occur in the next life when God's new creation is redeemed and restored. The writer of Hebrews brings the awesome presence of God back to the minds of his readers by comparing God's power at Mount Sinai to the destruction of the universe at the end of time.

At that time his voice shook the earth, but now he has promised, "Once more I will shake not only the earth but also the heavens." The words "once more" indicate the removing of what can be shaken—that is, created things—so that what cannot be shaken may remain. Therefore, since we are receiving a kingdom that cannot be shaken, let us be thankful, and so worship God acceptably with reverence and awe, for our "God is a consuming fire." (Hebrews 12:26–29) (NIV)

So at the present, only by the spiritual power of the revealed Word of God are we able to have a small glimpse of that which will be in the world to come.

While we do not look at the things which are seen, but at the things which are not seen. For the things which are seen are temporary, but the things which are not seen are eternal. (2 Corinthians 4:18)

The material universe may seem almost eternal from the human perspective, but nonetheless it is temporal in the state in which it now exists. It can and will be shaken and destroyed. It will not remain in its present condition. As human creatures we are enabled only to reason within this temporal existence. The unregenerate mind basically views this temporal world as a continuing city, unlike faithful Abraham.

For here we have no continuing city, but we seek the one to come. (Hebrews 13:14)

For he [Abraham] waited for the city which has foundations, whose builder and maker is God. (Hebrews 11:10)

Those who believe and trust in God understand by faith that the material universe is destructible and wearing out as we speak. True, the lifetime of a star may be billions of years, but it is still temporal and given enough time will succumb to it. This temporal, material universe will be destroyed by fire.

But the day of the Lord will come as a thief in the night, in which the heavens will pass away with a great noise, and the elements will melt with fervent heat; both the earth and the works that are in it will be burned up. Therefore, since all these things will be dissolved, what manner of persons ought you to be in holy conduct and godliness, looking for and hastening the coming of the day of God, because of which the heavens will be dissolved, being on fire, and the elements will melt with fervent heat? Nevertheless we, according to His promise, look for new heavens and a new earth in which righteousness dwells. (2 Peter 3:10–12)

It will be burned up, melt and dissolve, and then it will be restored. It will change from temporal and destructible to eternal and indestructible. In our present existence, the greatness of the Almighty can only be measured by the greatness of His creation. But all of the temporal creation is as nothing when compared to the power of God's existence. In fact, as the Creator observes all the wonders of His magnificent creation, He is so far superior that He must humble Himself to look upon it.

Who is like the Lord our God, Who dwells on high, who humbles Himself to behold the things that are in the heavens and in the earth? (Psalms 113:5–6)

Listen to an excerpt from the noted John Gill as he comments on Psalms 113:6.

The persons (of) the highest heavens, the angels whom he upholds in their beings, and admits into his presence; who always behold his face, and he beholds them, delights in their persons, and accepts their services; which, though pure and perfect, it is a condescension in him to do, since they are but creature services, and chargeable with folly and weakness; and who themselves are as nothing in comparison of him, and veil their faces before him (Job 4:18).

Thus says the Lord, your Redeemer, and He who formed you from the womb: "I am the Lord, who makes all things, who stretches out the heavens all alone, who spreads abroad the earth by Myself." (Isaiah 44:24)

GOD IS LOVE

Those who will enter into the eternal abode of bliss will be there because of love, both God's love and their own. If we lose sight of the fact that love is all encompassing in our earthly walk, we will lose sight of the fact that God is almighty. Without the realization of the love of God upon us we cannot truly know our Creator.

Beloved, let us love one another, for love is of God; and everyone who loves is born of God and knows God. He who does not love does not know God, for God is love. (1 John 4:7–8)

When we meditate on the eternal bliss of heaven, or how complete happiness could ever be accomplished for us, a spiritual mind will always conclude that it is because of the love of God. Although it is difficult to grasp, the fact is that God is love. John says everyone who loves is born of God and knows God. God does not just love—God is love! And all of creation was borne out of and sustained by His great love.

Millions have tried to explain or define love. Poems, songs and sermons, along with thousands and thousands of books have all been written trying to capture the essence of love. And the explanations and definitions are wide ranging. Next are listed most of the *Merriam-Webster Dictionary* definitions of love. (1) Strong affection for another arising out of kinship or personal ties maternal love for a child. (2) Attraction based on sexual desire: affection and tenderness felt by lovers (after all these years, they are still very much in love). (3) Affection based on admiration, benevolence, or common interests (love for his old schoolmates). (4) An assurance of affection (give her my love). (5) Warm attachment, enthusiasm, or devotion (love of the sea). (6) The object of attachment, devotion, or admiration (baseball was his first love). (7) A beloved person: darling—often used as a term of endearment. (8) Used as an informal term of address by the British (my love). (9) Unselfish loyal and benevolent concern for the good of another: such as the fatherly concern of God for humankind, brotherly concern for others. (10) A person's adoration of God. (11) A god (such as Cupid or Eros) or personification of love. (12) An amorous episode: love affair. (13) The sexual embrace: copulation. (14) A score of zero (as in tennis).

Note: All of these definitions have something to do with the many ways the word *love* is used in the English language. However, only one definition fulfills the complete meaning of love as well as identifying its source. That definition is God. God showed His love by allowing His creation, both human and nonhuman, to have the opportunity to obtain eternal life, immortality, through Jesus, His Son.

But God demonstrates his own love for us in this: While we were still sinners, Christ died for us. (Romans 5:8) (NIV)

From the beginning of creation, the love of God toward His entire creation has been praised in thousands of tongues and languages, and it has been shown in a thousand other ways. Love begins with God. He is the only source of love. And God loves all of His creation! The culmination of His love for all His creation was in the act of giving His only begotten Son. God not only loved the world, but He so loved the world that He showed His love in the most profound way possible by giving the ultimate gift of His only Son in order that the love might be reciprocal.

For God so loved the world that He gave His only begotten Son, that whoever believes in Him should not perish but have everlasting life. (John 3:16)

God's love not only provides pardon from sin but also gives eternal life and a shared eternal inheritance that could only be obtained by a full father–child relationship in His human family.

The Spirit Himself bears witness with our spirit that we are children of God, and if children, then heirs—heirs of God and joint heirs with Christ, if indeed we suffer with Him, that we may also be glorified together. (Romans 8:16–17)

Humanity would be given an eternal abode of blissful infinite life by trusting in God's Son. They would not only be given immortality but would become joint heirs with the Son through faith in Him. Jesus in effect summed up God's love for His adopted human children with the following words. Those who never enter into a relationship with God through love will have missed it all!

Let not your heart be troubled; you believe in God, believe also in Me. In My Father's house are many mansions; if it were not so, I would have told you. I go to prepare a place for you." (John 14:1–2)

COMPLETE HAPPINESS

It is impossible for even the most spiritual mind to grasp the sheer awesomeness of eternal bliss. According to the *Merriam-Webster Dictionary*, the full meaning of *bliss* is <u>complete happiness</u>. This is unimaginable! The human mind has not, cannot, nor will it ever in this world, experience complete happiness. This can happen only through the power of God and Christ in the world to come. It's difficult if not impossible to even believe there could be a place or state where there can be complete happiness, a place where there is no pain or anxiety, a place where there is no thought of an impending mortal demise that can only end in death. Equally unimaginable is a place or state of unending joys, a place where human mortality will have been swallowed up with deathless immortality. Imagine the impossibility of nothing negative ever again being experienced or even coming to mind. In other words, imagine the possibility of nothing ever being able to detract from complete happiness. But this is the state in which Jesus and the New Testament writers speak of as heaven.

So when this corruptible has put on incorruption, and this mortal has put on immortality, then shall be brought to pass the saying that is written: "Death is swallowed up in victory." (I Corinthians 15:54)

According to God's Word, the next world will be all of these good things and much more, with nothing to hinder them! These statements of bliss are the promises of the Creator to the redeemed and restored creation. However, these promises can only be fulfilled when the *corruptible* mortal being has been transformed into an *incorruptible* immortal being. Yet the Bible clearly teaches complete happiness (bliss) will be the situation of redeemed humanity in the next world.

A blissful state cannot happen in this mortal existence. Nor will it immediately occur with the death of the body as many think. The disembodied state after physical death is not the final act of the redemptive process wrought in the redemptive work of Christ. In this life there can be a spiritual resurrection of the spirit/soul unto or toward eternal life. But complete happiness will occur only after the body is redeemed and rewards are given.

Keep yourselves in the love of God, looking for the mercy of our Lord Jesus Christ <u>unto eternal life</u>. (Jude 1:21)

In order to possess complete happiness there must be a resurrection of the body *into* eternal life. *Into* means we have passed from one place or state to another. This will be accomplished only by our mortal body becoming immortalized at the resurrection when Jesus comes back. This is the final act, the redemption of the body. The eternal bliss to come in the next age will be predicated completely on the redemption of the mortal body into immortality and eternal life.

Then Peter said, "See, we have left all and followed You." So He said to them, "Assuredly, I say to you, there is no one who has left house or parents or brothers or wife or children, for the sake of the kingdom of God, who shall not receive many times more in this present time, and in the age to come eternal life." (Luke 18:28–30)

The transition of mortality into immortality is the consummation of the glory that shall be revealed in the children of God. This is when the saved truly become children of God.

For we know that the whole creation groans and labors with birth pangs together until now. Not only that, but we also who have the first-fruits of the Spirit, even we ourselves groan within ourselves, eagerly waiting for the adoption, the redemption of our body. (Romans 8:22–23)

So we can never be completely happy in a disembodied state between this life and the next, meaning before the resurrection of the body.

For we know that if the earthly tent [our body] we live in is destroyed, we have a building from God, an eternal house in heaven, not built by human hands. Meanwhile we groan, longing to be clothed instead with our heavenly dwelling, because when we are clothed, we will not be found naked. For while we are in this tent, we groan and are burdened, because <u>we do not wish to be unclothed but to be clothed instead with our heavenly dwelling, so that what is mortal may be swallowed up by life</u>. Now the one who has <u>fashioned us for this very purpose</u> is God, who has given us the Spirit as a deposit, guaranteeing what is to come. (2 Corinthians 5:1–5)

Of course the mortal bodies of God's children can only be redeemed by the atoning merits of the blood of Christ. God, through Christ, has fashioned us for this very purpose. The word *redeem* means to be bought back. Not only has God fashioned us for this very purpose (to be changed into an immortal being), but He has also guaranteed it will happen unless we depart from His mercy. This guarantee is made by giving His people a portion of His Holy Spirit as a deposit or down payment on the redemption that is to come at the resurrection.

Who hath also sealed us, and given the earnest of the Spirit in our hearts. (1 Corinthians 1:22)

This is the eternal life Jesus talked about that will abide in those who believe in Him. It begins with a heart filled with gratitude toward God. We are changed from the inside out: first the inside, the renewing of the mind, then the outside, the redemption of the body.

For this corruptible must put on incorruption, and this mortal must put on immortality. So when this corruptible has put on incorruption, and this mortal has put on immortality, then shall be brought to pass the saying that is written: "Death is swallowed up in victory." "O Death, where is your sting? O Hades, where is your victory?" (1 Corinthians 15:53–55)

Only when the body is redeemed is "Death is swallowed up in victory" and, therefore, complete contentment and happiness will be accomplished for the children of God forever. Only then will the complete story of God's love be known by His people. Because only then will it be revealed what we shall be, that which could have only been made possible by the infinite love of our Creator and heavenly Father. God's children will only inherit His kingdom because they are His children.

Behold what manner of love the Father has bestowed on us, that we should be called children of God! Therefore the world does not know us, because it did not know Him. Beloved, now we are children of God; and it has not yet been revealed what we shall be, but we know that when He is revealed, we shall be like Him, for we shall see Him as He is. (1 John 3:1–2)

Chapter 1 was entitled "Childhood Thoughts." There I discussed my thoughts as a child in connection with God's judgment on the world. I wrote about how I had imagined it to be. But later, as I began to examine the scriptures in a more careful and detailed way, I realized much of my thinking was conceived of many centuries of traditional beliefs. I now also believe much of the current religious thinking about heaven (eternal bliss) is from that same source. Only as born again children of God will the Father begin to reveal His will to us.

CHILDREN OF GOD

Beloved, now we are <u>children of God</u>; and it has not yet been revealed what we shall be, but we know that when He is revealed, we shall be like Him, for we shall see Him as He is. (1 John 3:2)

As I have previously talked about, it is unimaginably difficult to wrap our mental fingers around the concept of eternity and the eternal bliss that awaits those who are in Christ. In order to imagine an eternity of bliss, I think we must somehow be able to conceive of God's love in enabling us to become His children and being able to share His inheritance with His only begotten Son. This is unspeakable! But it is true.

As a young man I was sometimes stimulated to think in a somewhat deeper way by reading early American and English literature. One night, while I feebly pondered thoughts of what eternity might be like, I wrote a short poem in order to convey my feelings on the subject. The title I gave the poem was simply "Eternity." In it was the following line:

"How could one imagine or halfway comprehend,

That eternity is time itself and that it could never end?"

I still ponder this question. The human mind simply cannot conceive of anything never ending! We cannot think of existence without time. But, on the other hand, how is it possible to think in terms of the complete end of things like time and space? As mortals, we are caught up in the dilemma of trying to answer questions that are unanswerable to us. There are questions to which we can find no real answers while existing in this present material universe, in our mortal state of being while immersed in our finite system of time or duration. But as I discussed in a previous chapter, we can be assured this present system of duration called time is not the system that will govern our future world. Our understanding of these kinds of things will never be realized until death is swallowed up in victory.

John writes, "it has not yet been revealed what we shall be." We cannot know in our temporal existence what we shall be, or how it can happen. This is yet to be revealed, but it will be revealed. John further writes, "but we know that when He is revealed, we shall be like Him." And we should find comfort in this thought, catching a small glimpse of eternity by faith. We have hope because by that faith we know we shall be like Him. And it is also within this promise that we should be brought to the realization that immortal bliss is beyond our present mortal comprehension. But we can know we are God's children!

So in Christ Jesus you are all children of God through faith, for all of you who were baptized into Christ have clothed yourselves with Christ. (Galatians 3:26–27) (NIV)

As adopted children of God in this life, and with our natural minds having been transformed and spiritually regenerated to know much more than in our previous natural and unregenerate state, we still only catch a glimpse of eternal bliss. And even though we now live in the flesh, we have been given the ability to surrender our will to God's will through Jesus, creating a spiritual, parent–child relationship with the Father. By surrendering to God's will for our life, we do not have to walk after the flesh any longer. Still, for the present we are limited in our ability to gaze beyond this veil of tears into eternity. But we can be assured of this one thing. *Beloved, now we are children of God.*

John tells us in our present state as children of God, our future state has yet to be completely revealed to us: *it has not yet been revealed what we shall be.* We can know, however, by John's words, that when Jesus is revealed, *we will be like him.* Then we will know. By understanding that *now we are children of God* we can begin to visualize how our present kinship to the Father may relate to our future state of being like His Son. Our present state of being now the children of God has everything to do with being like Jesus in the hereafter.

For both He [Jesus] who sanctifies and those who are being sanctified are all of one, for which reason He is not ashamed to call them brethren. (Hebrews 2:11)

In order to know what causes this son and daughter relationship with God the Father, we need to look at the things that have been revealed about it to us in His Word. One of the first things we must understand is that there is no partiality with God. Any thought to the contrary is a reflection on the justice, kindness and mercy of a loving Creator.

Then Peter opened his mouth and said: "In truth I perceive that God shows no partiality. But in every nation whoever fears Him and works righteousness is accepted by Him." (Acts 10:34–35)

It should be easy to see God is not partial because of race, sex, personality, etc. Only God has the power to determine these created characteristics. He gives us our gender, color of skin and all the determining factors of how we look and who we are. He created the master plan of our DNA. How foolish to think God the Creator would show partiality toward us for being simply as we were created to be. The scriptures are very clear on this point. We also cannot be partial in our judgment of others and be pleasing to God.

There is neither Jew nor Greek, there is neither slave nor free, there is neither male nor female; for you are all one in Christ Jesus. (Galatians 3:28)

God determines our physical and biological characteristics. He brings us into existence at the proper time that serves His purpose. And He gives us the abilities to fulfill the purpose He has for us. But after He creates us, He allows us the opportunity to choose how we use our abilities. We can either reject or accept the eternal life He offers. Eternal life is given to those who accept the salvation that is in His Son. So God does accept some to be His children, while rejecting others. And the acceptance or rejection is never because God is partial.

GOD CHOOSES HIS CHILDREN

We do not choose God, but rather He chooses us. But we do make a choice as to whether to serve Him. This, however, is not always the teaching of some professed Christians. As discussed previously, some teach God actually shows partiality in connection with eternal salvation. This is the conclusion one must draw if God elects some to salvation while denying it to others, without any power of choice on the part of the individual. This is absolutely contrary to what the Bible teaches. The idea that humanity has no choice in its own eternal destiny is without any scriptural basis and casts a negative shadow on the love of God as well.

Actually the scriptures teach the exact opposite. We have been created and given the opportunity to choose our own eternal destiny. Even as Joshua set before Israel a choice, we are all given a choice by a loving, merciful and just Creator.

And if it seems evil to you to serve the Lord, <u>choose for yourselves</u> this day whom you will serve, whether the gods which your fathers served that were on the other side of the River, or the gods of the Amorites, in whose land you dwell. But as for me and my house, we will serve the Lord. (Joshua 24:15)

In Joshua's case, he made the choice to serve the Lord. The children of Israel did not first choose the Lord, but rather the Lord had first chosen them to be His people. But in order for them to enter Canaan, the land of milk and honey, they had to make a choice whether to trust the Lord and follow His counsel or forfeit this glorious inheritance. Today is no different. God has chosen those who will be resurrected spiritually to reign with His Son, to inherit a glorious inheritance as children of the Most High.

Isolating certain verses or passages in the Bible and then not accepting others may make the Bible seem to teach an idea it really doesn't teach. This is true in connection with the erroneous idea that humans have no free will to choose eternal life. There are several often-used scriptures given by those who advocate this particular doctrine of God's foreordination—that is, not having a choice or free will. Let's look at a few of them. The first example is Jesus speaking to His disciples in John's writing.

You did not choose Me, but I chose you. (John 15:16a)

Usually only this (a) part of the verse is quoted by proponents of this no choice argument. And by only using a part of the verse, it could mean almost anything. They argue by Jesus saying I chose you, His disciples had no choice in their eternal destination. But He continues by saying, "and appointed you that you should go and bear fruit, and that your fruit should remain, that whatever you ask the Father in My name He may give you" (John 15:16b). But notice carefully what else Jesus says to His handpicked disciples in the remainder of this same verse. He is talking about selecting them for a special spiritual work, to go and bear fruit. He chose them for this work rather than them having chosen Him.

Another familiar scripture used by those in opposition to free will is found in the book of Acts.

Now when the Gentiles heard this, they were glad and glorified the word of the Lord. And <u>as many as had been appointed to eternal life believed</u>. (Acts 13:48)

Once again, many times only part of the passage is quoted or read. In this instance it is the (b) part. The no choice advocates jump on the part that says, "And as many as had been appointed to eternal life believed." Again, this verse in isolation might seem to imply the absence of a choice by the Gentiles subsequent to hearing the gospel of Christ. The argument would be that they believed only because they had already been chosen or appointed to eternal life, but they themselves had no choice in the matter.

Paul was preaching in a Jewish synagogue at Antioch in Pisidia when he spoke these words in Acts 13:48. He had preached at the same place the previous Sabbath. And at that time the Gentiles who were there and who had heard him preach Jesus wanted to hear more the next Sabbath. So the following Sabbath many Gentiles were in the audience. In fact, verse 44 says, "On the next Sabbath almost the whole city came together to hear the word of God." Because of this, the Jews of the synagogue, who had invited Paul to speak, became envious and contradicting and blaspheming, they opposed the things spoken by Paul. The envy of the Jews was evidently because so many Gentiles of the city had come to hear the gospel of Jesus. But once again, when the context is carefully examined, this scripture does not teach the Gentiles were saved without making the choice to obey. Let's look at what led up to the statement in verse 48 by examining verse 46.

Then Paul and Barnabas grew bold and said, "It was necessary that the word of God should be spoken to you first; but since you reject it, and judge yourselves unworthy of everlasting life, behold, we turn to the Gentiles." (Acts 13:46)

This verse plainly states that the Jews rejected the word of God. It is impossible to reject something without having the choice to receive it. Paul says in Romans 1:16 that the gospel (that which was preached to these Jews) is the power of God unto salvation.

Last, notice two other passages listed in what follows, used by those who advocate the no choice idea. Both are found in the book of Romans. On first glance, and once again by isolating this passage, it may sound like God chooses who will be saved and lost without any choice on the part of the individual. However, it is easy to prove by the Bible that this is mistaken.

For whom He foreknew, He also predestined to be conformed to the image of His Son, that He might be the firstborn among many brethren. Moreover whom He predestined, these He also called; whom He called, these He also justified; and whom He justified, these He also glorified. (Romans 8:29–30)

You will say to me then, "Why does He still find fault, for who has resisted His will?" But indeed, O man, who are you to reply against God? Will the thing formed say to him who formed it, "Why have you made me like this?" Does not the potter have power over the clay, from the same lump to make one vessel for honor and another for dishonor? (Romans 9:19–21)

Are these passages really teaching God unmercifully chooses to condemn people without ever giving them any choice to accept or reject? Absolutely not! When we put these verses together in harmony with the rest of the scriptures we can easily see God does not show any partiality. Any thought to the contrary is a dark reflection on a just and merciful Creator.

Now, without taking a lot of time, let's look at the above two passages in Romans together with other scripture. Surely we need to consider the whole counsel of God before foolishly concluding God shows partiality in the eternal damnation of a vast swath of the human race.

For whom He foreknew, He also predestined to be conformed to the image of His Son, that He might be the firstborn among many brethren. Who are those whom God foreknew? Of course God knows all things and therefore would know the future in connection to the salvation or condemnation of the whole world. But here only a particular part of saved humanity is under consideration. These were those whom God foreknew would choose to serve Him by faith in His Son and accepting Jesus as the sacrifice for their sins. Even if these were predestined without choice, and clearly they are not, this verse only speaks of those who would be saved. The lost are not under consideration here. God's foreknowledge has nothing to do with causing the salvation of those in mind. Rather, because of His foreknowledge, he was able to see the choice made by those foreknown and therefore subsequently able to predetermine they would be conformed to the image of His Son.

It's easy to miss what is said in the last part of this verse, "that He might be the firstborn among many brethren." This is the thing God predetermined or predestinated. God did not predestinate who would be saved, but that those who would be saved would be conformed to the image of Jesus. In this He also predestinated those whom He foreknew would become brethren (brothers and sisters) with His only begotten Son; Jesus being the firstborn, with many spiritual siblings to follow. The Bible talks a lot about the glory that will be revealed in these sons and daughters of God. To charge God with the kind of partiality expressed by the no choice proponents would fly in the face of almost everything Jesus taught while He walked on the earth. It would contradict every example of love and justice the Savior stood for. And Jesus taught us that without doubt, "I and my Father are one" (John 30:1).

Without free will on the part of an individual, partiality would be exactly what God would be guilty of. Almighty God would never be the cause of eternal destruction of anyone by not allowing them a choice in the matter. If this was the case, then absolutely no one would have any recourse in their disposition toward God's will. They would in effect be robotic, having no God-given will of their own. This is an absurd and dangerous doctrine.

So when Paul says "for whom He foreknew," he is talking about the infinite foreknowledge of God rather than the freedom of choice of God's created human creatures. Those whom He foreknew were at least a part of those who would be eventually saved eternally. But there was obviously a special group under consideration in this statement, and those being considered were to be conformed to the image of Jesus. But who were they?

But to all who did receive him [Jesus], who believed in his name, he gave the right to become children of God, who were born, not of blood, nor of the will of the flesh, nor of the will of man, but of God. (John 1:12–13)

This scripture goes a long way in the identification of "those whom He foreknew." God gave the right to become children of God to all those who would receive Jesus and believe in His name. These were not given the right to become children of God because of blood (physical descendants of Abraham). Neither were they given the right to become children of God because of willpower or fleshly ambition or any human endeavor, but because of God's purpose out of an abundance of His love and mercy. In other words, only those who will call Jesus Lord can call God Abba Father. We cannot be a true son and heir of the Father without being a brother to Jesus.

And because you are sons, God has sent forth the Spirit of His Son into your hearts, crying out, "Abba, Father!" Therefore you are no longer a slave but a son, and if a son, then an heir of God through Christ. (Galatians 4:6–7)

Notice the above verse talks of sonship before God sends "forth the Spirit of His Son into your hearts." This would in some way mean sonship occurs before a relationship with God is established. We do not possess the Holy Spirit of God prior to our being reconciled with Him through Christ. Our relationship with the Father is brought about only by our relationship with the Son. But because He knows beforehand those whom He foreknew, He can speak of those as His sons and daughters in the present tense. When God sends forth the Spirit of His Son into our hearts, our son/daughtership (spiritual child–parent relationship) is sealed with the Holy Spirit of promise.

Nevertheless, God's solid foundation stands firm, sealed with this inscription: "The Lord knows those who are his," and, "Everyone who confesses the name of the Lord must turn away from wickedness." (2 Timothy 2:19) (NIV)

The Father foreknew some would trust in Him, but only after hearing the word of truth (the gospel) and believing would those who trusted be sealed with the Holy Spirit of promise. Being sealed with the Holy Spirit of promise allows the transition from servants or slaves to children of God.

In Him you also trusted, after you heard the word of truth, the gospel of your salvation; in whom also, having believed, you were sealed with the Holy Spirit of promise. (Ephesians 1:13)

Therefore God, through His infinite wisdom and foreknowledge, foreknew those who would believe on the name of His Son, and would subsequently be given the right to become His children. And because He foreknew, He was able to predestine them to be conformed to the image of His Son.

Being children of God and joint heirs with Christ has everything to do with heaven—eternal bliss!

JUST A LITTLE WHILE LONGER

When He opened the fifth seal, I saw under the altar the souls of those who had been slain for the word of God and for the testimony which they held. And they cried with a loud voice, saying, "How long, O Lord, holy and true, until You judge and avenge our blood on those who dwell on the earth?" Then a white robe was given to each of them; and it was said to them that they should rest a little while longer, until both the number of their fellow servants and their brethren, who would be killed as they were, was completed. (Revelation 6:9–11)

This scripture seems to depict the intermediate condition of the disembodied souls of the righteous. They are shown as martyrs in waiting, asking how long until the judgment of the unredeemed. Until then they are given white robes that are symbolic of the righteousness of the saints. They are asked to rest until the completion of the judgment of their adversaries. I firmly believe immortality and eternal life are made available to all of the creation of God. It makes no sense that the God of love would create with a desire to destroy.

You alone are the LORD. You made the heavens, even the highest heavens, and all their starry host, the earth and all that is on it, the seas and all that is in them. You give life to everything, and the multitudes of heaven worship you. (Nehemiah 9:6)

Nothing of creation will survive without surrendering to the sovereign power of the Creator. It is God's desire for the complete salvation of all His creation.

The Lord is not slack concerning His promise, as some count slackness, but is longsuffering toward us, not willing that any should perish but that all should come to repentance. (2 Peter 3:9)

Humanity has been given temporary life for a test, a time to seek after God. It has been given a time to accept the eternal life He freely offers. Mortal humanity can choose immortality. The rest of the creation is innocent before the Creator. It has been subjected to the curse of man's sin, but subjected in *hope* of restoration. This is the desire of the Creator. It's that simple. Sadly, according to Jesus, not all of human creation will accept it. He seems to say the majority of humanity will take the road leading to destruction by rejecting God and the life He freely gives.

Enter through the narrow gate. For wide is the gate and broad is the road that leads to destruction, and many enter through it. But small is the gate and narrow the road that leads to life, and only a few find it. (Matthew 7:13–14)

Jesus is the straight and narrow way. He is the only one in whom the Father is well pleased. The natural creation began when the Lord God formed Adam from the dust of the ground. This was man's created body. God then breathed into his nostrils the breath of life and man became a living soul. God then commanded and tested the human will of man. Man sinned; the will of the flesh failed. The redemption process for man began when God beget a Son through humanity. God's Son was given life inherent. He became the source of life, able to give it to whomever would accept it.

Then Jesus answered and said to them, "Most assuredly, I say to you, the Son can do nothing of Himself, but what He sees the Father do; for whatever He does, the Son also does in like manner. For the Father loves the Son, and shows Him all things that He Himself does; and He will show Him greater works than these, that you may marvel. For as the Father raises the dead and gives life to them, even so the Son gives life to whom He will. For the Father judges no one, but has committed all judgment to the Son, that all should honor the Son just as they honor the Father. He who does not honor the Son does not honor the Father who sent Him." (John 5:19–23)

Only temporal life will abide in humanity without Christ. Adam was made physically alive by the creative power of God. But through the procreative power of God, He has given the Son power to give eternal life and the power of sonship to all who choose life through Jesus.

And so it is written, "The first man Adam became a living being." The last Adam became a life-giving spirit. (1 Corinthians 15:45)

However, at this present time the whole creation continues to groan, travailing in the destructive effects of mortality. But soon this episode of painful existence will be over for the faithful sons and daughters of the Almighty and for the whole creation as well. Those who seek immortality and eternal life will soon exit this existence and enter their immortal existence.

God "will repay each person according to what they have done." To those who by persistence in doing good seek glory, honor and immortality, he will give eternal life. But for those who are self-seeking and who reject the truth and follow evil, there will be wrath and anger. (Rom. 2:6–8) (NIV)

GOING HOME!

Heaven cannot be truly conveyed to the human mind. We, in our finite human bodies, are confined to the realm of our natural senses. Without being spiritually regenerated and enabled to walk by faith, we are limited solely to the physically seen and sensed world. So those desiring immortality must look beyond this temporal existence. This hope can only be achieved by making the decision to walk by faith by trusting in the merciful and loving power of an infinite Creator. Only then can the human will be relinquished to the will and power of sovereign deity. And God accepts this effort. He does so because in this surrender to Jesus His divine justice is completely satisfied. This is the power of a sinless human sacrifice. All those surrendering to God through Jesus will be saved.

There have been millions of attempts to paint mental pictures of heaven, the abode of God. All attempts have proved feeble. We can no more visualize eternal bliss in heaven than we can imagine the end of the universe. Symbolic phrases like "a street of pure gold" or "gates of pearl" may invoke certain emotions or feelings of heaven's value, but only in mortal terms. But gold and pearls can never offer the bliss (complete happiness) for which we sigh. The human heart yearns for more. It longs for understanding through transparency and for security without fear and without end. In the temporal tent we call our body, we groan. Everything about this naturally created existence is doomed to ruin without these three necessary things: faith, hope and charity.

However, only charity or love will remain as we pass from this existence into the hereafter. Our hope will be realized when we have obtained that for which we have hoped. And our faith will become unnecessary when we behold our eternal destiny. But our love for God and for one another will continue throughout eternity. Charity never fails!

But when completeness comes, what is in part disappears. When I was a child, I talked like a child, I thought like a child, I reasoned like a child. When I became a man, I put the ways of childhood behind me. For now we see only a reflection as in a mirror; then we shall see face to face. Now I know in part; then I shall know fully, even as I am fully known. And now these three remain: faith, hope and love. But the greatest of these is love. (1 Corinthians 13:10–13) (NIV)

Eternal life is a gift from God. And, although it is not earned, it will be accepted with obedient gratitude toward the only One who has the power to give it. We are saved by grace through faith. We are not saved by the power of our own works of righteousness. All our righteousness is as filthy rags before God.

But we are all like an unclean thing, and all our righteousness's are like filthy rags; we all fade as a leaf, and our iniquities, like the wind, have taken us away. (Isaiah 64:6)

But just because God will forgive our trespasses by the blood of Christ does not mean we can continue in sin without striving to live faithfully to the commands of God. This seems to be what a lot of people want to believe. The same condition of heart that caused the initial surrender to the lordship of Christ must continue. In Romans Paul makes clear with the complete sixth chapter that in conversion to Christ, the mind must be changed from living for self to living for God. The wages (the reaped harvest) of sin is the second death. It is not eternal life in torture or torment. It is death. The gift of God is eternal life. God freely gives life without end (immortality) to all who surrender in faith to the salvation God offers through Jesus. But heaven is more than life forever. It is a life of complete happiness forever. It is a life with great rewards forever. It is unending joys! It is complete happiness because we are the children of God!

CONCLUDING THOUGHT

The first time "reward" is mentioned in the Bible is in Genesis 15 as God speaks to Abram in a vision. (Abram's name was later changed to Abraham.)

After these things the word of the Lord came to Abram in a vision, saying, "Do not be afraid, Abram. I am your shield, your exceedingly great reward." (Genesis 15:1)

The reward to Abram from the Lord would begin by allowing Abram's barren wife Sarai to conceive and bear a son. Abraham's reward was the beginning of what would bring Jesus into the world and ultimately reward all those who were faithful as well. In due time, through his son Isaac, God would completely fulfill Abram's exceedingly great reward by the coming of God's Son into the world!

All of the rewards of heaven toward humanity, and for that matter all of creation, were to come as a result of God's promise to Abraham. This was because Jesus descended from Isaac.

Nor are they all children because they are the seed of Abraham; but, "In Isaac your seed shall be called." (Romans 9:7)

But the promise to bless the world through Abraham's posterity was conditional. It had no possibility of being fulfilled without Abraham's faithfulness to the Lord. Of course the Lord knew even before the obedience of Abraham's faith came to fruition that Abraham would be faithful. Paul spoke in the past tense in reference to the fulfillment of the promise, even before Abraham's faith was supremely tested in his willingness to sacrifice his son Isaac.

As it is written, "I have made you a father of many nations" in the presence of Him whom he believed—God, who gives life to the dead and calls those things which do not exist as though they did. (Romans 4:17)

Years ago as a young man I studied the Bible with an older preacher who was of a different religious persuasion than me. I knew he had a different view than I held with regard to the proper response of faith to the gospel message of Christ. When I asked him what he believed a person must do to be saved, he simply said, "Believe in God." It was not the answer I expected. I expected something more detailed. But I realized if he meant a faith that trusted in God and was willing to obey God, he was 100 percent correct.

The Lord does not have to wait for the outward response of faith to proclaim the blessedness of it. We do. But God must see that the faith generated toward His commands and promises is a faith, a given opportunity, which we will obey. He knows this because of the almighty power of His complete foreknowledge of all things. We as humans, not knowing the hearts and minds of others, cannot make honest judgments about motives. God can and does. He works all things according to the counsel of His own will. His judgments are true and merciful.

In Him also we have obtained an inheritance, being predestined according to the purpose of Him who works all things according to the counsel of His will. (Ephesians 1:11)

When God rewards the faithful, He will have a perfect knowledge of all of life's situations.

Oh, the depth of the riches both of the wisdom and knowledge of God! How unsearchable are His judgments and His ways past finding out! (Romans 11:33)

As I discussed in a previous chapter, the exit of the faithful from this time-oriented system of duration will cause us to finally live as God intended for His children. Mortality will be swallowed up by life. When Jesus comes back those who have been redeemed will be resurrected to immortality and those who have not physically died will be changed in a twinkling of an eye from mortal to immortal.

And just as we have borne the image of the earthly man, so shall we bear the image of the heavenly man. I declare to you, brothers and sisters, that flesh and blood cannot inherit the kingdom of God, nor does the perishable inherit the imperishable. Listen, I tell you a mystery: We will not all sleep, but we will all be changed—in a flash, in the twinkling of an eye, at the last trumpet. For the trumpet will sound, the dead will be raised imperishable, and we will be changed. For the perishable must clothe itself with the imperishable, and the mortal with immortality. (1 Corinthians 15:49–53) (NIV)

Those who are in the graves will not go before those who are alive and remain at the return of Jesus to the earth. They will be caught up together with them, to meet the Lord in the air, and will forever be with the Lord.

Then we who are alive and remain shall be caught up together with them in the clouds to meet the Lord in the air AND THUS WE SHALL ALWAYS BE WITH THE LORD! (1 Thessalonians 4:17)

THE END